From the Head to the Heart:

Moving from Biblical Concepts to Experiential Reality

Terry Stanley

From the Head to the Heart:
Moving from Biblical Concepts to Experiential Reality
Terry Stanley

To order additional copies of this book or for more information, visit us on the web at headtotheheartbook.com

ISBN: 978-1-312-25355-1
Copyright ©2014 Terry Stanley
Published by Canaan Publishing

All rights reserved. No part of this publication may be reproduced, stored in a retrieval system or transmitted in any form by any means, electronic, mechanical, photocopy, recording or otherwise without the prior permission of the author, except as provided by USA copyright law.

Scripture taken from the *NEW AMERICAN STANDARD BIBLE,*
© 1960, 1962, 1963, 1968, 1971, 1972, 1973, 1975, 1977, by The Lockman Foundation. Used by permission.

The Holy Bible, King James Version (KJV)

Printed in the United States of America

To the prisoners:

whose walls of confinement are self-created

Additional Books
By Terry Stanley

"The Way Church Was Meant to Be"

"Mysteries of the Kingdom"

Available at Barnes and Noble, Amazon, or Lulu.com

Contents

Foreword	7
Thou Shalt Not Feel	10
First Things Second	13
The Anatomy of Man	17
Unraveling a Mystery	34
Paradox	38
The Common Error	44
Separating Soul and Spirit	62
Becoming Who You Are	83
The False Self	98
Who is Grace?	112
Yielding the Heart	130
While We Look	151
Breaking Through	161
The Frequency of Repentance	175
A Tale of Two Cities	182
The Role of Knowledge	187
Milk and Meat	205
Activities of the Heart	209
The Lazy Heart	217
How Does God Get To Your Heart?	225
You'd Better Or Else	238

Acknowledgments

Thanks to Steve McCalip, Paul Smith, and Chad Oliver for their editing contributions. Their many hours of hard work made this book readable for all.

The following families have provided tremendous love and support throughout the writing process. Many have participated in meaningful conversations which have inspired content in this book.

In alphabetical order they are: Justin Bailey, The Edges, the Fattas, the Gosselins, the Gruwells, Pete Harmazimski, the Heekes, Brad Heilhecker, Trina Hinton, the McCalips, the McCardles, the McGees, the Greg Miller family, the Jeff Miller family, the Mark Miller family, the Myuses, the Olivers, John Pankey, the Paxsons, the Ringors, the Rusts, the Sabras, the Salgados, the Shannons, the Smiths, the Taylors, the Tumlinsons, the Whittakers, and the Witts. Thanks also to Tim Marks, who initiated the very first conversation with me concerning the head and the heart.

A very special thank you to Nanci, my amazing wife.

This book was written prayerfully. Anything written that is good, true, or helpful is of the Lord Jesus Christ and not from the author.

Foreword

By Steve McCalip

It was a just a simple meeting over breakfast in Houston in 2009 with someone I had never met but whose home church I was curious about. Separated from the body of Christ for over twenty years due to my peculiar, doctrinal beliefs and hard heart, I figured this would just be another meeting where, once this man figured out my beliefs and I his, we would go our separate ways and maybe even "get into it" a little bit- spiritual confrontation being the norm for me. But what I experienced for the first time in my life was a man who took genuine interest in who I was and my situation, a man of God who showed me extraordinary patience and a sincere love that wasn't based on traditional religion and supposed "essential" doctrine.

Terry Stanley values people far above any beliefs or group he is or ever has been a part of. I met a person who didn't even know me but who I could tell cared about me - and not out of some religious obligation. After I rattled off all my pet doctrines and divisive "truths," I anticipated his "Oh no!" response, but he gently disarmed me with love and said something like, "Man, that's okay with me."

When we were through eating breakfast, I was shocked that he wasn't ready to "write me off" concerning my unorthodox beliefs as I had experienced so many times over the years. Instead, we hugged, and for the first time in twenty years, I felt the Lord softening my heart as I cried out to him in my car all the way home. Suddenly, my doctrines and beliefs, which were basically my security and comfort, took a backseat to experiencing the love of Christ deep down inside my heart. Though truth still mattered greatly, I was genuinely more interested in loving my brother than arguing about truth. I felt as if I was born again "again."

God's irony in our lives is almost too much to believe at times. I am the last person I would have ever imagined to be writing a foreword to this book because I would have dismissed this kind of writing five years ago as a subject I wasn't at all interested in and probably felt I already knew the concepts of. "Believe with the heart?-Love from the heart?" Sure, I know those things, and which Christian doesn't? The reality was that I had not experienced the power of love, the intricacies of it, and the "height, the depth, and the breadth" of it as Paul described. Those things could not be experienced through my cranium.

But that dismissal of knowing was the very problem in and of itself that this book deals with. I knew "about" it but didn't believe it with my heart, for if I did, I would have been living in truth and love instead of just truth. I would have been practicing that first commandment instead of just agreeing with it and writing it off as grade-school stuff. Thus, speaking the truth in love wasn't something I was good at even though I understood and knew (and said I believed) that we should do that very thing. Faith works by love, not by head knowledge and right doctrine. My faith wasn't working as it should though my doctrine was ironclad in many areas. The solution wasn't reading another book or listening to some new teacher. It was love. It was suffering. It was brokenness.

If the Lord is "all or nothing" about anything, it is the subject of our hearts. He says we will find him *daily* when we search for him with ALL of our hearts. Love works, and it will always work when our hearts are given to it.

The scourge of modern Christianity, especially in America, is that most of us are far too often relating to each other and to the Lord through our heads and not our hearts, and if there is one thing that will derail us in our relationships with each other and the Lord, *it is that very thing*. Terry has always practiced helping many of us in our fellowship in Houston see this very thing - that it is our hearts which we constantly need to monitor in our daily walk. He is a rare gift to the body of Christ who has been helping me and others to "keep ourselves in the love of God" (Jude 21).

What the body of Christ needs is some effective tools for recognizing when we are in "in our heads" instead of our hearts. But more importantly, the body needs to know how to move "from the head to the heart," and that is what Brother Terry has devoted his entire walk to doing. This book is replete with practical examples and helpful analogies to exercise our hearts, to help them "move over" from theory to reality. It is, I believe, probably the most thorough book on the human heart you will ever read, yet it is written with a simplicity and godly sincerity that is hard to find. It is a work based on twenty-five years of Terry's personal walk with the Lord and his leadership in the church. It is a book whose teachings have been practiced and proven on the hearts of many men and women whose struggles kept them in the merry-go-round of flesh, soul, and spirit.

One of the shortest distances we can travel can also be the longest trip we ever take - the eighteen inches from the head to the heart. That eighteen inches is the most important distance we can go when we get saved, but it is also a path that must be travelled daily, even moment by moment, if we desire to walk according to the Spirit and not our flesh. There aren't many books that will help guide you in this inner journey- none to the extent that you will soon read here. If we truly want to be men and women after God's own heart, we must dedicate ourselves to living from the heart, to worshipping from the heart, to loving from the heart.

There is really only one commandment: to love the Lord and each other with all our hearts. In order to do that with sincerity and reality, we must recognize when we are loving from "the head" and not the heart. We must "exercise our senses" and seek the Lord to discern soul (flesh) and spirit (heart). This lifestyle comes at a high cost. As Terry said, every move of the heart toward the Lord and each other *costs us* something. It costs constant humility and daily sacrifice. It costs the willingness to change our strongly-held beliefs if need be. Our Father's business can be an elusive thing at times, but Brother Terry has helped us tremendously to do the very thing that has to be done, to do the one thing that matters most-to love the Lord with *all our heart*, soul, mind, and spirit, and to love our neighbor as ourselves.

Thou Shalt Not Feel

It is a common problem: You know the truth in your head, but how to get the truth from your head to your heart is a different story.

We are totally saturated with biblical knowledge and facts. We know the exact chapter and verse of many of these truths, and many of us are exceptional at defending our theology. We can recite the historical evolution of our doctrines, and we can debunk theology that opposes our own by exposing its faulty origins. But when we are asked how our doctrines and theologies actually help us to fulfill the two greatest commandments of loving God and loving our neighbor as ourselves - well, we are not always sure how that applies.

The primary message of Jesus Christ is clear: He came to forgive sins. He taught us to have an intense love for God. He taught us to have a heart of radical forgiveness and love for others. We are invited to share and experience intimacy with our God on a daily basis, yet these are the things we are the least skilled at doing. We are much better at analyzing the scriptures and fervently defending the faith. We are much more comfortable with doing word-studies than we are at connecting with God in our hearts. Sadly, we are much better at doing things for God than knowing Him in intimacy.

It is the plague of modern, western man and the ancient Greek mind. We are very good at understanding concepts, but we are very poor at truly *seeing what is not seen* (2 Cor. 4:18). There is a vast difference between understanding a concept and experiencing the reality of that concept.

The word *doctrine* means "teaching." Teaching is good and essential, but we have changed the meaning of the word *doctrine* to "our strong opinions and positions on theology that we've decided not to change."

A Doctrine of Reaction

In our modern, Christian culture, we have collectively created a new doctrine. We have arrived at the conclusion that "Faith is not a feeling." However, it is with the heart that man believes and has faith (Rom. 10). And at the very same time, it is with the heart that we feel (Phil. 1:7). This seeming contradiction poses quite a problem.

The statement "Faith is not a feeling" is certainly a true statement. Faith is most definitely not a feeling. However, our constant need to emphatically declare that faith is not a feeling is born out of a reaction. Understandably, it is a reaction to fleshly emotionalism in the church. But our reactionary stance that faith is not a feeling has now created a new dilemma: Because we both believe and feel from our hearts, if we discount our feelings, we often avoid the realm of the heart and miss finding real faith in the process.

Many Christians have given up on feeling anything in their relationship with Christ. Experiencing a deep feeling of heartfelt joy, an inner peace that satisfies us completely, a fervent and intense heart of love, an extreme desire and daily passion for God, and a life of continually experiencing spiritual fulfillment are all extremely elusive to us.

We've all tasted moments of feeling and experiencing the presence of God, but it seems absolutely impossible to abide in God's presence on a daily basis. So we throw in the towel on the experiential and on healthy spiritual feelings and continue to emphatically declare that faith is not a feeling.

Disregarding the healthy feelings that should accompany real faith also has an undercurrent of justification. *We have justified our dryness.* We now make it quite alright to view the Christian life as only a life of duty and of "doing the right thing." We have decided that the life of faith is primarily a life of religious obligation and the keeping of rules. We have made our lack of experiential truth and experiential reality the accepted norm. We distract ourselves from intimacy with Christ and replace it with…anything else.

We have denied the validity of embracing the beautiful and wonderful emotions that are a part of love, joy, and spiritual peace. We have reduced Christianity to a mathematical equation.

For example, consider the popular teaching that declares "love is a choice." Love is never called a choice in scripture, but we declare it as though it were a biblical fact. For me personally, if loving me ever becomes a choice to my spouse or those I walk closely with, then I will politely respond with a "No thank you." I don't want someone to love me because they "should love me" or because it is the right choice to do so. Our God feels the same way. To love our King and the people He died for is much more than a mechanical, outward decision of "doing the right thing."

Jesus *felt compassion* many times in scripture (Matt. 9:36, Matt. 14:14, Matt. 18:27, Mk. 6:34, Lk. 7:13, Lk. 10:33, Lk. 15:20). We are to have His same experience. To love is to be moved deeply from within. When we love, certain choices will be a manifestation. Because of choices that *come out of* love, love can be observed outwardly. But love does not begin outwardly: Love begins inwardly - in the heart. Love is felt and it is experienced. As a result, love makes an outward choice and demonstrates itself out of a heartfelt experience.

To genuinely love or to receive love *feels* absolutely wonderful. This is not to say that love is only a feeling. But, to strip away from love the feelings that it evokes is to deny love's fullness and power. God is Spirit, and the fruit of His Spirit in our hearts is joy, peace, and love. These are all qualities of faith that are felt and experienced in the heart and soul of the inner man. They are more than feelings - they have substance, but they are, nonetheless, felt and experienced.

To a large degree, we have compartmentalized the emotional part of ourselves. We have become detached from the inner man - the place within us where true faith, power and love all originate.

As you journey to gain a deeper revelation of moving from the head to the heart, your Christian faith will become more real to you. You will soon find that your faith will become much more experiential, potent, and alive.

Questions for Understanding and Discussion

1. Why is there often an emphasis on head knowledge and intellectual learning, but things of the heart are neglected?
2. How can the statement "faith is not a feeling" be a cause for spiritual dysfunction?
3. Is it healthy for the Christian to feel spiritual emotions? Why or why not?

First Things Second

From the Head to the Heart is a sequel to a previous book, *Mysteries of the Kingdom*, which addressed foundational truth that is often lacking in many Christians' understanding. It explained the things that we should have heard from the beginning of our conversion to Christ. *Mysteries of the Kingdom* provided an explanation as to why many lack spiritual depth, experience instability in their walk, and have a general lack of passion for Jesus Christ.

From the Head to the Heart takes the next step. It not only addresses a very common problem experienced by many Christians, it also provides a healthy focus and a specific direction for the life of the Christian. In order to walk in a consistent depth of experience with Jesus Christ, you the reader will understand what you should "give yourself to" daily. You will understand the reasons why, and then learn how to actually do it.

> 2 Pet. 3:15-16 *"…just as also our beloved brother Paul, according to the wisdom given him, wrote to you, as also in all his letters, speaking in them of these things, in which are some things hard to understand…"*

The apostle Peter tells us that portions of Paul's letters are not easily understood. When a person is unfamiliar with certain unseen spiritual realities, those realities can seem foreign at first glance. However, just because an idea is new to you or it initially seems complex, does not mean it is not of God or not truth. The *application* of truth should always be simple, but the dynamics behind the application can sometimes be involved.

Because this book tackles the nuts and bolts of subjective spiritual dynamics that are not commonly discussed in Christianity, parts of this book may seem complicated. I therefore feel it necessary to frequently rephrase and reiterate key ideas and to express them in many different ways in order to uncover the truth behind the concepts presented. It is similar to holding up an object to the light and then turning it at different angles in order to see its many facets. Therefore, as you read (hopefully while in fellowship with the Holy Spirit), allow yourself to participate fully in the occasional repetitive nature of the paragraphs and the chapters.

On a personal note, I am still growing regarding the topics discussed in this book. This project became a learning experience for me, for it required me to revise my own theology in places as I compared my ideas with the entire canopy of scripture. I hope to always grow in more revelation of the inner workings of the heart. In many ways, this book chronicles the details of the last twenty-five years of my personal spiritual journey. Welcome to the very depths of my heart.

Accordingly, please bear with me, for I do not intend for this next statement to come across as arrogant. But my experience in communicating the ideas presented in this book to the majority of people is this: Often people think they fully understand the topic being discussed, but in reality they only see a small portion of it, or they don't really see it at all, but they think they do. We tend to place things we read or hear into slots and categories in our mind that already exist causing us to interpret and filter new information only through our previous understandings. This can cause us to miss the depth of the point when familiar language is presented. Just because we understand the words presented doesn't mean that we experience the depth of meaning behind those words. In fact, what you will discover is that many of the ideas in this book will not fit into any slot or category you currently have.

The Issue of Faith

Some readers' view of Christianity is largely centered around the issue of salvation. They may feel as though a person's salvation is ultimately the most important thing, and that after the pinnacle of salvation is achieved, then the life of the Christian is largely occupied with the duty of serving God, attending church, and living a good Christian life. This book takes a slightly different approach. Although salvation is of the upmost importance, it is the beginning point. It is the essential means to an end but is not the end itself. Salvation is only the first step that must be taken in order to achieve man's ultimate purpose. The apex of a man's purpose and highest calling is not that he is saved, but rather that he walks and grows in intimacy with Jesus Christ. Being saved is initially required to achieve this intimacy. Salvation deals with the "sin problem" and, therefore, serves as an *introduction* to a deeper life of faith and experience of Christ. To "know Christ" not only describes the fact that we have been saved, but it also describes our continual journey of plunging into the depths and riches of experiencing the living God. In addition, it is only intimacy with Christ that yields valid and legitimate Christian service and works that are both fruitful and wrought in God.

Because many subjects in this book deal with issues of the Christian walking daily in faith and in deepening his faith, it must be said upfront that only God is the author of our faith. Secondly, faith comes by hearing His word. Thirdly, you have already been given a measure of faith (Heb. 12:2, Rom. 10:17, Rom. 12:3). Having said that, the issues that involve moving from the head to the heart will lead you to *cooperate* with the measure of faith you have already been given. I also deal with topics that place you in a better posture internally to hear and receive the word of God in your heart which will also result in increasing your faith (Matt. 13:13).

Why All the Rhetoric in This Book?

In addressing one other type of Christian reader, there are many who approach the Christian life with a very straight forward style of simplicity. They shy away from spiritual complexities. When simplicity is the result of a heart that is filled with faith, it is to be applauded. For this kind of reader, the dissection of certain spiritual dynamics may actually cause unnecessary consternation. However, sometimes an overly simplistic approach is an avoidance of deeper things in the heart that should be addressed. At other times, a simplistic approach is the result of a lack of familiarity with deeper truths in scripture. If you find the discussions and topics presented to be initially wearisome, I encourage you to find endurance, for I will address many issues that will apply to every reader at one time or another. However, every Christian book is not written for every Christian. A particular book may not be helpful during every season of growth or at every stage of God's leading. During the early years of my faith, some Christian books made absolutely no sense to me at the time, but now those same books have become a treasure in my heart.

The Issue of Real Time

If a computer had the ability to track a freight train's current position in "real time," you could look at the computer screen and see a dot representing exactly where the train is at this very moment in time. Real time is now.

When we encounter spiritual truth, (whether in scripture, books, or hearing messages), we often observe the truth only as detached spectators. A common response may be, "I already agree with the truth I just heard, therefore, there is nothing else I need to do - next topic please." Or, "I agree with the truth I just heard, and I intend to apply it at some point in the future." However, scripture encourages us to respond quickly to God's promptings:

Mar 1:18 "Immediately they left their nets and followed Him."

When Jesus called His disciples to follow Him, the disciples didn't "ponder these things for a few days to consider them." Nor did they "spend time seeking God so they could learn to follow Him better." When God spoke to them and they heard His voice, they immediately responded. They quickly left their nets and followed Him. If God speaks to you through this book (or through anything), immediately put the book down and yield to the work of the Spirit in your heart (in real time). This book is not a novel. Don't just enjoy truth for the sake of enjoyment. Your religious flesh will want to taste and savor the truth, rejoice with it, and say, "That was really good" but you will remain *unchanged*. If you encounter too many truths without stopping to allow the Spirit to do real work in your heart, you will soon forget the truth you've heard, and the birds of the air will eat the seeds that have been sown in your heart (Luke 8:5). Make it a practice to frequently stop whatever you are doing to reconnect and receive from God. Read prayerfully and slowly, allowing the Holy Spirit to minister change into your life.

I will also warn you upfront about the danger of methodology. At times you may be tempted to take some of the ideas in this book and turn them into a systematic procedure or a formula for growth. That is not my intention in presenting these truths. Nothing can become a substitute for a relationship of devotion to Jesus Christ. There is no methodology or certain procedure for a relationship. In other words, allow God to use this book in your life (as He leads you), but be careful of building a system from the ideas on these pages. Otherwise, you will only wind up with more head knowledge which would be the opposite of the intended purpose of this book.

The Anatomy of Man Chapter

"The Anatomy of Man" chapter is the next chapter in the book. It is primarily a discussion of important terminology and definitions which are critical in understanding the remaining chapters. "The Anatomy of Man" chapter can be "dry" to read; parts of that chapter may be difficult to get through. I encourage you to find the fortitude and patience to read it because it will provide a good foundation for the rest of the book. It will also provide for a good foundation in understanding spiritual dynamics that commonly occur within yourself and all people. There are also diagrams and charts that will help you to visualize the concepts we will discuss later. I think you will find most of the remaining chapters to be inspirational and practical in application. However, if you find "The Anatomy of Man" too tedious to get through, then feel free to only use that chapter as a reference of terminology while reading the rest of the book.

A final thought before I continue. There is no condemnation for those in Jesus Christ (Rom. 8:1). There will be times while reading that you may be tempted to feel discouraged. Many of the ideas I will discuss will be challenging. Some of them will be foreign. You may realize that you have been unsuccessful with many of the concepts in this book at one time or another. Growth is a process, and Jesus Christ is the author and finisher of our faith. The blood of Jesus Christ has washed you clean from all of your sins even if you are not walking in a full experience of Him. If you have put your faith in Jesus Christ, then you are cleansed, accepted, forgiven, incredibly valued, and loved by God - no matter what.

Questions for Understanding and Discussion

1. Why is it important to not initially assume or gloss over seemingly familiar subjects?
2. Are complex spiritual truths always to be rejected? Why?
3. What role does salvation play in the life of the Christian?
4. If God is the author of faith, how does the Christian participate with faith and why is it important?
5. When is simplicity positive and when can it be negative?

The Anatomy of Man

The purpose of this chapter is to define important terms and to introduce the fundamental dynamics of a person's makeup. Some readers will find this chapter interesting and very helpful; other readers will find it laborious and tedious. The practical applications and import of this chapter will be provided throughout the rest of the book.

The Bible is not a science book, nor is the anatomy of man presented in scripture as a perfect diagram. To interpret scripture in such a way that creates formulas and schematics can be problematic at times. Occasionally, there is some overlap in the use of terms that define man's anatomy. Having said that, there are also hundreds of verses that describe man's anatomy very consistently which allows for a reasonably clear picture.

The conclusions and definitions in this chapter come from a variety of sources. The primary source is from scripture. Other past influences are from authors such as Watchman Nee and Dan Stone. Personal mentors, dialogue with peers, and personal experience were also influential.

> *1 Th. 5:23 "Now may the God of peace Himself sanctify you entirely; and may your spirit and soul and body be preserved complete, without blame at the coming of our Lord Jesus Christ."*

This particular verse is clear in describing three of the four major parts of man's anatomy: the *spirit, soul, and body*. There are also other places in scripture that support the naming of these parts as such (Heb. 4:12, 2 Cor. 4:16, Gen 2:7, Zech 12:1).

In identifying the fourth major part of man's anatomy, *the heart,* Jesus quotes Deuteronomy in both Mk. 12:30 and in Lk. 10:27:

> *"And you shall love the Lord your God with all your heart, and with all your soul, and with all your mind, and with all your strength."*

These verses and many others confirm to us that the anatomy of man consists of the body, soul, heart, and spirit. We will discuss these beginning with the outermost part and work our way toward the innermost part.

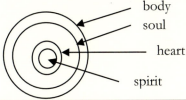

The First Organ - The Body

The body is the most easily understood part of man's anatomy. The body is obviously physical in nature and is visible. It was created from the dust of the ground (Gen. 2:7). It has various needs and wants in order to keep itself alive. The basic and most primary goal of the body *is survival.* In order to survive, the body has the needs of food, safety, and reproduction (it's survival in the sense of continuation). If the body is submitted to the Spirit of God, it can be used of God and is, therefore, called "an instrument of righteousness" (Rom. 6:13). If it is not submitted to the Spirit of God, it is called "the flesh" (Rom. 8:13).

The body's primary goal of survival is directly related to the base and carnal nature of the flesh.

The Second Organ - The Soul

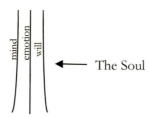

The soul is deeper than the physical body. The soul is the primary place of experience. Multiple scriptures describe the soul as the mind, the will, and the emotions.[1] The soul is the result of the body receiving the breath of life from God:

Gen. 2:7"And the Lord God formed man of the dust of the ground, and breathed into his nostrils the breath of life; and man became a living soul."

When God breathed spirit into man's body and caused his body to come alive, the result was that he became a living soul. Adam began to *experience* being alive.

When we say that the soul is the mind, will and emotions, we are saying that the soul is what you are thinking, feeling, and choosing in any given moment. Feelings, thoughts, and what choices you are making can all change from moment to moment. In the morning you might feel happy, but in the evening you might feel sad. You might have thoughts and plans to go shopping. After you finish your shopping, you start to think about what you will cook for supper. You may decide to cook hamburgers, but then you change your mind and you make a salad instead. During a worship meeting, you may experience love and thankfulness for God. When the meeting is over, you may experience anxiety about a task you have to do for work the next day.

Your most evident feelings, thoughts, and choices are all experiences occurring in your soul. When you think a thought, you experience it. When you feel an emotion, you experience it. And when you have a certain desire or want, you experience that desire or want.

When you just read the previous sentence in the paragraph above, you read those words at a certain moment in time. During that moment you had a certain experience in your soul. That moment is now gone. You are now in a new moment in time. What you are feeling or thinking right now during this new moment is now a new experience in your soul. Now that moment is gone and you now have a new thought and possibly a new emotion which is now the current experience in your soul. This is very important to understand because it directly relates to you walking after the spirit or after the flesh as we will soon see.

In the next three sections, we will further break down the soul and explain its three elements. We will then continue to define the broader four parts of man by discussing the heart and then the spirit.

The Intellect - The Mind of the Soul

Throughout the course of life, we learn many facts, gather large amounts of information, and accumulate many memories. The brain, which is part of the body, stores all of this information like files in the memory banks of a computer. Just like a computer stores files on its hard drive, the brain is a storage place for files. When a certain memory file is accessed from your brain, it becomes a current thought that you experience which we call "your mind."

Scripture tell us that we must "renew our minds" (Rom. 12:2). Our minds need to be renewed because many of the files that are stored in our brains were taught to us and were learned before our spirits were washed and made new. Most of your memories, thoughts you have about life, and how you perceive and define truth were all programmed and recorded during the time before you came to faith in Jesus Christ. As you experienced life during this time, you learned many things and created many files. During this time when your experience was not of God, you created many memory files that were not based in God's truth. You learned an entire framework and sets of information concerning what you thought was truth and what you thought life was all about. However, because the majority of what you learned life was about was taught to you and experienced during the time you did not know Jesus Christ, many of the files stored in your brain are corrupt and bad files. This is why your mind must be renewed. Your bad files must be updated with new ones.

For example, before you came to Christ, you may have erroneously believed that money was one of life's greatest pursuits. Or maybe you thought that impressing your friends was extremely important. You may have experienced that authority figures were abusive or negative in some way. You probably were taught and believed that you were more loved and valued when you did things well, but when you "blew it," you were not as acceptable or valued. Even though you are now a Christian and you have a new spirit, many corrupt files are still stored in your brain.

Many of these incorrect files you have were created during your childhood. Oftentimes, the earlier the memory file, the more pervasive and foundational it is to your overall approach and view of life. Things we learn during the formative years often guide our general grid for all of life. These very early files provide the primary framework from which we process and interpret truth, perceptions, and feelings.

Even though you now have been born of God and you have a new spirit that is washed and joined with God's Spirit, you still have old thoughts that come up in your mind that are false. *To renew your mind is to replace your old files with truth.* As the files in your brain become updated and renewed, you have the potential to have truth in your mind. Although every file in your brain is not a bad file (Many are benign, serving only a neutral purpose of basic functioning), the only way to know what is real and what is true is from scripture and from the Spirit of God.

Do not confuse the mind with the brain. The mind (which is one of three elements of the soul) is only the "viewer" of the current file being accessed from the brain. The mind can be an expression of the flesh or of the Spirit. As we will see in a future chapter, the Spirit of God can access files in the brain and bring them into our minds. If this is the case, then the file from the brain *is of the spirit.* However, if you are not submitted to the Spirit of God and you are accessing files in your brain independent of God (even if they are renewed files that are true), then the thoughts in your mind *are of the flesh.*

When we use the phrase *our head* in this book, it is understood that we are talking about thoughts in the mind that are being accessed from stored memory in our brain that are not being accessed or prompted by the Spirit.

The Emotions – The Feelings of the Soul

Just like the mind, the emotions or the feelings that are currently being experienced in the soul are either an expression of the flesh or an expression of the Spirit:

> *Gal. 5:19-21 "Now the deeds of the flesh are evident, which are: immorality, impurity, sensuality, idolatry, sorcery, enmities, strife, jealousy, outbursts of anger, disputes, dissensions, factions, envying, drunkenness, carousing, and things like these..."*

There are fleshly emotions that coincide with sensuality, jealousy, outbursts of anger, envying and "things like these." There are also fleshly emotions that correspond with lust, greed, selfishness, hate, etc. There is a vast array of emotions that accompany the flesh.

Many times there are extreme and powerful emotions attached to certain memory files you have stored in your brain. Emotions can be extremely powerful, and they can seem very real. Although it "is true" that you are experiencing the emotions, many times you mistakenly believe that your emotions define what the truth actually is. It is important to know that even though you feel strongly about certain things, and even though many of your feelings seem like they are indeed the truth, many of them are simply false and errant feelings that are not based in reality.

Have you ever experienced a vivid and powerful dream? Perhaps you've dreamed you were falling, you were shot with a gun, or your spouse was unfaithful. Powerful dreams can produce powerful emotions within the dream. You may have even awakened after a dream still experiencing the emotions from the dream. Even though the dream was not real at all, you experience real emotions in your soul sometimes hours after the dream is over. Many of the corrupt files that you have stored in your brain also produce emotions in you that are simply not based in anything that is real.

Gal. 5:22-23 "But the fruit of the Spirit is love, joy, peace, patience, kindness, goodness, faithfulness, gentleness, self-control..."

We also see that certain emotions can come from the Spirit of God such as the emotions that accompany love, joy, peace, etc. The emotions that come from God are emotions that are of the truth. For example, your life may outwardly be in shambles, and there may be utter turmoil all around you, but the emotions that come from God will be peace, a sense of calm, confidence in Him, and safety. Although it may be a reality that your situation in life is negative or not ideal, it is a false emotion to feel as though God has turned His back on you. In the midst of turmoil, an emotion based in truth would be an experience of peace because it is truth that God has not forsaken you during this difficult time.

If someone attacks you or accuses you sharply, the emotions of the flesh will speak to you that you are belittled, accused, rejected, or hated. However, in that situation, the emotions that come from the Spirit will be of comfort, love for your attacker, compassion, peace, and reassurance that you are loved. Note that these are more than just emotions. The fruit of the Spirit is substance, but there are healthy and correct emotions that accompany the substance and truth of the Spirit.

The Will – The Wants, Desires, and Choices of the Soul

The third element of the soul is the will. Your will is also a part of your experience- along with your mind and emotions. Your will is what you are wanting, desiring, craving, and longing for. Your will also expresses what you are currently choosing in any given moment. Just like your mind and your emotions, your will can be an expression of the Spirit of God or it can be an expression of the flesh.

Jn. 1:13 "...nor of the will of the flesh nor of the will of man, but of God."

Just like the mind and the emotions, the experience of your will can change from moment to moment. If, for example, you create a specific plan to tell a lie, your will is currently not the will of God. During this experience of your will to lie, you have the option to submit your will to God. This will begin the process of actually changing your will to being aligned with God's will.

The Third Organ - The Heart

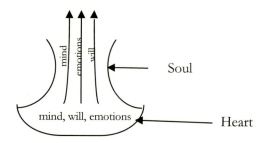

Deeper than the soul is the heart. The word "heart" appears in scripture 726 times. The heart possesses the same attributes as the soul - but on a much deeper level.[2] There are many verses that make a distinction between the soul and the heart.[3]

As we begin to discuss the elements of the heart, it will be helpful in your understanding to realize two things upfront. First, although the heart is a separate and deeper place than the soul, the things that fill the heart in any given moment *almost always fill the soul as well*. The second thing to realize is that there can be exceptions to this. At times conflict between the soul and the heart can exist in which the experience in the soul is not expressing what is truly filling the heart. Just like the soul, the heart can be filled with and express either the flesh or the Spirit.

The Mind of the Heart

Ps. 64:6 "...for the inward thought and the heart of a man are deep."

The things of the heart are frequently expressed as current thoughts in the mind (soul) as well. When a particular desire, want, feeling, fear, emotion, etc. is filling the heart, a file in the brain is accessed to express it. For example, you may have a desire in your heart to love and care for someone. Suddenly, the thought comes up in your mind to bake that person a cake or do something else that expresses that kindness you feel for him or her. The thought you have in your mind to bake that person a cake is a file that you have in your brain that matches and can express the desire you have in your heart.

Many times there are no words or actions that can adequately express what we feel in our hearts towards others. When you feel very deeply about someone or something and you cannot express it adequately, it is because there is no file available in your brain that matches the true impulse that is deep in the heart.

The Emotions of the Heart

The emotions in the heart are also normally expressed in the soul as well. We will see throughout many discussions in this book that our emotions can be valuable indicators of heart belief, but they cannot be trusted as defining what truth is (This is also true concerning thoughts in the mind).

> *1 Sam. 28:5 "When Saul saw the camp of the Philistines, he was afraid and his heart trembled greatly."*

> *Ps. 33:21 "For our heart rejoices in Him, because we trust in His holy name."*

Emotions stemming from the heart are very deep and can be very moving. Fleshly, primitive emotions such as fear, anger, lust, and pride can evolve and morph into many varieties; therefore, they disguise themselves in the heart. Holy and pure emotions of the Spirit that accompany love, joy, peace, trust, and faith are elating, encouraging, and empowering.

The Will of the Heart

> *Pro. 20:5 "A plan in the heart of a man is like deep water…"*

> *Ps. 40:8 "I delight to do Your will, O my God; Your Law is within my heart."*

Again, just like the mind and emotions of the heart, the will of the heart can be of the flesh or of the spirit. Again, the will in the heart is commonly expressed and experienced in the soul as well.

Unique Functions of the Heart

So far, we have explained that the heart is separate from the soul. The mind, will, and emotions of the heart are deeper than the mind, will, and emotions of the soul. However, the contents of the heart are normally and frequently expressed in the soul as well, although there can be a disconnect at times. There is also a very specific set of functions we see the heart performing in scripture. The functions that are unique to the heart are: *believing, trusting, doubting, fearing, hardening, opening, or closing.* We do not see scriptures that describe the soul as performing these functions.

Below are samples of scripture that show the unique functions of the heart.

Rom. 10:9,10 "...that if you confess with your mouth Jesus as Lord, and believe in your heart that God raised Him from the dead, you will be saved; for with the heart a person believes, resulting in righteousness, and with the mouth he confesses, resulting in salvation."

Pro. 3:5 "Trust in the Lord with all your heart..."

With the heart, we believe and trust.

Mk. 11:23 "Truly I say to you, whoever says to this mountain, 'Be taken up and cast into the sea,' and does not doubt in his heart, but believes that what he says is going to happen, it will be granted him."

With the heart, we can doubt.

2 Cor. 6:11 "Our mouth has spoken freely to you, O Corinthians, our heart is opened wide."

The heart can be opened.

1 Jo 3:17 "But whoever has the world's goods, and sees his brother in need and closes his heart against him, how does the love of God abide in him?"

The heart can be closed.

We will practically apply these unique functions throughout the book because the heart plays a very key role in experiencing the reality of spiritual things.

The Fourth Organ - The Spirit

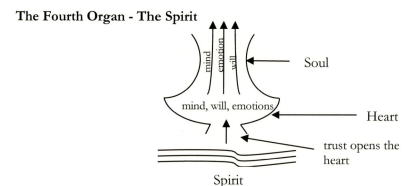

There are two references to "the spirit" is scripture (not including demonic spirits). One is the human spirit or the spirit of man. The second is the Holy

Spirit or the Spirit of God. The human spirit is designated by "a little s". The Spirit of God is spelled with "a big S". We will address both.

Your human spirit is at the deepest center of your innermost being. Your spirit is the core of who you really are. It is ultimately the driving force behind your life choices and your experience. It is the source of strength and power, the wellspring of life that fills the Christian, and it is the ultimate motivating and driving force of all human beings.

Before you submitted your life to Jesus Christ, your human spirit was not of God. Your spirit was unclean and sinful. Other terms that are also used to describe the condition of the human spirit before conversion to Christ are: *dead, darkened, alienated, separated from God, and un-regenerated* (Gen. 2:16-17, Eph. 2:1, 3-5, Jn. 8:44, Rom. 1:28-32, Tit. 3:3-6). Before you came to Christ, you were engaged in selfishness and evil continually because of the condition of your spirit. In fact, before you were a Christian, your unrighteous spirit was an ally of Satan in which he utilized to manipulate you and deceive you. You were enslaved to the evil one and to the power of sin because of the condition of your human spirit:

> *Jn. 8:44 "You are of your father the devil, and you want to do the desires of your father..."*

When you submitted your life to Jesus Christ and trusted in Him for the forgiveness of sins, your spirit was washed. When you submitted your life to Christ, you were regenerated or "made alive," and your human spirit became completely clean. Thus, you became a new person. (1 Cor. 15:22, 2 Cor. 5:21, Rom. 3:28, Heb. 12:23, Jn. 17:21, 1 Cor. 1:30):

> *1 Cor. 6:17 "But the one who joins himself to the Lord is one spirit with Him."*

If you are a Christian, then your human spirit has become one with the Spirit of Christ Himself. When you were born again, you were born of the Spirit of God. At the point you submitted to the Lordship and authority of Jesus Christ and trusted in His blood to wash you of your sins, your human spirit became intermingled or meshed with the Spirit of God.

Let's look again at the verse in Mark 12:

> *Mk. 12:30 "And you shall love the Lord your God with all your heart, and with all your soul, and with all your mind, and with all your strength."*

Notice that this verse does not mention loving God with your spirit. This is because your spirit is not a place of choosing. Your spirit is either in one of two *conditions* that cannot be changed. It is not in a state of change as the soul or heart can be. It is either in the condition that it is darkened and opposed to God, or it is in the condition that it is righteous and loves God. If you are walking *after your spirit* as a Christian, then you will experience love for God and the fruit of the Spirit.

[**Very Important note:** Many times in the New Testament, the translators freely interchange the words "spirit" (little "s") and "Spirit" (big "S"). Again, big "S" being God's Spirit and little "s" referring to our human spirit. Either use is often interchangeable because we have become one with God in our human spirit. We can refer to His Spirit inside us, or we can refer to our human spirit which has now taken on His qualities because we have become meshed and intertwined with Him in our spirit. However, we ourselves are certainly not God, nor do we share in His actual deity although we do share in His righteous nature. In many chapters and topics throughout this book, "the spirit" or "the Spirit"(little "s" or "big S") are also frequently used interchangeably as they are in scripture as well. At times I may specifically refer to your spirit (little "s") when speaking in context of the body, soul, and heart. Or, at times I may refer to the Spirit (big "S") when placing a specific emphasis on Christ who lives in you. Either way, the terms are interchangeable for the born-again believer. However, they are not interchangeable for the non-Christian, as the human spirit of the unbeliever has not been made one with God's Spirit.]

The spirit is the most rarely understood and often the most ignored part of man. The vast majority of people live from only their soul or from their heart filled with the flesh. Rarely, if ever, do people live from their spirit. Although the spirit of a person influences, affects, and guides the general course of life for people (often without awareness), it is very rarely focused upon as a place to consciously live from and experience daily - much less moment by moment. The exception to this concerning non-Christians are those who purposely engage in spiritualism and witchcraft.

If and when the spirit is contacted by the majority of Christians, it provides for an *extremely* special and powerful experience, yet the spirit is often encountered "hit and miss" as an accidental occurrence and is not contacted in a conscious way. Therefore, there is not usually understanding as to the reason for periodic times of powerful experience. The reason for most Christians' lack of depth, inspiration, creativity, revelation, faithfulness, daily joy, perseverance, insight, and a general lack of intimacy with Christ is because they have not learned to live from their spirit. Those whom the Lord uses in the most effective ways with fruit that remains are those who learn to live from their spirit and not from their natural soul life.

The proper and intended order of flow is this: The spirit should fill the heart, which will then be experienced in the soul. Finally, the soul is expressed through the body with words and actions. Therefore, the whole anatomy of man is to be filled with the Spirit and all parts are in agreement. The heart, soul, and body are the container or "vessel" for the Spirit to live and express His life through. However, due to various deceptions, erroneous teaching in the church, a lack of understanding, and damage in the minds and emotions of many Christians, the intended order is hindered, and there is a frequent disconnect.

Comparing the Soul and the Heart

In the next couple of sections, we will help reinforce your understanding with a discussion of additional dynamics of the interaction of soul and heart and how they relate to one another.

We've mentioned that the soul normally expresses what is filling the heart. The soul and heart work very closely together. There are thirty-four places in scripture that speak of them together in the same verse (yet separating them). In addition, we also see scriptures that describe how they function together.

> *Matt. 12:34 "...For the mouth speaks out of that which fills the heart."*

In the verse above, we see that when we speak, we are speaking from what is in our hearts. The impulse from the heart quickly becomes an experienced thought in the soul which the body then expresses through speech.

> *Heb. 4:12 "For the word of God is living and active and sharper than any two-edged sword, and piercing as far as the division of soul and spirit, of both joints and marrow, and able to judge the thoughts and intentions of the heart."*

We can see from the verse above that as the word of God separates what is soul from what is spirit, it also judges and discerns the things that originate from the heart. The soul experience originates from what begins in the heart.

As we briefly mentioned before, disconnects can exist in the soul expressing what is in the heart. This can happen if there are walls in the heart (a specific type of heart decision), patterns of avoidance, deceptions, unresolved pain, legalism, fear, darkness, judgments, trauma, or delusion. *No one is perfectly healthy.* Therefore, the thoughts in the mind will not always accurately represent that which is in the heart. We can deceive ourselves by distracting our minds away from what is truly in our hearts – especially in areas of pain, guilt, and shame. This is referred to as "suppression." Deeper patterns of suppression can become repression in which we become completely unconscious of a particular event or of what we feel concerning an issue. When there are things in the heart that we are unaware of or that are undealt with, we live from only the shallow place of the soul in relating to those particular life situations.

An example will help to clarify a disconnect between the heart and soul: Your mind may consist of a certain set of thoughts on a matter (soul), but if you were to explore your deeper heart, you may see a different set of thoughts than what is currently in your mind (a type of double-mindedness). Perhaps if someone asked you the question, "What do you think about Brother Joe?" You may quickly reply, "I think Brother Joe is a fine brother!" The thoughts you have in your mind that Brother Joe is a fine brother may be your current and honest thoughts experienced in your soul. However, if you were to spend some time exploring the deeper thoughts in your heart concerning Brother Joe, you might find that in the depths of your heart, you really think Brother Joe is self-centered and lazy. For one reason or another, you could not or would not face what was really in your heart concerning Brother Joe. At the point in time that you expose the thoughts in your heart concerning Brother Joe, you soul quickly experiences those same thoughts and joins with the heart in agreement.

To use another example: When deciding what you want for lunch, you may see that you want to eat pizza (the experience of your will in your soul). However, the deeper will in your heart may be that you want to lose weight. During your initial check to see what it is you want to eat, you may only see that you want pizza. But if you were to slow down, and really find the deeper will of your heart, you may see that what you really want is a healthy salad.

In the same way, you may have feelings or emotions that are present in your soul, but really another set of emotions is deeper in the heart. At times you may experience temporary or shallow feelings of happiness, but deeper in your heart may abide feelings of despair concerning your true situation in life. Deeper feelings of guilt, fear, pride, etc. can be filling our hearts while we distract our souls with shallower thoughts and short-lived pleasures.

Because there can be a difference in the experience of the soul and the experience in the heart, it can also work to our benefit. During a certain part of your day, your heart may be filled with the Spirit of God and the love of God. As the day continues, you may need to focus your shallower mind on work, think through certain tasks, or do some problem-solving. If your deeper heart experience is of the spirit, even though you may be focusing your shallower mind (soul) with work, you are not necessarily breaking fellowship with God.

Even though the soul may shallowly experience a separate set of thoughts, emotions, and desires apart from the heart, it is the deeper experience in the heart which continually colors and ultimately affects our daily life. That which fills the heart is always our pervasive experience – although we may not always have a cognitive awareness of it. This is a difficult dynamic to put into words. We can put on a happy attitude in the shallowness of our soul and yet really, deep down, the sadness that is present in our hearts "colors" our entire experience of all things. Although we experience the effects of this, we may not have clarity as to what we are always actually experiencing in the heart unless we actually "look" and allow the Lord to search our heart (Jer. 17:9).

The Heart is the Gatekeeper to the Spirit

As we previously mentioned, there are additional and unique attributes of the heart that are not characteristics of the soul such as opening, closing, believing, trusting, and doubting; we can also see that *the heart is the gatekeeper to the spirit*. The soul does not perform this function.

The biblical definition of *belief* always includes trust in the heart. It is not the soul that believes, but it is the heart (Rom. 10:9). Because the heart is deeper than the soul, yet not as deep as the spirit, the heart functions as the link between the soul and the spirit. When the heart yields to the spirit in trusting belief, the gate of the heart is opened for the spirit to fill the heart. When the heart is filled with the Spirit of God, it overflows into the experience of the soul very easily, as most things do. Very often, if there is any disconnect between the heart and soul because of the deceptions of the flesh, the healthy link will be restored between the heart and soul as the heart is filled with the Spirit.

Trust is more than knowing the truth in the heart. *Trust is an action in the heart that yields or gives up its current belief and then clings to something else for dependency (preferably Christ).* We will explore this dynamic thoroughly in future chapters.

If you are familiar with David's Tabernacle or Solomon's Temple during the Old Testament period, each provides a picture for us to gain more insight. The body and the experiences in the soul are represented by the outer court. The Holy place represents the heart. The Holy of Holies or "the most Holy place " is represented by the spirit.

By observing Mark 15:38, and 2 Corinthians 3:15-16, we see that the veil between your heart and the spirit has been torn and taken away (the veil between the Holy Place and the Holy of Holies). This is extremely significant in that we now have access to the Spirit of God in our hearts at any time.

Revelation and Hearing God's Voice

What does it mean exactly to "receive a revelation from God?" At times, the Spirit may directly access a file from our brain and pull it directly into our mind. Or, the Spirit may immediately insert a new thought into your mind that was not previously a file stored in your brain. When either of these occurs, we say that we "heard God's voice" or that we "received a revelation" directly from God. This can be an exhilarating experience. Suddenly in an instant, your understanding is enlightened on a particular matter. Like a flash of lightning, you suddenly "see" what can take an hour to explain to someone else. When the Spirit reveals something to the mind of your heart and soul, He will usually also provide you with the power to change your heart (if applicable) at the same time He grants you understanding. Revelation from God and hearing His voice is truly an amazing experience. Sadly, many Christians live only from revelation to revelation. They become addicted to the elation of seeing new things and the change that it brings, yet they do not know how to daily walk after the Spirit as we will soon see. Walking after the Spirit is like "walking in constant revelation" that never stops.

Walking After the Flesh

A simple definition of "the flesh" is this: the flesh is the body, soul, and heart in a state of independence and autonomy from the Spirit.

Your heart is the gatekeeper which either yields the soul and body to the spirit, or the heart chooses to keep the vessel unbelieving and independent. There are other ways we could describe walking after the flesh for purposes of understanding. Walking after the flesh could be described as "walking after your body" (although this is not scriptural language, but only to clarify). Other ways to describe walking after the flesh would be to say that we are walking independently of God, having an unbelieving heart, allowing the heart to be filled with the flesh, or walking shallowly while we independently access the files stored in our brains. Scripturally speaking, we can also call this "leaning to your own understanding" (Prov. 3:5).

In the case of nonbelievers, they are continually walking after their flesh, for they have no other choice. Even if the non-Christian's heart is filled with his human spirit, he continues to live in unrighteousness because the unbeliever's spirit is unregenerate and unrighteous. If the born-again Christian is ever allowing his spirit to fill his heart, then he experiences life, joy, peace, love, and righteousness because of the new condition of his cleansed, human spirit.

Many Christians have an overly narrow view of what it means to walk after the flesh. Often when the phrase "walking after the flesh" is heard, many Christians take it to only mean specifically having an outburst of anger or losing control in some way. Although walking after the flesh certainly includes outbursts of anger or losing self-control, it is much broader than that:

> *Gal. 5:19 "Now the deeds of the flesh are evident, which are: immorality, impurity, sensuality, idolatry, sorcery, enmities, strife, jealousy, outbursts of anger, disputes, dissentions, factions, envying, drunkenness, carousing, and things like these..."*

The deeds of the flesh are not the flesh itself. The deeds of the flesh are only the *deeds* or outward manifestations of the flesh. The deeds of the flesh are what the body will do, what the soul will experience, and what the heart will be filled with if the heart does not open its gate to trust and submission to the Spirit. As the body, soul, and heart are in a state of independence from the Spirit, the motivations of the flesh to protect and satisfy itself manifest with various impulses in your mind, emotions, and will.

If a Christian is walking after his flesh, he will eventually and sometimes immediately do things that are on the list in Galatians 5:19. However, many times Christians are walking after the flesh, and they are hiding the fact that they are - even from themselves. Christians can be totally selfish or miserable inside and all the while they are suppressing these attitudes and not showing it outwardly. Many Christians have learned how to outwardly behave in a manner acceptable to others, while inwardly they are judgmental, self-righteous, proud, empty, miserable, etc. We often fool ourselves and others by "Christianizing" the flesh.

Therefore, we must realize that the list referenced in Galatians 5:19 is not an all-inclusive list. Paul concludes the list with *"and things like these."* You can display similar acts or do things that are variations of the things on the Galatians list that are not specifically included, and you will be manifesting the results of walking after the flesh.

Walking After the Spirit

If the body, soul, and heart are submitted to the Spirit of God (via the gateway of the heart), then the body is not "the flesh". Rather, the body becomes an instrument of righteousness (Rom. 6:13). In this state of submission and being yielded, the body becomes an instrument or tool to be used of the Lord. When we are submitted to Christ, we can be used of God to accomplish His purposes on Earth. If we are not submitted to Christ in any given moment, we are selfish and independent; therefore, we are only seeking our own desires - the desires of the flesh.

The flesh fills the experience of the heart and soul when we walk after the flesh. In the same way, when we walk after the Spirit, the Spirit fills the experience of the heart and soul. Experiencing the Spirit in your heart and in your soul is wonderfully fulfilling. Having the thoughts of God in our minds, experiencing His feelings of joy and love, and having our will totally in line with His is *the most fulfilling, satisfying, and exhilarating experience a human being can possibly have* (Jn. 7:38, Eph. 3:8, 19).

Walking after the Spirit is very often misunderstood. It is commonly thought of as "being good". Walking after the Spirit is not shallowly having a good attitude or behaving nicely. Nor is it simply thinking thoughts about God. It has nothing to do with outward good behavior, having a sweet disposition, or behaving pleasantly. It has nothing to do with reading your Bible or going to church meetings. The flesh is very much able to mimic all of these attributes.

Many Christians also think of walking after the Spirit as another thing on the list of Christian things they should be doing such as reading their Bibles, witnessing, praying, etc.

Walking after the Spirit is not at all *just another thing* we should make sure we are doing. Walking after the Spirit is *the only thing* we are to be doing.

Walking after the Spirit is a heart dynamic of complete trust and spiritual depth. It is the result of being in a humble and yielded posture in your heart that produces a dependence that the flesh cannot imitate. As we walk after the Spirit, revelation from God becomes a very frequent occurrence, but it is a by-product and secondary to the intimacy with Christ you are experiencing. Walking after the Spirit is more like "walking in revelation" or "walking in hearing God's voice" as opposed to experiencing a periodic revelation or hearing God's voice sporadically.

Walking after the Spirit has become a cliché in many Christian circles that substitutes the reality of its true meaning for only a shallow idea. *To walk after the Spirit is to share the life of another while we are unaware and unconscious of self.* Again, walking after the Spirit is more than believing the truth in the heart. Walking after the Spirit is yielding to and trusting in another person, for the Lord is the Spirit (2 Cor. 3:17).

This book discusses walking after the Spirit in great depth and how vitally important it is for the entire Christian experience and service to God.

Concluding the Anatomy of Man

Be advised that the gaining of knowledge is always a double-edged sword. If submitted and released, knowledge can be used for good. Knowledge can also be used for bad (against yourself and others) as a tool of the flesh. Concerning the knowledge provided in this chapter, you should not constantly analyze yourself to judge whether or not you are experiencing the flesh or the Spirit. This would be a fleshly use of the knowledge you have just gained. Your focus is to always be on Christ Himself with heart submission and love to Him. Only then will the result be that you trust Him in your heart and experience Him in your soul. You also cannot determine the heart of another person, decide where that person is walking, or even make it your business unless the Spirit of God reveals this to you.

Perhaps the definitions of body, soul, spirit, heart, and walking after the Spirit or flesh have spawned more questions for you. Many of your questions will be answered, practical applications will be offered, and more clarification will come from the chapters that follow.

Notes:

[Do not confuse "being in the flesh" or "being in the Spirit" with "walking after the flesh" or "walking after the Spirit." If the Spirit of God is in you (which is true for all Christians), then you are always "in the Spirit", but you are not always *walking* after the Spirit (Romans 8)].

[1] A sample of scriptures describing soul as mind, will, or emotions: Ps.27:12, Ps. 41:2, Ezek.16:27, Deut. 21:14, Ps. 35:25, Num. 30:2, I Chr.. 22:19, Jer. 44:14, Job 6:7, Song 1:7, Luke 1:46, Job 33:20, 2 Sam. 5:8, Zech. 11:8, Deut. 6:5, Job 10:1, Ps. 107:18, Ps. 119:20, Prov. 16:24, Ezek. 24:25, Prov. 19:2, Ps. 13:2, Ps. 139:14, Lam. 3:20, Prov. 2:10, Prov. 3:21,22 Prov. 24:14.

[2] A sample of scriptures using the heart as mind, will, or emotions: Jn. 14:27, Lk. 9:47, Act 11:23, Ex. 7:14, Ex. 35:5, Deu. 2:30, Ps. 17:10, Ps. 19:8, Ps. 27:3, Ps. 33:11, Ps. 38:8, Ps. 49:3, Heb. 4:12, Act. 8:2, Ecc. 8:5, Ecc. 9:7, Jer. 30:24, Jer. 49:16, Lk. 1:51, Lk. 2:19, Lk. 12:45, Jn. 14:1, Jn. 16:22, Act 8:22, Rom 9:2, Rom 10:6, Jas 3:14, Rev 18:7.

[3] A sample of scriptures that distinguish heart from soul: Deu. 4:29, Deu. 10:12, Deu. 11:13, Deu. 11:18, Deu. 13:3, Deu. 26:16, Deu. 30:2, Deu. 30:6, Deu. 30:10, Jos. 22:5, 1 Sam. 2:35, 1Ki. 2:4, 1Ki. 8:48, 2 Ki. 23:3, 2 Ki. 23:25, 1Ch. 22:19, 2 Ch. 6:38, 2 Ch. 15:12, 2 Ch. 34:31, Jer. 32:41, Act. 4:32.

Body	Soul	Heart	Spirit
The outer man	The shallower inner man	The deeper inner man	The innermost man
The outer court	The outer court	The holy place	The most holy place
The human body which includes the brain.	The thoughts in the mind, the feelings in the emotions, the desire in the will.	Deeper thoughts, emotions, and will.	The deepest part of a person. The driving force of our life.
Also called "your members"	The obvious experience of mind, emotions, and will.	Deeper place of experience of mind, emotions, and will.	Same as the Spirit of Christ who is in us. Our true self (we are not Christ, but hidden in Him.)
Is an instrument of righteousness if submitted to the spirit.	Filled with the spirit if heart is filled with the spirit.	Gatekeeper to whole person being filled with spirit	Not in a state of change. Righteous and perfected if regenerated.
Called "the flesh" if not submitted (yielded and presented) – its natural state by default.	Is filled with what is filling the heart – flesh by default as heart is not yielded.	Is unbelieving and not trusting in the spirit by default.	Not in a state of change. Dead, sinful nature, an ally of Satan if not regenerated.

Questions for Understanding and Discussion

1. List the four parts of man.
2. List the elements that make up the soul.
3. List the elements that make up the heart.
4. How are the heart and the soul different?
5. Name some things that the heart does that the soul does not.
6. Describe the spirit.
7. What does it mean to say that the heart is "the gatekeeper to the spirit," and why is this the case?
8. What does it mean to "walk after the flesh?"
9. What does it mean to "walk after the Spirit?"

Unraveling a Mystery

What are we asking exactly when we pose the question, "How do I get the knowledge that is in my head into my heart?"

Are we saying that we believe things in our head, but we don't really believe them in our heart? Or are we possibly saying we know certain facts to be true, but we really don't experience them or walk in them?

Getting biblical information from your head into your heart is actually the process of transferring truth from thoughts in your mind into your *daily experience.*

We all know that we can read a book about skydiving and thereby have plenty of concepts in our minds about skydiving. These concepts will give us the thoughts that skydiving is exhilarating, a bit scary, perhaps something to be pursued, perhaps something to be avoided.

But it is an entirely different thing to actually jump out of an airplane.

The experience of skydiving, feeling the rush of excitement upon stepping out into the air, feeling the intense wind in your face, seeing the earth rising to meet you, and feeling the calm and quiet of floating under your open parachute, is nothing like concepts we may have in our minds about skydiving from only reading about it.

The same idea is true about knowing your spouse. If you had never met your spouse, you could read stories about him or her or even memorize a detailed biography about your mate, but it would never be an adequate substitute for actually experiencing your spouse as a real person. Could the written words or even the best biography replace one moment of embrace?

This same principle applies to the things of God. We all have plenty of concepts about God, but experiencing, tasting, and knowing Him is a completely different thing altogether.

We see from "The Anatomy of Man" chapter and in the verses of 1 Th. 5:23 and Mark 12:30 that man consists of spirit, soul, heart, and body. The soul is the experience you have in your mind, will, and emotions. The heart is your deeper experience (also your mind, will, and emotions). In addition, your heart is the place where you believe. This teaching is foundational and very important to understand as I discuss the next topic.

Many Christians simply do not experience true intimacy with God on a frequent basis, if ever. The reason for this lies with the fact that your heart and soul are separate "organs" from your spirit. So, as you attempt to move biblical truth from your thoughts into the depths of your daily experience – you restrict yourselves if you stay within the organs of your soul and heart rather than going to the source of spiritual experience; your spirit.

Only in the spirit is there found the true reality of spiritual things. Spiritual experience is only in the spirit while soulish experience is in the soul. Going to the spirit is like actually going skydiving. Going to the spirit is like actually encountering your spouse. You cannot fully experience things of the spirit by remaining in the realms of the soul or heart.

Even if you are fully aware of a biblical truth in your mind, even if you believe it completely in the depths of your heart, you will not experience the reality of it unless you find the spirit.

These ideas will become much clearer to you as we explore them more thoroughly throughout this chapter and in following chapters.

Psychology Offers No Permanent Solution

The word *psychology* comes from the Greek word *psyche* which is translated as the word *soul* in the New Testament. Psychology is literally the study of the soul or the study of the mind, will, and emotions.

The practice of psychology will often attempt to bridge the gap between the mind, will, and emotions. Through targeted dialogue, regression, and cognitive techniques, psychology attempts to heal the emotions and restore errant memories in order to develop better coping skills. One could surmise that the ultimate goal of psychology is healing and restoration by either replacing lies with truth or by working objective truth into the daily experience of the patient. In other words, psychology often attempts to get truth from the head and into the heart.

However, psychology leaves out the absolute, most important element in its overall philosophy. Psychology, by definition, only deals within the realm of the soul. It completely omits the spirit – the source of life and truth (for the Christian). The spirit is rarely understood and even more rarely discerned and separated from that which is soul; by non–Christians and Christians alike.

Reroute

The title of this book is actually a misnomer. You cannot go from "your head to your heart" and experience spiritual things. The correct path is from the head to the spirit, and then the result will be true experience of spiritual things in the heart and in the soul. In order to experience and live out the biblical truths you have in your head, you must leave the realm of your soul and heart and go to the spirit. The result will be true spiritual experience within the heart and the soul. We will discuss how to do this in detail in future chapters.

Remaining only within the realm of the soul and heart results in spiritual death, misery, striving, self-effort, hypocrisy, religion, emptiness, self-righteousness, obligation, rule-keeping, frustration, and spiritual dryness. Also, if you attempt to skip going to the spirit first, you can easily err by producing false, emotional "experiences" of God. These fabricated experiences will lead you astray (Col. 2:18), and these activities are currently rampant in the church. Christians also try to replicate and re-create past experiences with God because they so desperately want to feel and experience what they experienced last week or last year. If you attempt to re-create spiritual experience at an emotional level, the result will be shallow and false. Any manipulation of the emotions in order to experience the things of God will only be a short-lived production.

The large majority of Christians try to live the Christian life from the soul and heart without going to the spirit. They do this primarily because of self-reliance which we will discuss in future chapters. Many Christians actually do find their spirit at times, but they don't know why, how, or exactly what has taken place. When a Christian occasionally contacts his spirit, he or she often describes it as "an intimate encounter with God," or "God was pouring His Spirit out," or "I sensed His presence." It is also for this reason that many Christians experience periodic "breakthroughs" with God in certain areas, but they are only short-lived. We may touch the spirit during times of revelation, but we then err by gravitating back to the soul in order to live and walk out the very revelation we gained from the spirit. Living from the soul never works because there is "no good thing" within your flesh (Rom. 7:18). If we learn to walk and live from our spirit instead of our soul, we can actually live daily encountering His intimacy and sensing and knowing His presence.

Some soulish Christians are constantly longing for more, wanting a touch from God, hoping for a rare spiritual encounter of His presence, and thirsting for His intimacy. This beggarly position constantly pleads with God to "Please let us experience Your presence." Yet, there is never a moving over in the heart into a position of *trust* - the actual doorway to the spirit. We will also discuss this idea in great detail in future chapters.

There is no fault in wanting and hoping for more of God. To long for more of God is an excellent place to start. But to stay solely in the place of longing for more keeps you in your soul only. We must move on to actually *having* and experiencing God which involves faith. There is a huge difference between wanting and actually having - a difference in grasping for more and actually learning to enjoy the more. And a difference in spending most of the moments of your day hoping and praying for more rather than learning to bask in, receive, and to savor what has already been given to you.

Thus, the following cycle is common for many Christians:

1. Hope is kindled for intimacy and a connection with God. As a result, you long for, hope, and want more experience with God.
2. The true depth and frequency of this need largely goes unmet.
3. Because of the unmet need, you choose to fill yourself with other alternatives:
   a. Focusing outwardly by doing things for God in Christian service in order to feel pleasing to God and alleviate guilt. This produces false intimacy.
   b. Occupying yourself with biblical concepts and theology to substitute intimate relationship.

      c. Giving up to some degree on intimate experience of God and become resigned to living dry and empty while distracting yourself with the affairs of everyday life.
4. Due to a life crisis (either large or small), a breakthrough encounter of experiencing God becomes a new motivation to repeat this cycle.

This cycle is really the only thing that is available to you if you stay within your own mind, will and emotions only. A frequent practice of leaving the soul and going to the spirit is the only solution that can break the cycle.

As your heart becomes yielded and submitted to the spirit, the spirit then fills the heart along with the mind, will, and emotions. But the spirit cannot fill the mind, will, and emotions if you stay within the realm of your own mind, will, and emotions only. It is like desperately trying to fill a bucket with water by searching for water only within the dry bucket. The bucket must be lowered into the well of water below.

If you do not leave the soul and heart and actually go to the spirit, you are still operating only within yourself - and there is no life in yourself. None. Only the Spirit of God has life within Himself, and there are no shortcuts (Jn. 5:26). The only way we can experience the things of God is to go to God who is the Spirit. Staying within the realm of the soul and heart and not going to the spirit leaves us with only a self-improvement plan, self-effort, concept Christianity, and false emotions.

Questions for Understanding and Discussion

1. What are we really saying when we say "Move from the head to the heart"?
2. What is the most important step in moving from the head to the heart when desiring to experience spiritual truths?
3. Why is psychology lacking and inadequate?
4. Why is this book title a misnomer?
5. Briefly describe the cycle that results from not regularly accessing the spirit.

Paradox

As we delve into the many topics and dynamics that involve moving from the head and into the heart, we must take a brief aside in this chapter and discuss an issue of responsibility on the part of every believer.

We know that God is the author and the perfecter of faith (Heb. 12:2). He also began a good work in us and He will finish it (Phil 1:6). Yet at the very same time, there are plenty of scriptures that command us to do something ourselves in order to cooperate with the growth process. We are told to humble ourselves (James 4:10), to fight the fight of faith (1 Tim. 6:12), to give ourselves to believing God (John 14:1), and to walk after the Spirit (Rom. 8:4).

If faith begins and ends with God, and He is the one working within us in order to perfect us, yet we are told to humble ourselves, trust Him, and make good choices – then who is ultimately responsible for our growth?

Does God do it all for us? Yes, He absolutely does.

>*Phl 2:13 "…for it is God who is at work in you, both to will and to work for His good pleasure."*

Does God do it all for us? No, He absolutely does not.

>*Gal 5:16 "But I say, walk by the Spirit, and you will not carry out the desire of the flesh."*

Predisposed Theology

Very often our theology is affected by our predispositions. If you have a talent for being a good cook, you will probably like cooking. If you are good at fixing mechanical things and working with your hands, you will probably have an affinity towards those activities. I am not a good basketball player. I was cut from the basketball team in the 7th grade. I, therefore, despise the sport and see no purpose for its existence. We tend to agree with, support, and promote ideas and activities we are successful at.

If you have had little success in experiencing God in your heart or walking after the Spirit, then you will tend to develop and cling to theologies that negate or disregard such a practice. Many people find themselves frustrated concerning activities that involve unseen, spiritual experience. Perhaps you've tried to give yourself to things like walking after the Spirit, humbling yourself, opening your heart to God, or experiencing His love - but you've been mostly unsuccessful. It would not be uncommon for you to ignore the many verses in scripture that describe our personal involvement in these activities. You will tend to want to "make it okay" that you don't experience God very often by emphasizing some other aspect of Christianity. The problem with emphasizing things like Christian service, apologetics, or theology is that healthy expressions of these things only come from truly encountering and experiencing Jesus Christ (John 15:5).

Only to the degree that you've experienced the Spirit of God are you able to discern, recognize, and apply truth. It is the Spirit of God who illuminates truth to you (Eph. 1:17). Even if you have a thorough knowledge of the scripture, without adequate experience of the Spirit, your fleshly mind will incorrectly handle and misapply the word of truth.

For example, within many countries and cultures of the world there are phrases and language expressions that are specific to that certain country or culture. Many of these expressions and customs could not possibly be understood by someone unless that person has lived in that country and has experienced the culture firsthand. The same is true for the things of God. Unless you've spent time in the heavenly country of God's Spirit, you will misuse and misappropriate the scriptures to fit into your limited knowledge grid that is biased, influenced, and restricted to only what you have already been exposed to. Many of the great truths in scripture are not fully understood until you have tasted and experienced them.

Paradox Invites Error

Let's look at a real example. There are large numbers of Christians who focus heavily on the truth concerning the "sovereignty of God." Biblically, it is accurate to say that God is completely sovereign. God sees all things, knows all things, and He allows and causes many things to happen. He has known the end of time since the beginning of time. A common problem, however, with the "sovereignty of God only" paradigm is that it tends to ignore seemingly opposite truths. While God is all knowing (even knowing how we will choose before we choose, 1 Pet. 1:2), it is also a fact that we freely choose out of our own free will and He does not cause or force our choice. To say that God *causes* us to choose what we choose actually changes the definition of the word "choice." If this were the case, then multiple scriptures that instruct us to choose in some way would simply be a farce.

God is also not the author of sin (James 1:13). If we sin, God has not caused us to choose sin or rebellion.

So herein lies the root of a very common problem: When two seemingly opposing truths both remain true at the same time, it is referred to as a paradox. Without becoming too philosophical, consider the next two sentences: *The following sentence is true. The previous sentence is false.* Stop and think about those two sentences just for a minute. If the first sentence is true, then the second sentence is true. Yet, if the second sentence is true, it requires the first sentence to be false; thus, it negates the truth of second sentence! This kind of paradox involves circular reasoning. Another example of paradox is referred to as the paradox of value. The paradox of value states that *"the more valuable an item is, the more expensive it is to purchase."* Diamonds, gold, expensive cars, and fancy houses are all of high value and, therefore, expensive to purchase. However, water is more valuable and precious than any diamond or mansion. You must have water or you will die. Yet, water is very inexpensive to purchase. Therefore, it is true that items of great value are costly. It is also true that the priceless commodity of water is cheap.

The problem with understanding and applying truths that are paradoxical is that if you embrace only one to be true, *then you have to reject the other* – even though it may be true as well. If you embrace both as true, then you seemingly have a contradiction.

There is no contradiction in scripture, yet scripture is full of paradox. Some examples would be these: We are made strong through weakness. We receive through giving. We gain by losing. We live by dying. God finished all things on the cross, yet we do not see all things finished. We are in Christ and seated at the right hand of the Father, yet we are in a body and our feet are on the Earth. Jesus is fully a man and He is fully God. All Christians have been fully sanctified, yet all Christians are in the process of sanctification. Christians can sin, yet it is impossible for a Christian to sin[2] (1 Jn. 3:9, see note).

Paradoxes such as these have no problem existing within the spiritual realm, yet they break the rules of life here on earth and seemingly contradict themselves.

Abraham's Paradox

Consider the account of Abraham and Isaac (Gen. 22). God's promise to Abraham was that he would multiply Abraham's descendants as vast as the stars in heaven and as the sand on the seashore through Abraham's son Isaac – then God told Abraham to kill Isaac!

At this point, Abraham had a paradox in front of him. God promised that He would use Isaac to increase his descendants and to bless the nations. That was a true statement because it was a promise from God. God also told Abraham to sacrifice Isaac by killing Isaac. If Abraham killed Isaac, then how could the promise have been fulfilled? Abraham had to obey God which meant that he had to kill Isaac. Yet, it remained a fact that God would bless Abraham through Isaac. Both were true at the same time. In order to embrace both realities, Abraham had to come to a completely *irrational* conclusion: He concluded that God would have to raise the dead (Heb. 11:17-19). Abraham embraced both truths at the same time which forced him to *trust* God.

When we attempt to understand one side of a spiritual truth and embrace it, our limited human logic causes us to reject the other side of the paradox. The spiritual realm exists outside of time. It is not governed by the rules and laws that govern Earth. When we try to understand a spiritual paradox given the limited cognitive abilities of our brain, and then apply and enforce the laws that exist on Earth, we can only arrive at the following logic: "Both cannot be true at the same time. If one side of the argument is true, the other side must be false."

The *rejection* of spiritual paradox leads to spiritual error.

> *Mat 11:25 "At that time Jesus said, "I praise You, Father, Lord of heaven and earth, that You have hidden these things from the wise and intelligent and have revealed them to infants."*

Abraham had to trust God in order to hold to both truths, but the wise and intelligent prefer not to trust. They would much rather understand.

Let's revisit our opening discussion concerning the sovereignty of God. To embrace only the truth that God has to do everything in you and that you have no responsibility for your growth will lead to passivity in your heart. Why bother to humble yourself, to yield yourself, and give your heart to trusting God if He is the only one that can cause these things to happen in you?

God commands you to believe the truth. He doesn't make you believe. He has given you a "measure of faith," yet it is your place to cooperate with the faith He has already given you. Both dynamics are true. You must employ your faith on a daily basis in order to actively believe God in your heart. He has given you His Spirit. Yet it is up to you to yield to His Spirit. It is your responsibility to humble yourself, not God's responsibility.[1]

> *1Ti 6:12 "Fight the good fight of faith; take hold of the eternal life to which you were called..."*

> *Jud 1:20-21 "But you, beloved, building yourselves up on your most holy faith, praying in the Holy Spirit, keep yourselves in the love of God..."*

> *Jhn 14:1 "Do not let your heart be troubled; believe in God, believe also in Me."*

> *Act 8:37 "And Philip said, "If you believe with all your heart, you may." And he answered and said, "I believe that Jesus Christ is the Son of God."*

> *Pro 4:23 "Watch over your heart with all diligence, for from it flow the springs of life."*

> *Pro 3:5 "Trust in the LORD with all your heart and do not lean on your own understanding."*

It is true that God has given us a measure of faith. He began the faith that is in us and He is perfecting it. But we can choose to not cooperate. We can harden our hearts and give ourselves to not cooperating with what He is doing in us (Heb. 3:12).

"Choice" is an important word. There are many paths you can choose for the course of your life. We know that Jesus Christ is the only true path. But there are many paths of emphasis you can choose even within Christianity. As a

Christian, what should you be about doing? How should you spend your time? What is the correct focus of a Christian to be?

Many times, the rejection of certain biblical paradoxes affects how and what we choose on a daily basis. It is extremely common today for Christians to have an incorrect focus and to wind up on a path that misses the point of what Christ taught.

Common errant pursuits within Christianity include:

1. Multiple forms of legalism in order to feel right and pleasing to God.
2. An emphasis on doing things for God rather than knowing Him.
3. A focus on growing through head knowledge rather than experiential relationship.
4. A pursuit of spiritual experiences and spiritual manifestations which are separate from experiencing and knowing the person of Jesus Christ and Him alone. For example: pursuing signs and wonders, spiritual gifts, healings, demonstrations and miracles. These are merely manifestations of God and can easily distract us from pursuing God Himself.
5. There is a new emphasis in Christianity on not being religious in the traditional sense but missing the person of Jesus Christ in the process. This reactionary focus is common in some emergent church models and post-modern philosophy.

Simple and undistracted devotion to Christ is rarely satisfying enough for the majority of Christians (2 Cor. 11:3). When we are not encountering the Lord Himself in a real and life-giving way on a daily basis, it quickly leads to playing ball in the wrong ball park. Christians are constantly tempted to want other things within the Christian experience besides Jesus Christ alone. These temptations are often hard to resist because they are so much easier than learning to live from the Spirit. The easy way is seldom the right way. Your heart needs a daily, uncomplicated focus. Your heart needs a path that leads to life.

Notes:

[1](Ex 10:3 Lev 16:29, Lev 16:31, Lev 23:27, Lev 23:29, Lev 23:32, Num. 29:7, Num. 30:13, 2Ch 7:14, 2Ch 33:23, 2Ch 36:12, Ezra 8:21, Pro 6:3, Pro 16:19, Isa 58:5, Isa 66:2, Zeph. 2:3, Jam 4:10, 1Pe 3:8, 1Pe 5:5, 1Pe 5:6).

[2] 1 John 3:9 *"...he cannot sin."* This verse is referring to our spirit that cannot sin. Your spirit is born of God, and it has the seed of God within it, therefore, it cannot sin. Hebrews 12:23 also uses this same language by saying *"spirits of righteous men made perfect."* However, in viewing the person as a whole (body, soul, and spirit), we most certainly can sin (1 Jhn 1:10). We sin if we walk after the flesh and not the Spirit, and we are accountable for choosing to do so. Yet, it is not our spirit who is sinning if we sin (Rom. 7:17, 20).

Questions for Understanding and Discussion

1. What is a paradox?
2. Why is it important to be able to embrace paradox in scripture?
3. Do you have any role in your spiritual growth?

The Common Error

Romans 10:9-10 "That if you confess with your mouth Jesus as Lord, and **believe in your heart** *that God raised Him from the dead, you will be saved; for* **with the heart a person believes**, *resulting in righteousness, and with the mouth he confesses, resulting in salvation."*

From this verse we see that it is with your heart that you believe. You cannot believe with your head. Your head is where you exercise your intellect, logic, reason, memory, rationale, and cognitive thought. It is the part of your thinking that you would use to solve a math problem, calculate a percentage, or recite facts and truths that you have memorized.

Your head can only agree that a certain fact is true. When you come to the conclusion that certain information is true in your head, you arrive at what is called "a decision." Your head can only conclude or decide that something is true and then retain that true concept. Other ways of stating this would be to say that "You have agreed with a certain fact" or "You have decided that certain information is correct."

Agreeing that a concept is true is not the same thing as faith in the heart. To believe with the heart is something entirely different than only deciding that a concept is true. To decide that something is true in your head is only the first step before you go on to actually believe it in the deeper place of the heart.

When you hear a new piece of information, you first decide whether or not it is true in your mind. If you agree that the statement is a true statement, you mentally make a decision that the statement is true. If you don't agree that the statement is true, then you mentally decide that the statement is false. Another way to describe this is using the word "acceptance." You either accept something as being true or not true. However, once you accept or decide that a statement is a true statement, you must take an additional step to actually "believe" with your heart.

With the head we decide. With the heart we believe.

Decisions Become Our Camouflage

Because you have made decisions in your head that certain things are true, your thoughts cause you to deceive yourself into thinking that those concepts are being believed in your heart. You may often think that you believe something because you have made a decision that it is a true statement, but if you are like the rest of us, you have fooled yourself in many areas.

We fool ourselves with biblical facts. We think we believe them, but often we really do not. Many times we only agree that the concept is true with our heads. We've "decided" that it is true, but we do not believe it with our hearts.

One of the biggest hindrances to our growth as Christians is having a focus on the decisions of truth we have made in our head instead of looking to see what our real heart belief is in the moment. We use the facts in our head as *evidence* of belief, but they are not. What is really in our heart is the true evidence of belief. When we look at the statements of fact in our head for evidence of belief, and we see that we mentally agree with it, it allows for the false beliefs in the heart to remain undealt with. Therefore, the "beliefs" we have in our head don't match up with our entire inner experience. When there is a discrepancy between what we agree with in our heads and what we are truly believing in our hearts, it leads to hypocrisy and many outward choices that betray our mental assertions.

How Can We Know What Is Really In Our Hearts?

> *Jer. 17:9-10 "The heart is deceitful above all things, and desperately wicked: who can know it? I the Lord search the heart, I try the reins, even to give every man according to his ways, and according to the fruit of his doings."*

Because we cannot take the concepts we have in our heads as evidence of heart belief, we must look elsewhere to determine what is really in our hearts. How can you possibly know if the correct concepts in your head are being believed with your heart? It is the Lord who reveals to us what is in our hearts. He does this in a number of ways, and we will explore some of them in depth.

Certainly one way to tell what is really being believed in your heart is by observing your choosing patterns. If you consistently make choices that betray what you supposedly believe, then it is evidence that your healthy mental assertions are being trumped by a deeper heart belief.

Another indication of what your heart is really believing is to observe "your current experience." The feelings you are having and the emotions you are experiencing are strong indicators of true, current heart beliefs.

A third way to know what is really in your heart is by God showing you by direct revelation. Many times God will directly reveal to you what you really believe in your heart. Often when He shows you this, He will also give you the power to change and repent as well.

Scripture is a fourth way that God will show you what you truly believe in your heart. The scripture is God's objective truth that cuts through the lies we often have in our own soul.

And lastly, another excellent way God reveals your true heart beliefs is through the body of Christ. As you walk closely with others in a tightly knit community of people, then your heart is revealed and exposed concerning what you believe in many ways. It is extremely rare for Christians in western cultures to live as closely knit with each other and with consistent vulnerability as God intends. Many Christians believe they are experiencing community life together because they are a member of a local church or even because they belong to a small group. However, attending a meeting once or twice a week is one thing (even if people are vulnerable during the meeting), but sharing life together is entirely different. There is something about daily living together in which the seemingly small and routine situations of life expose our hearts and provide opportunity for love, forgiveness, and change.

The Exposing Nature of Cost

As just mentioned, our choosing patterns reveal what our heart is currently believing. When we have a choice in front of us that will "cost us something," it often exposes our true heart belief. Your response to the cost of a choice frequently reveals what is really in your heart.

For example, you may tell yourself that you will pay off your credit card bill next month. You may be fully convinced that you will do so. However, when you actually sit down to write the check to the credit card company, you suddenly realize that you really need the money for something else. So, you end up writing a check for only the minimum monthly payment again. This reveals that you had a decision in your mind that you should pay off the credit card, but you had no conviction of heart to pay off the card. It was easy to say, "I will pay off the card" when the cost was not in front of you. But when the actual cost was staring you in the face, it revealed that your true heart belief was that the money would be better spent on other things.

You may have a "belief" that it is good to help people in need. But when an actual person is in front of you, and he is really in desperate need of your time, financial help, or your labor, you will suddenly see what you truly believe in your heart concerning the matter. You may have only had a decision in your head that said, "It is good to help people in need." Decisions in the head are worth something, but not very much.

You can decide with your head that stray animals should have a good home. But when a wet and smelly dog is on your doorstep, the sudden cost to you reveals what you really believe in your heart. Your true heart belief may be that your personal convenience is currently more important to you than taking in a stray dog into your home.

Perhaps you can think of certain standards or principles in life that you agree with or have decided are true, but if you really think about it, have those particular ideas really required anything of you? If those ideas actually showed up on your front door and began to cost you something, would you still agree with them?

Let's say for just a minute that you agree with the fact that you should eat more vegetables than junk food. Yet, you observe that your practice is to eat more junk food than vegetables. You may mentally agree with the fact that vegetables are better for you than junk food. You may have even decided that since vegetables are better for you, then you will eat more vegetables. However, *it costs nothing* for you to only agree with this fact in your mind. When it comes down to you actually choosing to eat vegetables over junk food on a regular basis, you have to believe that statement with your heart, not just in your head because it will now cost you something. To make a change in your regular eating habits will affect your life and your daily experience.

Even while you may totally agree with the fact in your head that you should eat vegetables instead of junk food, the real belief in your heart may possibly be something like this: "junk food tastes better, is more comforting, and is more satisfying to me than eating vegetables." If this is really what is in your heart, then your true belief is that there is more benefit to you in the moment from eating junk food than from eating vegetables. This is your true heart belief, whether you know it or not, while the entire time you have an opposite statement abiding in your head that you have decided is true - that you should eat vegetables instead of junk food. When you *continually focus on the decision* you've made in your head, *it keeps you from dealing* with what is really in your heart. Instead, observe your choices to explore what is really in your heart on various issues.

We have thousands of factual truths in our heads that we agree with and have decided are true, yet they cost us nothing. When a statement begins to actually cost you something, then your heart suddenly gets involved, not just your head. Only your heart will *feel* the pain of the cost.

The things of God are no different. You may mentally agree with many truths in scripture, but there are conflicting things that are really in your heart that you do not see. As long as the fact in your head doesn't require something of you or cost you something, you are perfectly fine to say you "believe it." But as soon as a biblical truth starts to actually cost you something, you will realize that you never really believed it in the first place. *You will ultimately choose, experience, and live out what is filling your heart.* For the most part, people wind up choosing and living the kind of life that they ultimately want deep in their hearts.

> *Luk 12:34 "For where your treasure is, there your heart will be also."*

This is a strange phenomenon. Many people have patterns of difficulty, trauma, loss, and turmoil in their lives, but many times it is because they actually prefer, want, or expect this kind of life deep in their hearts.

I knew a man once whose philosophy was, "Life is hard and full of pain." So guess what? His life was continually hard and full of pain. We make many small and unnoticeable choices over and over again out of the things that fill our hearts. Our choices then mushroom into lifestyles and patterns that match what we truly believe.

Moving Over and Paying the Price

Every day you make simple choices such as what clothes you will wear, how fast you will drive, what kind of work you will do that day, how you will speak to people, what you will have for lunch, and what time you will go to bed. Most of your everyday choices are simple intellectual and rational choices. But there is another type of choice you can make.

When the Bible says to "believe with your heart," it is saying that you must make a certain type of *inner* choice - a heart choice.

> *Acts 8:37 "And Philip said, "If you believe with all your heart, you may." And he answered and said, "I believe that Jesus Christ is the Son of God."*

A heart choice of believing is a choice of both "yielding" and "trusting." *Yielding* is giving up or letting go of what you currently believe. *Trusting* is grasping or holding onto something as your source. If you are trusting in your weekly paycheck to sustain you, then you are grasping or holding on to that check in your heart. In order to change your heart and instead believe God as your sustainer, then you must *yield* or let go of your current trust in the paycheck and then *trust* or cling to God as your source. In order to believe God, therefore, we must first yield what we currently believe and then hold on to and depend completely on Jesus Christ.

When we agree with a fact in our head, to actually believe it with our heart requires that we "move over" inside of ourselves. The moving over process includes both yielding and trusting in the heart. Have you ever heard initially some new piece of news, and you didn't really believe it at first? But later, you moved over inside yourself to actually believe it? When you moved over on the inside is when you actually trusted in that truth in your heart. Perhaps someone told you some really bad news about a loved one, and at first you refused to believe it. But later, you moved over to believe that it was true. If the news was particularly difficult or painful, then you probably experienced powerful emotions at the moment you moved over. Emotions are often evidence of heart belief.

To believe something new that you currently don't believe, you must surrender the current belief that is in your heart (yielding) and exchange it for the new belief that you will cling to (trusting). This is why it costs you to believe. When you yield, you pay a price. *The cost for you to believe will always be the price you have to pay to give up your current belief.*

Many times you really don't know what you truly believe in your heart. Or, at times you may be unwilling to pay the price of giving up your current belief. You probably almost always have good intentions, but to replace your current beliefs is sometimes too high of a price to pay.

I've met non-Christians who will emphatically say they believe that "Jesus is Lord." They will agree this is a fact, and they will not deny it. But when the conversation begins to shift to "Jesus being *their* Lord," they suddenly start to back pedal. When people's so called "beliefs" begin to actually require something of them, it exposes what they really believe.

Many times we hold heart beliefs that keep us walking after the flesh and keep us with a hard heart toward God or other people. Many times these heart beliefs are very ferociously protected. Often unconsciously, we run the other way when we smell even the slightest whiff in the air that would require us to yield our heart beliefs. Here are a few common fleshly heart beliefs that I've observed either in myself or others that have been heavily guarded and costly for people to let go of:

> God is unjust. God is unloving. Men are abusive. Men are selfish. Fathers leave you. Women are not trustworthy. Mothers are dishonest. I am flawed, unlovable and undesirable.

Well-fortified heart beliefs such as these serve to protect us from ever being wounded again. We must risk our safety by yielding and giving up the lies we believe in order to replace those lies with truth in the heart.

Your Belief System is Actually a Decision Matrix

We often hear of the term "belief system." Your belief system is often used to describe the set of beliefs you hold, how those beliefs fit together, and why you believe the things you do. Many times our system of beliefs does not consist of beliefs at all, but rather it is a group of decisions in our heads.

In our heads, we have decided that many things are true. But we may not have necessarily believed all of those things in our hearts. Christianity is not a belief system - it is a condition. To be a Christian means that the Spirit of the Lord Jesus Christ Himself is living inside of you. To be a Christian means that "who you were" has died and that "who you are" is washed and made totally clean. This is not a decision in the Christian's head, but rather a state of condition the Christian is in.

Christianity is about walking in a daily intimate encounter with the true and living God. Simply holding to a list of ideas in your head about what the Bible says and doesn't say isn't worth a lot. Many people's "Christianity" is only a hobby. It's a hobby of ideas, a hobby of strong opinions, and a preoccupation with biblical philosophies.

A Common "Belief"

Perhaps you agree in your mind with the fact that God loves you with unconditional love. Let's say that you agree with that fact 100%. You might even tell other people that it is absolutely true that God loves us with unconditional love. You could probably preach a sermon on it.

However, you may feel closer to God and more aware of His love for you when you are making good choices. If you make bad choices in your life or if you blatantly commit a sin, then you may not experience His love very much at all. You may not experience His love or His nearness until your guilt has subsided from your bad choices.

In addition, you may at times feel like God is somewhat distant from you or is not quite as pleased with you when you observe negative circumstances in your life. If your car breaks down, if you get sick, or if you are suffering in some way, you may feel as though God were punishing you a little, has taken His hand of mercy off of you, or that He is displeased with you on some level.

On the other hand, you may feel as though the Lord is more pleased with you and that He is delighted in you when you have evidence that things are going well for you in your life. When you are healthy and you feel good, when you have good relationships, when you have plenty of money, when you have no problems, when the world is smiling at you and the sun is shining on you – you may feel as though God were smiling at you and shining on you, too. But you might feel that He smiles at you a little less during times of suffering, pain, and sin. Are you really sure you believe His love is unconditional?

Your feelings change depending on your circumstances. When things are great and you feel good about yourself, you feel like God feels good about you too. When things are bad and you feel badly about yourself, you project those feelings onto God toward you.

We are all aware of the roller-coaster ride of our feelings. Because our feelings change and our feelings come and go, our Christian culture has again decided that "We can't trust our feelings." This is a true statement in one sense, but it is totally and completely false in another.

Feelings. Nothing More Than Feelings?

It is certainly true that you cannot trust your feelings to dictate the facts. Your various feelings do not change God's truth.

However, your feelings and what you are currently experiencing are indicators. The feelings you are having, whether they are feelings of joy, depression, hate, or peace, are the reality of "your current experience." Your current experience is an indication of where you are in your heart and what you are really believing in any given moment. I am not addressing the facts you have in your head. I know you probably have most of those straight. What I am addressing is the belief you currently have in your heart in any given moment. Don't confuse the two.

We see from "The Anatomy of Man" chapter that the nature of the heart is such that it is possible to believe something in one moment, but not in the next moment. This is not usually true with concepts in our heads. Once we have decided in our heads that something is true, we tend to maintain that decision (although it is possible to "change our minds" or learn a new truth). However, unlike the head, the experience of the heart and soul can change frequently.

"Your experience" is a moment by moment thing. To illustrate this, I will use the example of a marriage relationship. It may be true that you "love" your spouse. You may love them very deeply. But "love" is not always filling your heart and your soul toward them. At times you may experience anger, extreme frustration, or even hatred toward your spouse, the same persons that you "love." Yes, you love your spouse. But you are not always actively engaged in "loving" them. Sometimes you are selfish. Sometimes you are not putting them first. Sometimes they have deeply offended you and you are angry or hurt. Love is not always what is filling your heart. If you have ever experienced rage toward your spouse, love is not what is in your heart toward them in those moments - even though you have a decision in your head "that you love your spouse."

You cannot have two things in your heart at once (Matt. 6:24, 1 Jn. 4:20). You cannot have love filling your heart for your spouse and selfishness, anger, or unforgiveness at the same time. This is why a decision or a commitment to someone is never good enough. If you say to your spouse, "I'm committed to you, I've married you, I love you," but you continually act hatefully and selfishly toward them, you will destroy the relationship. Love is much more than a commitment and an outward choice. Love is something of the heart.

To abide in love is to continue to yield our hearts to see the value and the treasure that a person is. "To love" your spouse is to renew your heart continually toward them, many times a day. We are to live "falling in love" with our spouse often and frequently. If we do this in our hearts, it will manifest itself with wonderful outward choices. But it must start in the heart for it to be real.

Heart Belief Can Change Often

Because what fills the heart can change, and because we also believe with our hearts, we can move in and out of true heart belief, even though the concepts in our heads remain consistent.

You may have the concept straight in your head that God loves you unconditionally, and you may believe it in your heart at times, but when certain things happen in life that are a trigger for you to feel as though God were distant, putting up with you, or punishing you, they are indicators that what *was* in your heart is now *no longer* in your heart. Your heart belief has now changed, which is revealed by your current emotions and your current inner experience – all the while you may have the concept of God's unconditional love very clear in your mind.

Just like we should change what is in our hearts when we have hate or selfishness toward our spouses, we should change what is in our hearts toward the Lord when our experience is indicating that we are not believing the truth on a heart level.

> Jer 11:20 "But, O Lord of hosts, who judges righteously, Who tries the feelings and the heart…"

We said earlier that your inner experience is an indicator of where you are in your heart and what you are really believing in any given moment.

It is a settled fact that God actually lives in you and that you are in Him. This became a fact when you first believed on Jesus Christ and became a Christian. He is always in you. He has joined Himself to your human spirit. You are one with Christ. When you became a Christian, you also were placed in Christ. You are seated with Him in the heavenly places (Eph 2:6). These are the facts. And it is good that you have decided that these facts are true in your head. Facts are true whether you feel them or not. Facts are true whether you are experiencing them or not. *But mentally holding on to facts is not the same as faith.*

Sometimes you experience and feel as though the facts are true and sometimes you do not. We often say in Christian circles that "feelings come and go." But again, this kind of statement does not recognize the importance of experience as being an indicator of heart belief. Yes, feelings do come and go. And usually it is because the faith in your heart has come and gone.

When you are having the experience that Christ is in you, your heart experience is agreeing with the established fact that you agree with in your head. However, when you are not experiencing the fact that Christ is in you, your lack of experience of that truth indicates that you are not believing the truth in your heart in those moments - although your current feelings and experience do not change the truth that Christ is in you. Although this fact is true whether you believe it or not, as far as you are concerned, this true concept is only in your head when your experience is not lining up. It is not in your heart.

Resting on your concepts is not enough. You can say to your spouse, "I am committed to you, for you are my spouse," but if love is not filling your heart or you are acting selfishly toward them, then your "commitment" is doing very little for your spouse in that moment.

We do the same with God. Because we have a commitment to Him, we allow unbelief or apathy to be in our hearts, and we think nothing of it. We rest on our prior good decisions and our prior commitments. Past decisions do not excuse this present moment, just like in any committed relationship. If love is not what is in your heart, you must change what is in your heart. You must change your heart so that your experience will line up with what you agree with is the truth. Your spouse will appreciate this, too.

You agree with the fact that God will never leave you or forsake you, yet you feel distant from Him at times. You agree with the statement that God loves you unconditionally, yet you are more aware of His love at certain times than you are at other times.

Circumstances Expose Our Heart

It is an important first step to acknowledge that you may only *sometimes* believe with your heart all of the various facts that are in your head. When certain circumstances in your life arise, or your situation suddenly changes, it usually doesn't change your heart beliefs - it only *exposes* what you have really been believing all along in your heart. Hypocrisy occurs when our unbelieving hearts are revealed to us by God, and we then allow the heart belief to remain without repentance. Mental assertions that coexist with conflicting heart beliefs yield hypocritical practices.

Let's go back to our example of the unconditional love of God. You agree with the concept that God loves you unconditionally. In other words, there are no conditions or set of circumstances that could possibly change His love for you. Yet, if you sin or make a lot of really bad choices, you feel like you are in the dog house.

When your circumstances change and then your experience changes in your heart, they often reveal your true heart belief – that you were only trusting in your circumstances the whole time. God is purifying us and correcting our hearts through the trials of life and through the changing of circumstances. He is gently exposing our hearts to us over and over again in order to lead us to a deeper level of repentance.

Emotions Are Not the Goal

I want to make it very clear that *feeling certain emotions is never the goal.* If feeling a certain way or having certain emotions becomes your goal, you will never be in the truth. You will only be double minded, unstable, and you will be tossed like the waves of the ocean (Jas 1:6-8).

The point is that *emotions are often indicators* of what you are really believing in your heart in any given moment. They are a by-product of heart belief. If your emotions are not lining up with the truth, your heart is not believing the truth. The truth is currently only in your head. Remember, it is "with the heart that man believes" (Rom 10:10). When the heart is truly believing God and trusting Him, the heart is filled with the experience of God which then overflows into the soul as well. Therefore, when your emotions are betraying your head knowledge, you are not believing the truth in that particular moment. When your heart believes what your head knows is true, your emotions will follow.

A High Price to Pay

We said earlier that to truly believe from our hearts, it will cost us something. Heart belief requires something of us – every time. This is the reason why many times the truth is only in our heads and not in our hearts. We are often unwilling to pay the price of heart belief. It will cost us something to "move over" in our hearts to really believe God. It will require something of us. It is often painful and it is often fearful to our flesh to believe God.

Again, looking at our ongoing example of God's unconditional love - let's say that you have correctly decided in your mind that God loves you unconditionally. Next, you sin horribly which causes you to experience being in the doghouse of guilt. This is an indicator that you are possibly unwilling to pay the price of what it will cost you to believe God's love during these moments of guilt and shame.

What does it require of you to believe His unconditional love for you if you are drowning in the ocean of guilt?[3]

It requires humility.

Humility can be a very painful price to pay. It requires tremendous humility and it requires becoming small to believe and receive the unconditional love of God for us in the middle of our sinfulness. Humility requires us to "let God love on us" when we actually deserve His rejection. In fact, it costs us everything to allow God to lavish His love on us when we know deep in our hearts that we deserve nothing less than total rejection and utter shame.

We are disgusted with ourselves and we hate ourselves at times. We feel like we just can't get it together - ever. We want to throw ourselves away. During this time, God is pulling you toward Him and longing for you to be near Him *even more* (Lk. 15:20, Rom. 6:1). He wants to comfort you. Sin has beaten you up and you are in need of extra tenderness and love from your Father. Will you humble yourself completely and break down in order to receive? Or, will you hold on to your current heart belief that you must reap what you truly deserve – rejection and separation? You must move over in your heart, pay the price, and yield your wrong belief (that feels so right) in order to trust and cling to your loving Father. It is risky and painful.

Mental agreement is cheap. Heart belief will always have to pay a price.

Many times when agnostics or atheists come face to face with death, they start praying and calling out to God. Sometimes they are in pain (Pain and suffering gets to our hearts and causes us to abandon the shallow and empty concepts in our heads. Suffering is one of the quickest ways to the heart – discussed in a later chapter). When actually faced with the certainty of death, suffering, and hell, many times the unbelieving person will abandon the convenience of their unbelief and choose to humble themselves. When there is "hell to pay," suddenly the luxury of unbelief is too costly.

I related the following story in the previous book, *Mysteries of the Kingdom*, but I will revisit it here from a different perspective.

There once was a man who fastened a tight rope across a water fall. As a crowd gathered around, he asked them a question: "How many of you believe that I can walk across the tightrope and not fall?" About half of the crowd raised their hands. The man quickly scaled the ladder leading up to the tightrope. He then carefully placed his feet on to the rope and proceeded to walk across the chasm, and crashing water below, with minimal effort. He made his way back to the crowd, climbed down the ladder, and bowed his head as the crowd applauded.

Next, the man rolled out a wheelbarrow. He asked the crowd, "How many of you believe that I can walk across the tight rope while pushing this wheelbarrow?"

After witnessing the skill of the man as he walked the tight rope the first time, well over half the crowd now raised their hands. A particular lady in the front row of the crowd had her hand enthusiastically raised. The man pointed to her and said, "Ma'am, since you believe that I can do this, please now…take your seat inside the wheelbarrow while I push it across the waterfall."

Everyone believed the man could push the wheelbarrow across the tightrope while it was cheap to believe it. But when their so called belief actually required something of them, it was exposed for what it was – only mental agreement. What was really in their hearts was some degree of doubt.

If a member of the crowd really believed fully in their heart that the man could push the wheelbarrow across the tightrope and in no way would they possibly fall, they could get in the wheelbarrow and actually enjoy the ride with no thought of fear.

We Are Commanded To Believe, Not Decide

Why is it so common for new converts to Christianity to fall away in their faith shortly after their so called conversion? We have preached that the unsaved should make "decisions for Christ." This phrase is found nowhere in scripture. On the contrary, the Bible tells us "to believe" on the Lord Jesus Christ. Only in heart belief is there power to weather the storms of life that require difficult choices. Only heart belief produces the experience of what we say we believe.

To simply make a decision that something is true does not necessarily change your heart belief. A decision that you have made in the past gives you no power for this present moment. Because you've decided that "something is true" at one time in your life leaves you with no current inner strength to live it out in the heat of the battle. This is why so many new converts don't finish their race. This is why so many Christians live powerless lives of defeat with a lukewarm Christianity. They have certainly made a decision for Christ. They have certainly decided that many things are true about God, but they have no conviction of heart. Many do not find a daily, trusting faith that is of the heart and that encounters the living God. You must learn to believe in your heart, right now, and in this present moment in order for your concepts to do you any good.

A decision is very similar to "a commitment." A commitment is simply a decision with longevity attached. Jesus Christ never asked anyone to make a commitment to Him. He only commands that we believe Him.[2] Believing God from the heart versus making a commitment are vastly different things. One has power - the other only has intentions. However good intentions may be, they are still only intentions. Without the power of heart belief, intentions are nothing. I can intend to jump out of an airplane and skydive, but until I do, I am still in the airplane.

We are having altar calls all over the world inviting people to make commitments to Christ. A commitment to Christ or a decision to follow Christ is usually a shallow choice in the soul. It is often a decision in people's flesh to follow God which is impossible to accomplish for the long term. The flesh cannot follow God. All it can do is get sick of a particular lifestyle, turn over a new leaf, have good intentions, and try harder to live better. The flesh can only make a commitment, then recommit, then recommit again. We don't need to rededicate our lives to Christ. *We need to believe the gospel.*

When someone believes Jesus Christ from the heart, it costs them everything. It cost them everything else they believe. When someone believes Jesus Christ from the heart, it is accompanied with a humble and broken contrition. Only then can true transformation take place in the inner man. At the point of total abandoned heart belief, the Holy Spirit joins to the human spirit, and a person is changed forever.

We have settled for a passionless "robot Christianity." We go through the motions of religious duty and say we are loving God. Love is passionate. Love is intense. Love is wild. Love is abandoned. Love is fervent. Love is from the heart (1 Pet. 1:22).

We have justified a Christianity of mundane ritual. We justify our dryness and call it "devotion." God is not a duty or an obligation. Our wonderful, beautiful, and magnificent Savior is not a "should" or a "have to." He is not a weekly church service or a commitment. He is not a life style of rules to make you feel righteous about yourself in order to alleviate your guilt.

God commands you to believe Him. He warns strongly against unbelief. Depression, selfishness, anger, hate, and all the other deeds of the flesh are not some kind of spiritual merry-go-round that we get on by accident and then have to wait for it to magically let us off. We can choose to have the joy of the Lord in any moment. We choose everything that fills our hearts whether it is good or bad. We choose to believe and we choose not to believe.

Belief Versus Faith

As discussed earlier, it is important not to confuse concepts in the head with having true faith. The action of believing is accomplished within the heart, not the head. While a concept may be held as true in the head, the heart may not always agree.

The word *believe* comes from the Greek word *pisteuo* in the New Testament. The ending of the Greek word *pisteuo* designates it as being a verb. Therefore, *pisteuo* is an action word. Another way to describe the word *pisteuo* in English would be to say that it is "the action of believing." The word *pisteuo* occurs 248 times in the New Testament. Here we see an example of *pisteuo*, the action word:

> *Mar 1:15 "and saying, "The time is fulfilled, and the kingdom of God is at hand; repent and believe in the gospel."*

The word "believe" is found in many popular verses in the New Testament. Some verses communicate the idea that "to believe" is not only a one-time action but an ongoing action that we are to do.

When we examine the word faith in scripture, we see a slightly different meaning. The word faith is translated from the Greek word *pistis*. *Pistis* is actually a noun, not a verb like *pisteuo* (believe). Because *faith* is a noun, *faith* is something that you possess or have.

In light of the word *believe* which is an action word, another way to describe the word *faith* would be to use the word *belief*. *Believe* is something you do, while *belief* is where you wind up. The action of believing moves you from one place to another. Faith or belief is the position your heart is in as a result of believing.

When you are in a believing posture in your heart, you wind up "seeing" what is not seen – you, therefore, have belief, or we could say that you are "of faith." When your heart is in a believing posture, you know certain things to be true because you are experiencing and tasting the reality of those things in the moment. When your heart is believing, you can look in your heart to see what your heart is currently seeing as opposed to searching the files in your brain to see what you agree with or to see what decisions you have made in the past regarding certain issues. When you have faith, you have internal evidence in the moment. Therefore, faith is substance. Thus, we read from Hebrews 11:1 in the King James translation:

"Now faith is the substance of things hoped for, the evidence of things not seen."

Faith becomes a commodity or substance in the heart that is usable. However, faith only comes from the action of yielding your heart to God and trusting in Him. The trusting action in the heart is the action of believing. The result of believing is that you wind up with "belief." Very often the word *belief* is confused with concepts in the mind without the reality of faith in the heart.

It should be noted that *believe (pisteuo)* and *faith (pistis)* both come from the same root word *(peitho)* meaning "to be persuaded, to yield to, to trust."

We will discuss in detail the actual action of believing and trusting in the heart in future chapters. But we have touched on it to some degree in this chapter. There is an action of letting go in the heart. The letting go action we are doing is releasing our current belief and replacing it with another. The moving over and yielding we must do in our hearts in order to believe is necessary because we are currently grasping something else that is not the object of our desired belief. There is always something being believed in the heart. Many times deep-rooted beliefs and positions of the heart are masked by our more noble concepts that are in the head. It will always cost us to trust in our hearts because we have to release our current beliefs in order to grasp new ones.

A Process For Believing

Your heart is very similar to a cup that has capacity (refer to the illustration of the heart in "Anatomy of Man"). When you have an incorrect belief in your heart, it is like a cup with sand filling it. When you try to believe the truth without removing the sand that is in the cup, the new truth only becomes a shallow belief on top. It will not remain or have much depth as long as the incorrect belief is still there underneath - what you really believe remains at the core. You must remove the incorrect belief first in order to make room for the new belief to take hold in your cup with any degree of depth. Depending on the subject matter, some correct beliefs cannot exist at all within the heart while there remains a conflicting belief hidden below.

You must see clearly what your real and current belief truly is before you can remove it. This is part of the repentance process.

Here is a list of sample questions that may help you find your current heart beliefs in the particular area of God's love:

- When God looks at you right now in this very moment, how do you feel God feels about you?
- When you focus on God right now, do you feel that He desires intimacy with you?
- As you look at God in this very moment, what is His attitude towards you?
- Is God waiting for you to get it together in some way?
- Should you be doing something more in order for Him to be totally delighted in you?
- As God looks at you, is He impatiently tapping His foot with His arms folded?
- Is God tolerating you while He slowly shakes His head?
- Is He delighted in who you are and completely pleased with who you are in every way?
- Does God see you as having the same righteousness as Jesus His Son?
- Does God desire you as much as He does His Son Jesus?

Questions like these often reveal your true heart beliefs. Depending on the area or subject matter, different questions may need to be asked.

Even when people hear the truth and they actually realize that the current beliefs in their hearts do not agree with the truth, they erroneously try to place the correct belief on top of the incorrect belief. Instead, the incorrect belief must be forsaken and rooted out of the heart. You must empty the cup of the sand first, then the correct belief will not only be received much easier, but it will also tend to remain intact.

The removal of incorrect beliefs from the heart is not always an easy process. They are usually there for a reason. Occasionally, people can let go and forsake incorrect beliefs in the heart just by seeing them. But more often, the incorrect beliefs are tied to "emotional proof" that these lies are really the truth. Past experiences erroneously prove to us that our incorrect beliefs are facts.

For example, it is extremely common for most people to be raised in a household where acceptance and love were tied to performance. As a child, if you performed well, then you probably received some sort of affirmation. If you performed poorly, then you either didn't receive affirmation or you received disapproval, which your soul received as rejection. This teaches and trains the heart that love is conditional. Being raised in an environment where this particular cause and effect is repeated many times provides for a stimulus that "proves" to people that the lies they believe are actually the truth. It is especially difficult to remove lies when they were developed during the young formative years and then further reinforced throughout life outside the home.

To remove ingrained lies that are tied to emotional proof, it will ultimately require the work of the Spirit in your heart. A simple step in the direction of humility always cooperates with the work of the Spirit in your heart. While being in touch with the incorrect heart belief that you currently have, you should then realize that "You do not know" what the truth actually is. This helps to begin the removal process of the lie. Lies that are believed in the heart are fortified with pride, arrogance and positions of confidence. When you see a certain truth in God's word, yet your life experience and your damaged emotions tell you something contrary, you must remain in an arrogant and confident posture in order to maintain your position.

Let's practice the humble "I don't know" attitude. Consider the question "How do you feel God feels about you in this very moment?" Perhaps you believe that God is not totally pleased with you on some level. You may feel as if God only tolerates you, that He is not really pleased with who you are, or that He is waiting for you to get it together on some level. Your emotions and your life experience convince you that this is true. However, if you know your Bible, you are aware that this would be contrary to the core message of the gospel. We know from scripture that God's love is unconditional and that as a Christian, you have the very righteousness of Jesus Christ (2 Cor. 5:21, Rom. 3:21). The new person that you are in Christ has been cleansed, joined with God's Spirit, made acceptable, and is pleasing to God. This condition is wholly true - apart from what you do or do not do. If you encounter resistance to letting go of the lie that you are not pleasing to God on some level, then your first step is to find the humble position of "I don't really know what the truth is."

Compare your heart to a tightly clenched fist that is gripping your lie. Going to the humble position of not being so sure about your perception of the truth would be compared to relaxing your hand. The lie is still there in your hand, but now your heart is open, fingers relaxed, ready to replace the lie with the truth. Instead of trying to make the leap from lies directly to truth, you must go *from lies, to humility, then to truth*. Humbling yourself under the reality that your emotions are damaged and that your perceptions disagree with God's word will bring you to the fact that you really can't trust yourself. Are you sure that all of your emotions and feelings are actually lining up with the truth of God's word? Hint: the correct answer is "No."

Many times, asking someone to change an ingrained heart belief that is a lie is like asking someone to change their definition of the color blue to the color red. We look to our emotions as an extremely reliable source of evidence for what the truth is. If we "feel" that God is disappointed in us, then we believe that is the truth. However, we can never look to our emotions as the determining factor for what reality is. Emotions are only indicators of what you are believing.

Question: "Do you see that color on the wall?"
Response: "Yes, I see it."
Question: "What color is it?"
Response: "Blue."
Question: "That is not blue, it is red."
Response: "It most certainly is blue; I know what blue looks like."
Question: "I want you to trust me. Will you realize that your definition of the color blue has been incorrect all these years? You've been lied to. In fact, you do not know what blue actually looks like. You've been calling it the wrong thing."

This may seem like a silly example, but when incorrect heart beliefs are present, this dialogue is not far from being accurate. The beliefs we hold in our hearts shape how we view the world. They completely affect our experience in every way. The person who holds incorrect heart beliefs must pry their fingers open and release their strong position before the actual truth can be fully received.

Once you have humbled yourself and have released your strong position of "knowing," you are now a candidate for receiving the truth implanted in your heart. Releasing your lies will cost you something. It may cost you dearly. But after you have humbled yourself and have faced that "You really don't know for sure" - now it is much easier to simply accept and hold on to the truth of God's word.

"I don't know" is a good humble phrase that can help with any area of hardheartedness. Various deceptions, judgments on other people, unforgiveness from past hurts, and erroneous beliefs can all begin the process of dislodging from the heart as they are released from being grasped with the tight grip of arrogance.

In this chapter we have explored the difference between decisions we agree with in our head, as opposed to believing with the heart. In the next few chapters, we will see that to truly experience the reality of spiritual things in the heart, we must cling to more than just truth in the heart - we must trust in what is spirit.

Notes:
[1] Free Grace Bible Chapel, Ch 12, "Let Faith Be Faith".
[2] Mat 9:28, Mat 18:6, Mat 21:32, Mar 1:15, Mar 5:36, Lk 8:12, Lk 8:50, Lk 24:25, Jn 1:7, Jn 1:12, Jn 1:50, Jn 3:12, Jn 3:18, Jn 4:48, Jn 5:38, Jn 5:46, Jhn 5:47, Jn 6:29, Jn 8:46, Jn 14:1, Act 8:37, Rom 10:9,10, Pro 4:23, Pro 23:26, Pro 7:25, Pro 3:5 – not a complete list.
[3] Guilt concerning sin is not the same as Godly sorrow. Godly sorrow produces repentance and contrition which is a good thing (2 Cor. 7:10). Guilt has with it rejection and separation from God as though you were being punished or turned away from by God. Godly sorrow has with it the awareness

of God pulling you even closer to Him because of your sin, not pushing you away. The Father's heart is to have compassion and draw closer to you if you sin as in the Father's response to the lost son in the parable of the Prodigal Son.

Questions for Understanding and Discussion

1. What is the difference in a decision and in belief?
2. What part of you believes and what part decides?
3. What is a belief system often confused with?
4. Describe some ways in which God will show you what is in your heart.
5. What is the difference in yielding and trusting?
6. Why does it cost you something to believe?
7. What does it mean to "move over?"
8. What role do feelings and emotions have?
9. What is the difference between belief and faith?
10. Describe a process for believing truth when lies exist.

Separating Soul and Spirit

> *Heb. 4:12 "For the word of God is living and active and sharper than any two-edged sword, and piercing as far as the **division of soul and spirit**, of both joints and marrow, and able to judge the thoughts and intentions of the heart."*

Learning to recognize the difference between what is soul and what is spirit is another important beginning topic. Perhaps you've never thought about the difference. If you don't learn to separate the two, you will mistakenly live from your soul instead of your spirit. You will think that your own thoughts, feelings, and desires are worthy of some degree of trust and attention, rather than separating them from the Spirit and then submitting them to the Spirit.

Before we continue, we must clarify our terminology a little further. We see from "The Anatomy of Man" chapter that both the soul and the heart are the places of experience. The heart is a deeper place of experience and the soul is a shallower place of experience. The experience that originates deep in the heart normally and almost always fills the experience in the soul as well. Another distinction between the heart and the soul is that the heart is the place where we choose to trust and believe. Whatever is being believed in the heart, is experienced in the heart, which then also fills the experience in the soul. The experience of the heart and the soul can either be of the flesh or of the Spirit of God.

When the Spirit (big "S" or little "s", a distinction does not need to be made because your human spirit is one with God's Spirit) is filling the experience in the heart and soul, we simply say, "We are according the Spirit" or "walking after the Spirit" (Rom 8). We do not say, "The Spirit is now filling my heart and soul" – although this would be technically correct. Conversely, if the flesh is filling the heart and soul, then we simply say, "We are according to the flesh" or "walking after the flesh". We don't say, "The flesh is filling my heart and soul".

The terminology of "after," "according to," and "walking after" concerning the flesh and the spirit are all synonymous in scripture. To state it very clearly, when you are "after the Spirit," you experience emotions that are of the Spirit of God which are joy, peace, and the emotions that accompany love. Also, when you are "after the Spirit," you will have thoughts that are prompted by and initiated by the Spirit of God. Thirdly, when you are after the Spirit your will and your choices will reflect those that correspond with the Spirit of God. When you are after or according to the Spirit, your personal desires and wants will remain submitted to Christ. As a result, you will find your desires and your wants aligning with and being in tune with the will of your heavenly Father.

If you are after the flesh - your thoughts, emotions and wants will be of yourself (independent of God). The most obvious expressions of the flesh are all and every form of selfishness, lust, pride, and fear. There are thousands of variations of these and many are subtle. Many patterns of the flesh continually morph themselves and change their appearance in order to remain intact and to seem more palatable. Christian varieties of flesh can be more subversive and socially acceptable, but are still not of God. Self-righteousness, spiritual pride, legalism, religious ceremony, spiritual duty and obligation, doctrinal arrogance, fleshly loyalties, fleshly religious zeal, and inward passivity are just some of the more common characteristics of the Christian version of the flesh.

When we are not walking after the Spirit, we may also say that "we are soulish," "following after the soul," or "in our soul." The reason for this terminology is that, by default, if we are not walking after the Spirit, then what is being experienced in our soul is the flesh. When discussing the idea of separating what is soul from what is spirit, we should understand that it is the soul which is expressing the flesh *by default*- unless we are yielded to the spirit.

Therefore, the following terms can be used interchangeably: "following after your soul", "being in your soul", "soulish", "being after the flesh", "walking after the flesh", or "according to the flesh".

When unchecked, the natural tendency is for the soul to express the flesh. We must, therefore, separate soul from spirit.

As an important side note, we should realize that the soul is not always communicated in a negative light in scripture. It is the place of experience and is neutral in and of itself (although it must always be expressing either flesh or Spirit). [1] There are situations in scripture which reflect the fact that the Spirit can be filling the soul experience.

Again, we examine Hebrews 4:12:

> *"For the word of God is living and active and sharper than any two-edged sword, and piercing as far as the **division of soul and spirit**, of both joints and marrow, and able to judge the thoughts and intentions of the heart."*

It is not only biblically sound to say that we should separate soul from spirit, but it is also biblical to say that we should separate "the flesh" from "the spirit.":

> Gal 5:16 *"But I say, walk by the Spirit, and you will not carry out the desire of the flesh."*

> Gal 5:17 *"For the flesh sets its desire against the Spirit, and the Spirit against the flesh; for these are in opposition to one another..."*

To reiterate, we are saying the same thing when we say "We must separate soul from spirit" or when we say "We must separate flesh from spirit." This is true because, by default, the common way of living life is for the flesh to continually express itself through the soul. If the Spirit is expressing through the soul, then we will specifically say "We are walking after the Spirit."

To help clarify: A Christian's human spirit has become one with God's Spirit. When the heart submits to and trusts in the Spirit (or spirit, little "s" - it does not matter), the Spirit then fills the heart and the soul, resulting in an experience of intimacy with God in the mind, will, and emotions. This is when the Christian is according to the Spirit.

It is not common nor does it happen naturally for the Spirit of God to fill the soul in either the Christian or the non-Christian. The unregenerate and unsaved are continually living after the flesh - they have no other choice because they do not have the Spirit of God within them. At the same time, it is more common for the Christian to walk after the flesh than to walk after the Spirit. Understandably, this is a difficult statement for many to hear.

The Christian will often mask the flesh through a lifestyle of legalisms by suppressing the flesh rather than to truly walk after the Spirit. The fruit of the Spirit is clear. Rarely found is the true joy of the Spirit which is an intense and fervent love for God, and the peace of heaven that passes all understanding filling most Christians on a moment by moment basis. Yet Christians know how they should act, and Christians know that they should display the fruit of the Spirit, especially around other Christians. Therefore, Christians try to *act* sweet, kind, patient, and loving. Acting in this manner is not godly. The true fruit of the Spirit… is only of "the Spirit". Only as the Spirit of God is truly filling both heart and soul is the unmistakable and potent manifestations of the Spirit experienced and manifested.

To walk after the Spirit is a miracle. It is absolutely impossible for any human to replicate or imitate the kindness, patience, and love of God. However, it is extremely common for Christians to try to have a kind attitude while still in their flesh. They attempt to show love while still in their flesh. They try to replicate the peace of the Spirit when it is only their natural flesh behaving nicely. Even an unbeliever can be nice, show patience, donate his labor and time, and act peacefully. Scores of "good" Christians have trained their flesh to behave properly in most situations and to live a lifestyle of wholesome goodness. There are currently millions of Buddhists and Hindus who have thoroughly trained their flesh to behave nicely, exhibit extreme patience, and to continually engage in acts of kindness and service - who would utterly put to shame the vast majority of Christians in these areas.

The nice and sweet flesh of the Christian must die. The smiles and cheerfulness during the Christian meeting which is followed by gossip and contempt on the ride home from the meeting is a nauseating lie. This week alone there will be countless Christian service projects performed and endless hours of labor donated in the name of "good Christian deeds." Most of these will be done because "It's what Christians should do." They are all a worthless distraction from what is most important.

> Jas 4:9 *"Be miserable and mourn and weep; let your laughter be turned into mourning and your joy to gloom."*

Instead of acting polite and pleasant with nice smiles and sympathetic words, it would be much better to become miserable and weep so that you might find God.

On the surface, the Christian who is not according to the Spirit but is suppressing the flesh can look very similar to the Christian who is actually walking after the Spirit. However, the flesh can only be suppressed and hidden from view for so long. If you are around a Christian who is not according the Spirit for very long, the self-focused nature of their flesh will become manifest. This is a stark contrast to the humility, tenderness, and sweetness of Christ that gives life.

An Aside on Legalism

When we introduce the word *legalism*, certain ideas may come to mind. Perhaps the idea of legalism causes you to think of having to abide by strict codes of behavior. Legalism is much deeper and pervasive than only this common definition.

The term *legalist* or *legalism* is all and any form of *self-effort* that is an attempt to make one's self pleasing to God (whatever form it may take). The flesh adores legalism because the flesh always loves its own efforts. By conforming its efforts to some code of behavior, the flesh seeks to establish its own righteousness apart from God. The outward deeds that we do may or may not be pleasing to Him, yet *who we are* as Christians is always pleasing to Him. It is imperative that you separate *what you do* outwardly from *who you are* inwardly. Paul explains this in his Rom. 7 discourse:

> Rom. 7:20 *"But if I am doing the very thing I do not want, I am no longer the one doing it, but sin which dwells in me."*

We must identify with the spirit that we are, not the flesh that we can walk after. In other words, if you think that who you are is your flesh, then you will set yourself up for legalism. The real person that makes up who you are is only your righteous and cleansed spirit. The flesh is only your body acting independently of God. *The flesh is not you.* Much more discussion on this occurs in the chapter, "The False Self."

Even if you think that you are not a legalist, your flesh is certainly legalistic. All flesh is legalistic in some way because the flesh always seeks some way to appear good. However, because the flesh can never actually be good or godly, it vacillates between trying to keep the law or in rebelling against the law.

The flesh has its definition of what is good, moral, and right. It then attempts to attain to this standard that it has established for itself. When the flesh finally gets tired of trying to keep these standards (which it always does), it busts free from the constraint of its own laws and breaks them. Religious flesh is dishonest about its rebellion. It therefore ignores and hides its own rule-breaking, and then it justifies itself with spiritual reasoning. Even non-Christians who seem to be complete rebels and seem to be without any law are rebels for a reason. In order to be a rebel, you have to rebel against something. All rebels feel under some sort of law. This is why they constantly act out in rebellion against it. Most rebels are rebelling against the law of God that they know innately. The gospel sets us free from these patterns of death in our flesh.

The blood of Christ cleanses us utterly and completely. If you have put your trust in the blood of Jesus to cleanse you, you have all of the righteousness of God (2 Cr. 5:21). This is the constant condition that your spirit is in, and it does not change.

Gold is a naturally occurring element. It cannot be created by man, and its composition cannot be altered. You can place a bar of gold in any circumstance, and it will not cease to be gold. You can put it in water, lower its temperature, heat it up, shape it, cut it, or melt it - but it still remains gold. In the same way, once your human spirit has been cleansed by the blood of Christ, it is by nature *clean*. You can do good deeds, bad deeds, walk after your spirit, or walk after your flesh, yet no matter what you do, you will not be able to add to or take away from the righteousness that your spirit is (Although it is true that you can do outward deeds that are not pleasing to God, or you can do outward deeds that are pleasing to God). None of the deeds that you do can change the righteous condition of your spirit. *Who you are and what you do are two separate things.* Sometimes you do deeds that come out of the nature of your spirit (walking after the spirit), and sometimes you do not (walking after the flesh). Your spirit is the core essence of who you are. Legalism is an attempt to exert some kind of self-effort in order to appear or become more righteous and pleasing to God. A person who is walking in legalism is not understanding or believing the complete message of the gospel.

Your flesh comes up with its own ideas of what is righteous and what is unrighteous, based on input received through your physical senses and the way your mind interprets that input. The input for a particular person depends on how and when that person was raised, the culture of which he is a part of, his spiritual training (or lack of it), and the social norms and opinions of the group of people he spends time with. A man who lived in America during the 1920's would think it was not proper, even shameful to appear in public without wearing a hat. It is not acceptable to kill cows in India. Christians who lived in the New England colonies in early America were forbidden to participate in religious music because it produced a "dreamy" state. Many Christians consider some or all of the following practices to be wrong (the teachings of the particular Christian group determine the variety and extremity): various dietary restrictions, the consumption of alcohol, watching television or movies, various manners of dress, facial hair styles, women working or not, spanking or not spanking children, going to a doctor or not, the use of medicine, playing cards).

The list is endless. A gang member or mafia member may truly feel that by killing someone he is doing the right thing (based on the norms and values that are a part of his world view). The average German soldier in the 1940's believed that it was morally good and his patriotic, righteous duty to kill Jews.

All varieties of flesh agree with being good or moral in some way and then try to achieve living to that standard, whatever it may be. Other varieties of flesh live in rebellion against its own standards of what is moral, just, and right. If you are after the flesh, you only have one of two choices in any given moment: Try to keep whatever law you are under (whether God's or your own) or rebel against it. But all flesh, whether it is trying to attain to the standard it agrees with or rebel against the standard – it has its own interpretations of what right and wrong actually is.

The truth is that only Jesus Christ is righteousness. He is the actual definition of righteousness. Only having His Spirit inside us makes us righteous. And only walking after the Spirit is living out that righteousness. The Old Testament law is good and it is right. However, trying to live under it is impossible (Acts 15:10). This explains the purpose of God giving us the law. Its purpose was to expose the sinfulness of the flesh (Gal. 3:19, Gal 3:23-25). Some believe that God gave the law and expected man to live up to it. To the contrary, God gave the law to show man that he could not possibly live up to it, and there desperately need a Savior. In other words, God did not give the law as a means for man to become righteous, but as a means to show man that he is not righteous. Only when we walk after the Spirit are we outwardly fulfilling the law, because again, Jesus Christ fulfilled and continually fulfills the law (Rom. 13:8-10). When we are walking after the Spirit, Jesus Christ is living His life through us (the only man who has ever been able to keep the law of God).

Rom. 8:4 "...so that the requirement of the Law might be fulfilled in us, who do not walk according to the flesh but according to the Spirit."

The dangers of legalism were frequently addressed by Jesus and the apostle Paul because it destroys any possibility of intimacy with God. It hardens the heart and it increases our self-focus like a cancer. Yet, it has the appearance of Godliness which allows it to propagate and spread rampantly into the hearts of men.

The Default of Walking After the Flesh

Rarely does the Christian live from his spirit on a continual basis. The Spirit of Christ within the believer is more likely to be encountered (but not always) during the activities of church meetings, scripture reading, and prayer. However, when these kinds of activities cease, quite often the Spirit ceases to fill the experience of the believer (1 Cor. 3:3).

You may disagree that your default or natural tendency is to experience and express the flesh because of the fact that you are a Christian. However, it requires an active and frequent submission in the inner person to walk after the Spirit. It is a thorough and complete submission that not many find on a daily basis. The frequency of submission to actually live life walking after the Spirit is much more frequent than you may realize. Just because you have concepts that say "You are submitted to God in your life" does not mean that you are fully submitted to God in your heart throughout the many moments of your day.

The fruit of the Spirit experienced in our hearts is truly unmistakable. If most readers will be honest, it is the exception rather than the norm to experience an intimate connection and encounter with the true and living Spirit of God. However, every believer has truly encountered the Lord in a real way at least once, if not many times. Being aware of God or thinking thoughts about Him is much different than a complete submission in total trust and in real time.

I must remind you again that there is no condemnation for those who are in Christ. As a born again Christian, you are cleansed and justified, made wholly righteous before God even during times of walking after the flesh. You are justified by the blood of Christ through faith. You are not justified by walking after the Spirit. You are saved because of what Christ did, not because of what you do or how well you choose or by how much you humble yourself. However, to walk during the moments of your day with the clear and potent life of God filling your heart with His inexpressible joy, His peace that passes all understanding, and His love that deeply satisfies your thirsting heart is the purpose of your salvation. It is what God is calling you to - and nothing less. This is the only way to move from the head and into the heart. Knowing God is entirely different than "knowing about" God. Receiving His love is entirely different than knowing "that" He loves you.

Flesh or Spirit Expresses Through the Soul

An analogy may be helpful in understanding the issue of the flesh or the Spirit expressing through the soul. Pretend for a moment that we have two flashlights. Flashlight number one is bright and clear with a strong beam of light. This flashlight represents the Spirit. Flashlight number two is dull with a yellowish and sickly beam of light. This flashlight represents the flesh. We can choose to shine either flashlight through a piece of colored glass. The colored glass represents the soul. As we shine either flashlight through the glass, the result will be that both the characteristics of the flashlight and the characteristics of the colored glass will be manifest. The manifestation of either light shining through the colored glass is experienced within ourselves and expressed to others.

Flashlight number two will shine its weak and yellowish beam through the colored glass of our individual soul and express its fleshly characteristics through the individual vessel that we are. Our individual way of thinking, manner of feeling, methods in which we process information, styles of choosing, and individual personality will all come forth - but the energy shining through will be coming from the flesh of flashlight number two. Selfishness, independence from God, fear, pride, and lust will all be the driving forces; but will be processed and experienced based on your individual personality characteristics.

If we shine the flashlight of the Spirit of God through the colored glass of our soul, the Spirit will come forth through the same piece of glass but with a strong and powerful beam of light, love, joy, peace, and God's wisdom. The energy of God's Spirit will shine through you and express Himself through the individuality of your personality characteristics.

When the Spirit is filling your soul (walking after the Spirit), you will have a very different set of thoughts and emotions than when the flesh is filling your soul. However, some characteristics of your individual personality will remain whether you are after the flesh or after the Spirit. This is because the colored piece of glass up to this point has remained exactly the same. The difference is only the source of what is filling you and coming through you (life or death, i.e. Spirit or flesh).

For example, one personality type (the color of the glass lens) may be one of fervor and abandon. The personality of this person is that he lives with spontaneity and passion. If this kind of person is walking after the flesh, he will tend to live recklessly, lawlessly, and impulsively. However, if this kind of person is filled with the Spirit of God, he will experience freedom, he will love with intensity, and he will exhibit a contagious passion for God.

An entirely different person may have a personality of more calm, introspection, and reflection. If he is after the Spirit, he will display a depth and stillness that is unmoved by the changing affairs of everyday life. However, if this same person were to walk after his flesh, he may exhibit depression and an unhealthy introspection that is detached from those around him.

No matter the type of colored glass prism you are, the sweetness of Christ and the fruit of the Spirit will be evident in you and through you only as you are walking after the Spirit.

When we rely only on our own set of emotions, thoughts and desires *apart from* the Spirit of God, we are following after our own soul (flesh). When we are following after our own soul apart from God's Spirit, the flashlight of the flesh is shining through us.

We must learn to separate our flesh's feelings, thoughts, and will from that of the Spirit.

Not Separating Spirit and Soul is Dangerous

It is extremely common within the church for there to be many so-called spiritual revelations and insights that do not originate from the Spirit of God but are soulish in nature.

> *Col. 2:18-19 "Let no one keep defrauding you of your prize by delighting in self-abasement and the worship of the angels, taking his stand on visions he has seen, inflated*

without cause by his fleshly mind, and not holding fast to the head, from whom the entire body, being supplied and held together by the joints and ligaments, grows with a growth which is from God."

Just because we feel something or see something that seems spiritual doesn't mean at all that it is coming from the Spirit of God. Many supposed "words from the Lord" that people claim to hear are only fleshly and emotional words. Many so-called spiritual leadings and spiritual impressions actually come from the flesh. The flesh is quite able to generate beautiful imagery, deep heartfelt feelings, seemingly spiritual pictures, and biblical analogies.

A perplexing observation in this area is that many people never seem to learn a lesson from their repeated fleshly insights. When false "words from God," visions, prophecies and heartfelt impressions don't come to pass or bear fruit, the words that were spoken are easily swept under the rug by those who spoke them and also by those who heard them spoken. When someone delivers a prophetic word from God and it does not come to pass, it must be addressed and dealt with. The purpose is never to reject or attack the person who committed an error, but the intent should be to teach the one who erred. It is okay to make a mistake. It is perfectly fine to step out in faith and to "miss it." But it is not perfectly fine to allow for a willful continuation of soulish spiritualism. An unbridled so-called "hearing from God" and a seeing of visions that is really only coming from the flesh is damaging. We must learn to discern what is soul and what is spirit, both within ourselves and without. We must continually learn to sift and discern what is truly the voice of God and what are only voices in our head. If words from God are not from God, they only produce disappointment and disillusionment. Many have become shipwrecked in their faith from this practice in various groups.

True spiritual thoughts from God "taste" a certain way and bring with them a very specific type of peace. Emotions that are generated from the Spirit have a specific quality to them that are different from the emotions that come from our own soul apart from God. They are also always supported in scripture.

A submitted will that is empowered by the Spirit is much different than the will that is generated from our own self-effort. Emotions, thoughts, and desires of the will that are not spiritual are empty. They often have a characteristic of anxiety or stress about them, and self is always a component. Even fleshly emotions that feel like freedom or various experiences of life's pleasantries are tinted and colored with fleshly discontent. Only emotions and thoughts that are fruit from the Spirit of God are full of life and have the element of Holy Spirit joy. Spiritual experiences come from a different realm that is not of Earth. Your body of flesh is made from the dust of the ground. It is earthy. Its essence is made up of carbon molecules. The emotions and thoughts the flesh generates are severely limited and shallow. However, what is Spirit is Spirit. It is from a different place altogether that actually transcends the experience of the flesh.

John 3:6 "That which is born of the flesh is flesh, and that which is born of the Spirit is spirit."

Our emotions play a very powerful role in our lives. Emotions often drive much of our decision making, and we often don't even realize it. You very often do what you feel like doing and you think what you feel like thinking. The kind of job you have, the people you spend time with, when, what, and how much you eat, and the kind of house you live in are just a few of the many decisions you probably make that are emotion driven. The current car that you now drive was more than likely purchased from an emotional decision on some level. The feel, the look, the styling, the color, the year model, how your friends might think of you because you own it, or how you would feel about yourself while driving the particular model you chose are all emotional decisions. Yet, you probably used logic to justify your emotionally driven decision. At some point, perhaps the gas mileage and the quality of the car became part of the "smart decision" to purchase the certain car you have. Although you generated certain logical justifications to allow yourself to buy the car, the driving force behind your decisions was "how it made you feel." Emotions are usually first, and rational thought is a very quick second in order to support what we truly feel.

Often, our opinions on doctrine and theology are based upon what we feel. If we feel unworthy in God's eyes, then we will choose a theology to match. If we feel like God is not pleased with us on some level, then we will believe that we must do more for God - while finding scriptures that seem to support those feelings.

Emotions are not bad if they are filled with the Spirit. In the same way, concepts we have about the truth are not negative either if they are being prompted by the Spirit. Jesus was a man who felt very deep emotions (Isa. 53:3, Jn. 11:35, Mk. 6:34, Mt. 21:12), yet His emotions never dictated his decisions (Lk. 22:42).

Only as we are trained in discernment of what is soul (flesh) and spirit can we begin to separate and recognize the two. This comes from being exposed to the pure word of God, from revelation in the inner man, and from very large blocks of time soaking in God's presence.

Spirit is a Different Substance than Soul
In learning to separate spirit from soul (Heb. 12), we often confuse our own feelings and thoughts with being spirit, but often they are not the same.

When God speaks to us, whether through scripture, direct revelation, or through someone else, it divides what is of soul and what is of spirit. When God speaks to us, the word of God judges the thoughts and intentions of our heart. We may feel like our motives are pure, but God's word will teach us if our motives are pure or not. God's word clarifies what is of His Spirit and what is coming from ourselves or the flesh. Let's consider an example of how God's word can separate soul from spirit.

At times we may feel love for another person. But often our love is a self-serving love and is therefore being generated by the flesh. Our natural human love is really only deep sentiment. Sometimes our love is delivered only in order to make the other person *feel loved*. Also, we may care and we may feel very deeply at times, but our love apart from God's love is always conditional. Only when our love for others originates from the spirit is it not fleshly or "soulish." But how can we possibly tell the difference?

When we read and hear the true nature of godly love in scriptures such as this one: *"Whoever forces you to go one mile, go with him two." (Mat 5:41)*, it will often cut completely through so much of our fleshly varieties of love. The separation of our natural human love and love that comes from the Spirit of God is one example of the word of God separating what is soul from what is spirit.

We can easily go two miles with someone if we feel like we want to. Perhaps if the other person has been nice to us or if we will get some kind of personal payoff we will not mind at all going two miles for someone else. Our friends would even give us a nice pat on the back for being so loving as to go two miles with some person in need. But if someone were to literally "force you" to walk with them for a mile, you might not be so nice. Let's think about this.

Imagine for just a moment that you were being kidnapped. Your kidnapper then tied your hands behind your back. Next, you were made to walk a mile down the street while the hot sun beat down on your head and a loaded gun was held at your back. If you were really "forced" to go a mile, would you really want to go two miles? To rise above your natural feelings of hatred and injustice and to actually have a heart of love for your persecutor is completely impossible for you to do in your flesh and in your own strength. Jesus further exposes our fleshly and soulish love in verse 46:

> Matt. 5:46 *"For if you love those who love you, what reward do you have? Do not even the tax collectors do the same?"*

You have an opportunity to love from the Spirit quite often. You are "forced" and victimized all of the time. Harsh words from the ones you love wound your heart. Years of kindness and the laying down of your life for certain people can instantly be dismissed and forgotten by those very same people over even the smallest of misunderstandings. Your heart of generosity and good intentions has, in some situations, been mistakenly misinterpreted as actually being selfish and unloving. If you are old enough to read this book, you have already experienced plenty of betrayal, abuse, abandonment, and hurt. Yet, it is in these very situations of being persecuted that your love for others is truly measured. God's word separates what is soulish and fleshly love from love that is from His Spirit.

Luk 6:35 "But love your enemies, and do good, and lend, expecting nothing in return; and your reward will be great, and you will be sons of the Most High; for He Himself is kind to ungrateful and evil men."

Rom 5:8 "But God demonstrates His own love toward us, in that while we were yet sinners, Christ died for us."

Soulish love is not tested until pain, persecution, disappointment, hurt feelings, and rejection are present. The love that comes from God that is of the Spirit and that is not soulish love sees past the personal hurt and pain that is being delivered to you. Even in the very moment that Jesus was being tortured and beaten, He loved by saying, *"Father forgive them for they know not what they do."* Even when you were evil and ungrateful toward God, your Father was kind to you. Even when you were in the condition of being a hater of God, Christ died for you. If someone is in the very act of hating you, rejecting you, and mistreating you – God's kind of love has a moving compassion toward the one persecuting you.

The person who is treating you this way is hurting too. Your kidnappers need compassion. Christ loved you this way while you hated and rejected Him. This is the only kind of love that could have reached you before you were saved. This is the exact kind of love that saved you from your sins and eternity in hell.

In separating soul from spirit, it is critical to read God's word and to know it. It provides an excellent knowledge base on many levels for the Spirit to use and prompt us with. Knowing the scriptures not only teaches us specific truths and realities, but it also teaches us to know the flavor and the culture of spiritual things. When you have a solid knowledge base of scripture, your constant thoughts that are only natural, earthly, and fleshly are more easily checked by the Spirit within you.

Spirit is Deeper than Soul

Although the word of God is pivotal in separating soul from spirit, we must also learn to look in the proper place within ourselves to see the spirit and not the soul.

Most of the time, we are extremely aware of ourselves – we are aware of what we think, feel, and want. So much so, that it is our normal way of being. To become according to the Spirit, we must move out of this extreme self-awareness and into Christ awareness. In other words, Jesus Christ becomes our focus and then our life. This is not just a concept or an idea. We are to become primarily conscious of the person of Jesus Christ, and in real-time. He becomes our moment by moment experience.

The body is the shallowest of the parts that makeup man. The soul is deeper than the body, the heart deeper than the soul, and the spirit is deeper than the heart. When we encounter people in daily life, we can easily discern their outward and visible signs such as body language, their looks, whether they are smiling or frowning, etc.

It is more difficult to discern a person's soul. Do they feel sad or happy? Are they depressed, nervous, or anxious? Although the emotions of people are more hidden from view than the body, we can sometimes tell if their soul is experiencing happiness, anger, sadness, depression or joy. However, to discern the spirit of men requires spiritual discernment. As a born-again Christian, your spirit will often let you know when you come in contact with another Christian. Even though there are no outward signs or particular words spoken about Christ, your spirit will often bear witness that you are with a spiritual brother or sister.

All people are either of one spirit or another. All fruit and manifestations of men's hearts have spirit behind it (whether good or bad). All words spoken, things written, music, and teaching - all expressions that come from men have discernible spirit behind those expressions.

Lk. 9:54, 55 "When His disciples James and John saw this, they said, "Lord, do You want us to command fire to come down from heaven and consume them?" But He turned and rebuked them, and said, "You do not know what kind of spirit you are of."

Where to Look

You must always look deeper than only your thoughts or your feelings to find your spirit. Jesus tells us that our spirit is in our "innermost being." The King James translates innermost being as "belly." The Greek word for *belly* literally means "the body cavity."

Jhn 7:38-39 "He who believes in Me, as the Scripture said, 'From his innermost being will flow rivers of living water.'" But this He spoke of the Spirit, whom those who believed in Him were to receive; for the Spirit was not yet given, because Jesus was not yet glorified."

The Spirit of God is not located in your head. He lives deep within your innermost parts. You can actually find, look at, and focus on the Spirit of God inside of you. Once you are looking at Him, you can then transition from "looking at" to "looking to" the Spirit of God inside of you. "Looking to" is moving into a trusting posture.

2 Cr.13:5 "…Or do you not recognize this about yourselves, that Jesus Christ is in you…"

Gal. 2:20 "I have been crucified with Christ; and it is no longer I who live, but Christ lives in me; and the life which I now live in the flesh I live by faith in the Son of God, who loved me and gave Himself up for me."

> *Col. 1:27 "to whom God willed to make known what is the riches of the glory of this mystery among the Gentiles, which is Christ in you, the hope of glory."*
>
> *1Jn. 4:4 "You are from God, little children, and have overcome them; because greater is He who is in you than he who is in the world."*

To find your spirit is to find Jesus Christ inside of you. To recognize and become aware of Jesus Christ inside you is the same thing as recognizing and becoming aware of your spirit apart from your soul. This is an important step in separating soul from spirit. What "you" may be feeling and thinking is often different from what the Lord's mind and emotions are within you.

2 Cr. 13:5 tells you that as a born again Christian, you can recognize the Spirit of Christ within you. If you are not used to doing this, it may take you a little time. When most people first begin to look for Christ in them, they only see themselves. They see their own emotions, will, and thoughts. This is because they have lived their entire lives from their soul and have not learned to surrender and submit the heart to the Spirit which begins to make the distinction clear between soul and spirit. When the soul is allowed to remain dominant for very long, it suppresses and quenches the spirit which makes Him more difficult to discern.

Do not be discouraged. If you are a Christian, then the Spirit of Christ is in you. As you give yourself to looking at Him in you, you will become more aware of Him. It may take some time if your soul has been dominant. As you stay in that place of looking at Him, you will become more aware of Him than you are aware of yourself. Then, as you yield yourself to Him and trust Him completely, He will become your life.

When I say that "You can be aware of Him," I am not saying to merely think about Him, but rather you can actually begin to live life through Him. When you are after the Spirit you are sharing in His life and you are living through His very life. You can only experience the reality of the Spirit of God as you move over into trust and yield yourself completely to Him.

As mentioned before, the activities of prayer, scripture reading, and worship in song are helpful in learning to discern the Spirit of God. If you were to engage in prayer, you would suddenly realize that you are not praying to yourself, but your focus is on someone separate from you. Prayer is directed to a separate person than yourself.

Looking for Christ in you is very much the same as praying (1 Th. 5:17). You are focused on God while praying and you are looking for God. When you are being aware of Christ in you, you are doing the exact same thing – focusing on God and looking at God (but without the words of praying necessarily). Now would be a great time to spend some time in prayer while focusing your mind and thoughts on Christ. At some point during your prayer, stop talking *but still maintain your focus on Him.* You can also do the same activity with worship. It is more challenging to accomplish this during scripture reading because the mind can easily become focused on the concepts in scripture and not on Christ Himself. But, it can be done. It is a wonderful and necessary thing to grasp concepts in scripture. However, I would encourage you to always be moving in the direction of focusing on the person of Christ during all scripture reading. You will gain much more revelation this way. You will also begin to know Jesus Christ more deeply rather than just knowing more concepts "about" Him.

>1 Cor. 15:45 "So also it is written, "The first man, Adam, became a living soul." The last Adam became a life-giving spirit."

The life-giving Spirit of Christ is in you. This is not an analogy. This is not a word picture or an illustration. It is a reality. He is a Spirit who is physically dwelling in you. He is as much in you as any of your other organs are in you.

The Lord is the Spirit

>2 Cor. 3:17 "Now the Lord is the Spirit, and where the Spirit of the Lord is, there is liberty.

>1 Cor. 6:17 "But the one who joins himself to the Lord is one spirit with Him."

Jesus is the Spirit. And your spirit has become one spirit with His Spirit. To recognize the Spirit of Jesus Christ in you is the same thing as recognizing your spirit within you.

Humility Gets You Out of the Way
To recognize and find Christ in you, humility is required. If you are proud and full of yourself, all you will see when you look inside yourself is yourself. Humility is an extremely important component in all spiritual revelation, and we will discuss it often in many subjects. If you are not truly humble, your experience will be of your own soul and not the Spirit of Christ within you. In other words, if you are not humble, you will only be able to see your own thoughts, emotions, and will. You must decrease – extremely and more severely than you've ever thought, in order for the Spirit to become recognizable within you.

Humility is commonly a misunderstood subject. Many people believe they are humble because they focus on feeling badly about themselves. This is not humility at all, but another form of pride. Self-hatred, self-pity, and a constant feeling of low self-esteem are all having a focus on yourself instead of a focus on Jesus Christ. Any type of self-focus is not humility.

Without going into too much detail here because we will cover it thoroughly in other chapters, humility is becoming the small childlike person you truly are. It is letting go of your "grown up act." As you face the reality of your smallness and then focus on the living presence of the person of Christ, you will be able to more easily recognize His Spirit within you. God is a living Spirit inside you who is separate from your own thoughts and emotions.

> *Psa 131:2* "*Surely I have composed and quieted my soul; Like a weaned child rests against his mother, My soul is like a weaned child within me.*"

Looking for Jesus Christ within you is one and the same motion as quieting and stilling yourself. As you prayerfully look for the presence of Jesus Christ within you, you will automatically begin the process of quieting your own thoughts and emotions. Think about the last time another person stood in front of you and spoke to you. If you were truly listening to what he was saying, you would have had to stop yourself from talking and you would have stopped entertaining your own thoughts as you placed your focus on the other person. To listen to another who is separate from you requires you to shift your attention away from your own thoughts and feelings and place your focus whole heartedly upon another. If you have the skills of a good listener, you will become so focused on the other person that you will forget about yourself and become totally involved in the other person's words and emotions. This "becoming lost in another" results in a stilling and quieting of yourself.

Recognizing the Spirit of Christ within you by humbling yourself, quieting yourself, and shifting your attention to another person is foundational in separating soul from spirit. The Spirit of Christ is another person within you. Your own thoughts and feelings are soulish.

The Lord spoke all of creation and nature into existence. Nature is His word. Because of this, many spiritual truths are observed in the realities of nature. I often think of the separation of soul and spirit in the picture of a hurricane. The eye of a hurricane is perfectly still and calm. This is a picture of our spirit, the deepest place within us of total calm. The outer part of the hurricane is a storm. The soul is continually in a state of unrest and turmoil. Most people live from the unrest of their tumultuous souls. Bouncing from thought to thought, from feeling to feeling – only as stable as the world around them.

We become so accustomed to living from our own soul that to live from our spirit is a foreign concept. We depend on ourselves and trust in ourselves on a moment by moment basis. It's all we've known. To live from your own soul apart from Christ is as common and as easy as lifting your hand, batting an eye, or walking across the room. It is natural. It is the way most people, Christian or not, live all of the time. Living from the soul is all most people have ever known and will ever know. Living life from your soul while adding to it a Christian lifestyle with biblical concepts and truth is of little or no value. To live this way is actually somewhat miserable. It is also extremely unappealing to the non-Christian world to observe a Christian full of opinions but with no power.

You may have the idea that you depend on God. But true dependency on another person is something that is a position of the heart. Christ is a person.

To trust Him as another person apart from yourself will be a change in the posture of your heart. This is always something that you do now, in this moment, and in real time. Trusting Christ as another person is not an additional character quality that you try to incorporate into your personality and grow into slowly. You can always trust and submit to Jesus Christ right now in your heart.

Trust is not a mindset. Trust is not being in mental agreement with principles. Trusting God is not just reciting positive clichés such as "God will have to do it", "He will provide", or "God is good."

A true position of heart dependency on the Spirit would be similar to what you would feel if you were to allow yourself *to enjoy* another person carting you around in a wheel barrow. Even if the person were to take you across a tight rope strung over a water fall, you would put your heart and your life in his hands during that very moment.

If you were literally sitting in a wheelbarrow with someone else pushing you around, you wouldn't just say the words, "he will have to do it," but you will *feel him* "having to do it." You would actually be living through the person carrying the wheelbarrow. If your wheelbarrow pusher decides to go left, then you automatically go left with him because you already gave him control over you at a previous point in time. You don't look to see if you want to go left because you are already in a posture of trust. If he wants to stop in front of a tree to look at it for a while, then you would look at the tree also. His experience would become your experience as you lived through his will. The same is true as you yield yourself the Spirit of God within you.

Initially, such a situation would cause you to feel totally out of control. Of course, you could sit in the wheelbarrow and fight it the whole time while trying to remain in control. You may bark orders to the driver and tell him what to do while you gripped the sides of the wheelbarrow because you are afraid and are unwilling to trust. This is completely different from letting go and enjoying the ride. In order to enjoy the wheelbarrow ride, you would have to let go inside your heart and not just comply outwardly. Letting go is surrendering to the driver's will, His guidance, His eyes, His hands, and His feet on a moment by moment basis. When you find true heart felt trust and enjoyment of the ride, you will begin to "rest" in the One who is driving.

Resting in the Spirit is not a passive, checked-out activity. Nor is it relying on past decisions that are only concepts in your head. On the contrary, resting is a very active experience - because Christ Himself is active. He is taking His wheelbarrow in many different places. When you yourself have ceased from your own labors, self-efforts, initiations, all doing, and all trying to get somewhere – you will resolve yourself to being carried and led by the Spirit of Jesus Christ within you. It is exhilarating to ride in the wheelbarrow of Jesus Himself while He lives His life through your body.

Learning to discern and look at the Spirit of Christ inside of you is a first step. Before you can get into the wheelbarrow, you must know where it is and who is driving it. Once you find your wheelbarrow and driver you might say,

"Are you kidding - you want me to climb in there?" Yes, God is inviting you to climb in. As you see and focus on the Spirit of God in you, let go to Him. Climb in and let go to *His* impulses of what He is saying, doing, and thinking – as opposed to your own apart from Him.

Can you tell that you do not tend to live this way? When you have a thought, you think it through. When you have a feeling, you often do not deny it. If someone hurts you, you take it into account. When you want something to change, you often entertain the desire. Of course, overtly sinful feelings and ungodly desires you easily recognize as coming from yourself and not from God. But *all feelings and thoughts that come from yourself* are not God. Probably the majority of thoughts and feelings that come up in you are seemingly harmless and impotent (They do not seem like sin). However, if you stay within the realm of your own soul for very long, not only will you experience the dryness and death of your own soul, but also you will begin to manifest the more obvious deeds of the flesh as opportunity presents itself to expose your heart.

The less you live in a trusting posture that is focused and let go to the Spirit of Christ within you, the more comfortable and solidified you become in living in control while following after the impulses of your own soul.

We briefly mentioned earlier that when the soul has been allowed to live unchecked and un-submitted to the Spirit for very long, it suppresses the Spirit within you. As we see in Galatians 5, the flesh is opposed to the Spirit.

Gal. 5:17 "For the flesh sets its desire against the Spirit, and the Spirit against the flesh; for these are in opposition to one another…"

This is one of the reasons it can be difficult to recognize the Spirit within you. If you have lived after the flesh for very long by continually following the impulses of your soul, the Spirit becomes quenched and inhibited within you by the flesh. It is not that the flesh is stronger, but the flesh becomes dominant and solidified – even hiding the Spirit from you and deceiving you from hearing and believing God. The flesh is very deceitful and wicked (Heb. 3:13). Several sessions of brutal honesty with yourself, extreme humility, and brokenness will begin the healing process.

Separation by Submission

An additional key in separating your soul from the spirit is through submission. As you submit to the authority of Jesus Christ and subject your mind, emotions, and will to Him, it becomes much clearer what is of Him and what is of yourself.

Healthy submission of the soul begins with the fear of the Lord. We see four places in scripture that explain that the fear of the Lord is the beginning of wisdom (Job 28:28, Ps. 111:10, Pro.. 1:7, Pro. 9:10). To fear God is an excellent starting place that sets you on the path of wisdom. A healthy fear of God should be foundational in the life of the Christian. I discussed the fear of God thoroughly in the previous book, *Mysteries of the Kingdom*. It is one of two foundational pillars in the life of the Christian that keep us spiritually healthy. Do not confuse the fear of God with punishment, but rather a healthy fear of God consists of an extreme awe, a worshipful reverence, and a respect that completely silences the flesh.

The fear of God is the first step into a total submission of yourself to Christ. Once you get yourself out of the way, you can begin to hear and understand true wisdom that comes from God, the only One who is wise. I usually start out each day focusing on the power and authority of God. I submit myself to His authority in a humble, submitted fear of God.

As you begin to see God in His awesome power and authority, place yourself under Him and be quiet. A complete subjection of your will is *not initiating in nature* but is subdued. Submitting yourself under God is allowing yourself to be exposed. As you become vulnerable under His loving and tender scrutiny, open your heart completely to Him and let Him have His way, whatever that may be.

I encourage you to have extreme thoroughness in your submission. Even when you feel you are totally submitted to God, submit even more. As you continue to give yourself to surrender, your busy thoughts and self-initiations will slow down and calm substantially.

The Soulish Christian

We will conclude this chapter by listing a few characteristics of the Christian who tends to live from his soul as opposed to his spirit.

- Addicted to his own feelings and thoughts- does not deny his own impulses but values and treasures them.
- Talks too much. The spirit is concise in communication and is always mindful of the audience who is listening. The soulish Christian treasures the good feelings of release that comes from many words. When he feels the impulse to talk, overly explain, or he feels the itch to tell a story, he will not deny the impulse.
- Believes his emotions that result from life's circumstances. When the soulish Christian receives bad news or is having a bad day, the emotions that arise within his flesh are believed to be reality. The circumstances of life often change his understanding of the truth concerning who he is in Christ or how God feels about him.
- Impulsive in thought and deed. A soulish Christian rapidly says and does whatever pops into his mind without slowly considering a matter before God in submission to Him.
- Addicted to doing activities. The soulish Christian cannot be still. He must constantly be doing something. Projects, activities, and accomplishment have become his life.

- Insecure concerning others. The soulish Christian is frequently driven by the approval of others. Insecurities in this area cause him to act out in saying things that promote himself and make himself look better in the eyes of his peers. He is not content with only God's approval.
- Never satisfied. The soulish Christians is frequently on a hunt to satisfy his thirsty and wandering heart. His soul is constantly generating and creating new focuses and campaigns that will occupy him and bring him life and happiness.
- Addicted to depression, anxiety, excitement, and pleasure. The soulish Christian lives from his emotions in every way. He prefers his own feelings over God's truth and the feelings that come from the Spirit.
- Opinionated and given to causes and campaigns. The soulish Christian is often driven and consumed with "what is right" concerning their personally chosen self-righteous causes. The only "cause" of the Christian is to be Jesus Christ.
- Frequently offended, hurt, incredulous, or appalled. The soulish Christian is self-focused and volatile in his emotions. The smallest matter is a stimulus for an emotional reaction or meltdown.
- Overly obsessive and extreme in the flesh. The soulish Christian is frequently infatuated with anything other than Christ.
- Overly conservative and balanced in the flesh. The soulish Christian can worship at the altar of conservatism and a balanced lifestyle of safety and cautious traditions. The spiritual Christian, however, is obsessed with the Spirit of Jesus Christ and is extreme in passion and abandonment with fervent love. He is not careful in the flesh.

The list above was created from the author's own experience of being fleshly and soulish at times.

Any Christian can walk after the flesh at any time and become soulish. Yet, we are not to know one another "according to the flesh" (naturally), but we are to know one another, including our own selves, according to who we are spiritually (2 Cor. 5:16).

We will discover more in the following chapters how to discern what is soul from what is spirit, and more importantly, how to transition living from the soul to living from the spirit - the only path from the head to the heart.

Notes:

[1] In each and every moment, your soul is either experiencing the Spirit or the flesh. There is no other option. However, to constantly examine to see if you are experiencing the flesh or the Spirit is an activity of the flesh. The activity of scrutinizing yourself is a self-focus. When experiencing the Spirit, the focus is on Christ. Walking after the Spirit includes trusting God to let you know if you are after the flesh or not.

Questions for Understanding and Discussion

1. Why is it important to separate soul from spirit?
2. What do the phrases "after," "according to," and "walking after" refer to?
3. To "be soulish" is the same thing as what?
4. How could you describe the idea of legalism?
5. Describe how the flesh or spirit can be expressed through the soul.
6. In what ways is spirit different than soul?
7. What are some helpful ways to discern your spirit?
8. What role does humility play in separating soul from spirit?
9. What role does submission play in separating soul form spirit?
10. Describe characteristics of a Christian who is living only from their soul.

Becoming Who You Are

1Jo 3:1 "See how great a love the Father has bestowed on us, that we would be called children of God; and such we are."

Imagine for a moment that you are a student at a university. One day when you graduate from the university you are currently attending, you plan to become a doctor. You have always wanted to be a doctor, but for now you are a student in college.

The day finally comes for you to graduate. At this point you are no longer a student. You are now a doctor. You do not have to just think about what it would be like to actually be a doctor anymore. The reality is you are now a doctor.

While you were a student at the university, you lived the reality of being a student. You bought books. You carried those books to class. You studied. You listened to your professors. You took notes. You took tests. You spent time with other students like yourself. You saw the inside of a classroom daily. You smelled what the classroom smelled like. You saw, touched, and experienced everything that a student experiences. You thought of yourself as being a student and you identified with being a student because you were a student. During the time you were actually a student you could only "think about" being a doctor.

There is a difference in actually being something and in thinking about being something. Being something is experiential. While "you are" one particular thing, you can only "think about" being something else that you are not. You cannot experience something that you are not. You can only imagine it, project, or think *about* it.

If you are on a boat in the middle of the ocean, you can only think *about* being on dry land. While you may have concepts, thoughts, and imaginations about the dry land, your true experience is currently being at sea.

Who Are You Really?

If you are born again, in your spirit, there are certain things that are true about you. Let's list a few of those things:

- In your spirit you *are* a child of God (Jn 1:12).
- In your spirit you *are* totally clean and righteous (2 Cor. 5:21).
- In your spirit you *are* perfect (Heb. 12:23).
- In your spirit *who you are* cannot sin (1 Jn. 3:9).
- In your spirit you *are* justified with God (Rom. 5:1).

- In your spirit you *are* at peace with God (Rom. 5:1).
- In your spirit *who you are* hears God (Jn. 10:27).
- In your spirit *who you are* knows God (Heb. 8:11).
- In your spirit you *are* one with God (1 Cor. 6:17).
- In your spirit *who you are* is full of joy and love (Gal. 5:22, 1 Pet. 1:8).
- In your spirit *who you are* is always satisfied, fulfilled, and content (Jn. 6:35).
- In your spirit *who you are* is hidden in Christ (Col. 3:3).

When you became a Christian, God joined His Spirit to your human spirit, washed you, made you clean, and gave you His very quality and characteristic of righteousness. This one act made the entire list above true about you in your spirit. These many characteristics of your spirit will never change. They are true whether you feel them or not. They are true whether you believe them or not. They are true whether you are thinking about them or not. They are the condition of your spirit, your true self.

When you are feeling gloomy, your spirit remains joyful. When you are feeling depressed, your spirit remains full of hope. When you are feeling guilty, your spirit is still righteous. If you make a sinful and rebellious choice, your spirit is still righteous and submitted to God. When you are being selfish, you spirit remains full of love for others. Your spirit is hardwired or permanently fixed with the characteristics of righteousness that God gave you. Again this is true because at the point of your Christian conversion, your human spirit became meshed together with God's Spirit, both becoming one spirit. Your human spirit was washed and made alive in the instant you were joined with God's Spirit (1 Cor. 15:22, 1 Pet. 3:18, Eph. 2:5, Col. 2:13). This forever changed the ongoing condition of your human spirit.

God's forgiveness toward you is not just that He "decided that you are forgiven." You are not forgiven because "He is letting you slide." You are not forgiven because "God decided that you don't have to pay for your sins." You are forgiven because of a condition you are in.

It is very important to realize the qualities and characteristics about you that are always true concerning your spirit, no matter what you think, feel, experience, or believe in any given moment.

So why is it that you don't always experience, feel, and think what is true in your spirit? *It is because you are not always "according to" your spirit.*

In Romans chapter 8, Paul specifically uses the terminology of "being according to" or "being after" the flesh or the Spirit. The words *"according to"* are used in some translations of the Bible and the word "after" is used in other translations. Both words communicate the same idea.

When your heart does the action of believing and trusting God, you become according to the spirit. At this point, what is true in your spirit becomes the experience you have in your heart and in your soul. Another way to say it would be that when you are according to the Spirit, then it is the Spirit that is filling your heart. You then experience the things that are true in your spirit.

Whatever you are "according to" is what your experience is. If you are according to your flesh, then you will experience the things of the flesh. If you are according to the spirit, then you will experience the things of the spirit.

Your spirit is the core of who you are. It is the essence, the nature, and the driving force of your being. Before you became a Christian, your dead, unwashed, darkened spirit was who you were (Eph 2:1). But when you came to Christ and submitted to Him, your spirit was washed and changed (Heb. 12:23). Your new spirit is your true identity.

Your flesh continues to have its erroneous idea of who you really are. The flesh's idea of who you are is based upon the stored memories in your brain of "who you were." The flesh thinks that who you used to be is actually who you are now – *but this is not true*. When you walk after the flesh, you are living according to who your flesh thinks you are which is really based on who you were before you came to faith in Christ. That is a false identity. The more you walk after the flesh, the more you reinforce the false identity of the flesh. The reason for this is that as you experience the flesh, the flesh uses your experience as evidence against yourself to prove that who you were is actually who you are now. In other words, if you sin or have bad thoughts (walk after the flesh), the flesh says, "Ah ha, see? You have not changed!" When you think and feel things very strongly that are not God, you think they are coming from you, but they are not. They are coming from "the flesh" (Rom. 7:20) which is not you at all. You must continue to identify with the new spirit that you are, no matter what you feel, think, or do.

When you move from living out of head knowledge to actually trusting with your heart, you will leave being after or according to the flesh and become after or according to the Spirit. It is at this time that you actually begin to experience and taste *the reality* of who you truly are in your spirit.

Recall the example of the college student who became a doctor. In your spirit, you actually *are* all of the things in our previous list. When you are according to your flesh, you can only have a concept *about* who you are in your spirit. In other words, as a Christian, if you are according to your flesh, you will have ideas and concepts about what you are like in your spirit, but you will not be experiencing the reality of it.

The Soul Aligning with What is True in the Spirit

Let's look at an illustration to help describe the dynamics of how this works. When we examine the diagram below, we can see that the soul is not the same as the spirit. The lines in the soul are more spread out and the lines in the spirit are closer together. In other words, there are many things throughout the day that occur in your soul that do not line up or correspond with what is happening in your spirit. You constantly have thoughts, feelings, and wants that are not in agreement and have nothing to do at all with what is currently going on in your spirit. Your spirit has its own set of thoughts, feelings, and wants in any given moment, and your soul has a separate set.

soul   spirit

In the second illustration below, we can see that the soul is now lining up with the spirit, and they are now identical. As you give your soul to things that are already true in the spirit, the soul will line up or "plug in" to the spirit. You may also think of this analogy as two gears which are right next to each other yet spinning at different speeds. When the soul is independent of the spirit (which it is in this state naturally or by default), it cannot engage or experience the things of the Spirit. However, when both gears are spinning at the same speed, they can lock in together and become one unit. You must therefore "line-up" your soul with your spirit. This is accomplished in the heart (the place of belief) through surrender, trust, and in giving yourself to the things that are already true in your spirit. As a result, the soul will "line up with" or experience what has always been true all along in your spirit.

soul   spirit

When you agree in your heart with what has already been made true in your spirit and then humbly yield to the person of Christ, the soul begins to line up with the spirit and you become "after the spirit." The previous sentence should be re-read, understood, and put into practice.

There are many things that are true in your spirit that you can give your heart to in agreement. Refer to our list at the beginning of this chapter.

Mar. 12:30 "...and you shall love the Lord your God with all your heart, and with all your soul, and with all your mind, and with all your strength."

Rom. 3:10-12 "as it is written, 'There is none righteous, not even one; there is none who understands, there is none who seeks for God; all have turned aside, together they have become useless; there is none who does good, there is not even one."

Consider the two verses above. Jesus commands us to love God wholeheartedly, yet we see from Romans 3 that we don't love God at all. The Romans 3 verse is a description of all men apart from God (either a non-

Christian or the flesh of a Christian). Your flesh has absolutely no desire for God. When you come to Christ and are born again, your flesh does not change. Only your spirit is made new. Although as a Christian, your flesh remains in opposition to God, the Spirit of God within you is passionately in love with God – all of the time.

Even when the experience in your soul is emptiness, sin, and misery, at the very same time these negative things are occurring in your soul, your spirit is rejoicing, loving God, and on fire for Jesus Christ. As you cooperate and give your empty heart to the greatest commandment of loving God and submitting to the person of Christ, your soul will line up and then become filled with what is true in your spirit. The gears will lock together in place.

God the Father is in love with His Son Jesus. Jesus loves the Father. The Spirit loves the Father. Therefore, God loves God (Jn. 3:35, Jn. 14:31, 2 Cor. 3:17). The three persons of God are in perpetual, fervent, loving fellowship with each other. The very nature and essence of God is love. In your spirit, which has been completely joined and meshed with God's Spirit, you are constantly participating in this circle of sharing, exchange, and fellowship of love for God all of the time.

You Cannot Produce the Fruit of the Spirit

It is impossible for you to produce the fruit of the Spirit. The fruit of the Spirit is the fruit...*of the Spirit*. It is not the fruit *of you* or anything that your flesh can create or imitate. All you can do is first recognize in your spirit that the qualities of God's Spirit are true, and then yield to them.

You are not kind - only God is kind. You have no joy - only God is joy. You have no patience - only God is patient. You have no love - only God is love. Your flesh can and will try to mimic the fruit of the Spirit. It will try to act kind, force patience, and replicate kindness. It will try to love, but the flesh's love is only a sentimental, self-serving love. Your flesh will try to treat others with kindness in order to "produce an effect" in the other person and make them feel loved so that you can be said to be loving. In other words, the flesh is motivated to make others feel as though they have been treated kindly. It can never be kind out of a nature that loves because the flesh's nature is not love. The flesh will also attempt to act kind or loving as to relieve itself of its own guilt, but it cannot love with God's love because the flesh by nature is self-serving.

>*Eph. 5:9 "For the fruit of the Spirit is in all goodness and righteousness and truth;"*

Perhaps you often have the idea that your sins are forgiven, but you rarely experience the reality and the feelings of being totally without sin in God's eyes. For the concept to become experiential reality, you must *become*. You must become a doctor to experience the reality of being a doctor. When you are after the flesh, it is just like being a student who dreams of being a doctor. A student can't experience being a doctor - he can only imagine what it would be like. It is only a concept to him. While after the flesh, you can only have concepts and dream about things that are true in the Spirit, but you cannot experience them.

When a truth goes from your head to your heart, you are going from a concept in your brain to the reality of what is already true in your spirit. You are moving from an idea about something to an experiential reality that you are seeing, tasting, and touching. You are going from wanting something to be true to what is true. You are moving from "wanting to be" into "being." You are moving from trying into having. You are not making anything happen or making anything true. It already is true in your spirit. You are moving from a concept in your brain into your spirit where it is a reality. Once you are according to your spirit, you realize what is true and has been true all along because you observe it as real. In your spirit, you see and taste the reality of what and who you are.

> Matt. 18:3-4 "...truly I say to you, unless you are converted and become like children, you will not enter the kingdom of heaven. Whoever then humbles himself as this child, he is the greatest in the kingdom of heaven."

Humbling Yourself is Becoming Who You Really Are

In the spiritual realm, we are not capable of doing anything because we are powerless. The Spirit of God works through us with His power to accomplish everything in us and through us. In our flesh we have no ability to bear any fruit for God. Jesus said in John 15:5 *"...for apart from me you can do nothing."* We cannot create any true desire for God in our flesh because we have no true desire for holiness[1], for prayer, nor any ability to love God or anyone else. It is all Him both in us and through us. However, there is one thing that we do have the power to do: God has given us the power of choice to humble ourselves.

God commands you forty-nine times in scripture to humble yourself. This is something *you do*, not Him. God can orchestrate difficult situations in life in order to bring you to the edge of the cliff. But you must choose to jump off. When you humble yourself, the vessel that you are submits itself under God's power and authority in order for Him to strengthen you, encourage you, use you, and flow through you. We mentioned earlier that we have the power to choose. Our choice to genuinely say "Yes" to God in our hearts is the same choice we are making when we humble ourselves. We have been given the power and the choice to either say "Yes" or "No" to God in any given moment. Therefore, in any given moment, you are either humbling yourself before Him or you are refusing to do so.

In the verse above, we see that Jesus is telling us that *"unless you become little children, you will not enter the Kingdom."* Notice the word *become*. You must *become* like a little child. This is not just thinking like a child or acting like a child. This is not acting childish. You must *become* like a child in your inner attitude and disposition. When you become like a child, you humble yourself. When you do this, you are beginning to cooperate with what is true about who you are in your spirit. When you become like a child, you have entered into the very reality that is true about yourself in your spirit. Why? Because you are just like a child in your spirit.

When you become like a child, you are becoming many things. A child is dependent on his father. A child is vulnerable. A child is trusting. A child feels needy. A child is fully aware of his weakness. A child feels his weakness. A child feels his smallness. A child feels lost unless his father directs them. A child craves love. A child feels and experiences a real need to be taken care of. You already are all these things in your spirit. Therefore, to become like a child, you are becoming what you already are in your spirit – small and dependent on your Father.

When Jesus said we *"cannot enter the Kingdom unless we become like children,"* it is meant to be applied to Christians, not just non-Christians. This verse has mostly been used to describe the initial humbling an unsaved person must do in order to become a Christian. However, it is saying much more than that. As a Christian, although we are positionally saved and have therefore already entered the Kingdom, we are certainly not always experiencing the Kingdom. If you are experiencing anger, lust, or selfishness - the Kingdom of God is not filling your heart at that moment in time; thus, you are after the flesh.

> *Acts 14:22 "strengthening the souls of the disciples, encouraging them to continue in the faith, and saying, "Through many tribulations we must enter the kingdom of God."*

Entering the Kingdom of God is not just going to heaven when you die. As Christians, we are to enter the Kingdom often in our hearts and in our experience. We should continually move from being according to the flesh to being according to the Spirit. When we do so, we are entering the Kingdom in our hearts. When we move from the head to the heart, we are entering the Kingdom. When we move from having religious concepts to experiential reality of those concepts, we are entering the Kingdom of God. This process also cooperates with Jesus's prayer of *"Your Kingdom come on earth as it is in heaven" (Matt. 6:10).* When what is true in your spirit (the Kingdom) fills your heart, and therefore your soul and body, it is bringing the Kingdom that is in the spiritual realm into the realm of Earth where your soul and body are.

Again, in the passage in Matt. 18, Jesus uses the word *converted*. We have only thought of this word as referring to new converts. However, every time you move from the flesh to the Spirit you are changed. You "convert" when you humble yourself and trust God from the heart. It is the difference between night and day when you humble yourself and move from the flesh to the Spirit.

Only in your spirit are you alive because only in your spirit can you "be". If you are living from your head, it is as though you are living out of a bundle of reactions and programmed memory responses. To live out of your head is death. To live from your spirit is life and peace. *Being* is freedom. Living life only responding to stored memories is bondage.

The Exhaustion of the Flesh

Living out of your head and being after the flesh is completely exhausting and tiring. There is no true rest in this condition. Again, true rest only comes from *being*. Have you noticed how tiring your constant thinking is? *Being* on the other hand is like relaxing on a comfortable raft while you float down a peaceful river. With the cool breeze and the gentle sound of the water, you experience the enjoyment and rest of nature as you float weightlessly with no cares. Living out of your head, on the other hand, would be as though you felt compelled to stop all of this aimless floating around on a raft. You, therefore, get out of your peaceful raft and sit on the side of the riverbank. Next, you spend your afternoon figuring out the best route of the rafting trip, the potential dangers of rafting, your amount of provisions, and the exact spot on the river where you should arrive in order to camp that night. To live constantly problem solving, planning, preparing, and preventing is not really living at all.

All of the thinking that you do with your brain is done in patterns. Have you realized that you seem to have the same recurring problems in your life? Let's say that you have a particular problem or a set of problems. You think of possible solutions to your problems, but then you realize that your solutions will not work. Then you get discouraged and give up on finding a solution. After some time passes, and you have given up on finding any true solutions, you begin to focus again on the problems in your life. You try to think of possible solutions. You realize that those solutions will not work, so you again give up on any solutions. And then you repeat the entire cycle again and again.

Your mind is a prison. It is a prison of your thinking cycles. Some cycles are shorter than other cycles. Some cycles are sub-cycles that are layered within other cycles. Some of your cycles happen in a fraction of a second. Some last an hour, some a day, and some last for weeks.

When you get tired from the stress of certain thinking cycles, your mind goes to its escape files. "How nice it would be if only I could…," or "One day I will finally be able to…" You start to dream of an escape from all of your work and the daily problems in your mind. You start looking forward to the coming weekend's fun activities, maybe creating a room addition, asking for a raise from your boss, going fishing, playing golf, going shopping, or changing to a better job. You may start planning for your next vacation. Once the day finally comes and you are actually on vacation, you are stressed the entire time. You come back from your vacation even more tired than before you left. Now you need a rest from your vacation. Your escapes are only a distraction from the hamster wheel of your mind. But within the prison of your mind, you are only able to exchange one hamster wheel for another.

Thought is not of the same substance as *spirit*. You cannot make the prison of your mind better or improve it because as long as you stay in it, you are bound to the rules of the prison. Within the realm of your mind, the only thing you can do is to replace one set of thoughts with another set of thoughts. But you are still within the prison that is in your head.

Living only within the realm of your thoughts is like taking a beautiful wild animal that is made to hunt by instinct and then training it in a laboratory to only eat on command. Before being confined to the laboratory, the wild animal was living as it was intended to live – free, wild, passionate, and alive. However, when the impulses and instincts of the wild animal are denied and the animal is trained to eat only when the light in the lab tells it to eat, then the animal is denied the ability to live out of its created instinct, the very thing that makes it truly what it is. To deny the animal its instincts is to deny it of its very nature. Living from your head is much the same way. It is denying yourself to live out of who you really are in your spirit.

You may not even be aware how tired you actually are from living in the dryness of your mind prison. Where is the life? Where is your vitality and joy in the Spirit? Where is the refreshing living water that is Jesus Christ? He is certainly not found in your head. If you are living out of your head, then your experience is limited to only the thoughts that can be in your head. Only when living from your heart which is filled with the Spirit is there life.

Few Are Those Who Find It

> *Mat 7:14 "For the gate is small and the way is narrow that leads to life, and there are few who find it."*

This verse addresses more than just salvation for unbelievers. It addresses finding *the life* of God. The life of God is His vitality, His joy, His zeal, His fire, and His love. Jesus is the life. We are invited and called to have a daily and real encounter with the living God filling our hearts – where we actually find *the life* of God.

The life of God, the living water of spiritual vitality, is in you. He lives in the spirit of every born-again believer. The only way to break free from the prison of your own mind is to find the Spirit. The Spirit is the life of another – Jesus Christ.

The Spirit of God does not live in your body part we call your foot. He does not live in the body part we call your arm. He does not live in the body part we call your hand, nor in the body part we call your leg. *He does not live in the body part we call your brain.* He has joined Himself to your spirit.

The brain is just as much a part of your body as your elbow. The function of the elbow is to connect the forearm and the upper arm. The function of the brain is to store memory and generate thoughts, but it is not intended to be "lived from." It is intended only to "be accessed" (see "The Role of Knowledge" chapter). The body and brain are intended as a tool to be used by the Spirit. But this only comes from you yielding the body to Him via the heart (Rom 12:1).

Only when we are *being* who we are in Christ are we set free from this exhausting mind prison. When you are in a state of *being* instead of the state of constantly thinking, you will savor the rich experience of each moment and enjoy it to its fullest. Being who you are in Christ is living in the extreme sensation of joy and in the experience of love - instead of living in the prison of your mind and its cycles of thought.

Actually Becoming Who You Are

Jesus tells you to become a little child. You already are a little child in your spirit. It is the truth of who you are. The flesh has its idea of who you are. But the flesh's identity is a false self.

You could not truly become like a child if you were not one already. Because you already are childlike in your spirit, there is nothing to force or create. You are simply going to move over to what is *already true*. Finding the truth, however, can seem elusive or difficult especially if you have lived for years with your false identity of being a capable adult.

Humbling yourself and becoming like a child is letting go of your false self who is capable, adult, strong, and self-reliant. Your false, adult self feels big and in charge. Your true childlike self is very small, needy, and dependent. Your childlike heart is not far away.

Because humility and becoming childlike is something of the heart, you will need to look inside. A good place to start would be to begin to find any kind of need or hunger for God that you may have. Be very honest with yourself at this point. Do you need Him? Take a very long minute to see if you do. Don't allow your answer to remain only factual. Instead, allow yourself to actually feel your need for Him. Stay there for a while and let your need for Him get all over you. Bathe in it for several minutes. Sit in your weakness. Sit in your hunger. Perhaps you can face the fact that you don't know certain things. Maybe you are bluffing and pretending you are more capable than you really are (maybe at work). Maybe you act like you know things that you don't really know around certain people. Perhaps you wear an attitude of confidence that is shallow or false at certain times or in specific settings. Be honest. Isn't it true that you really aren't who others think you are?

This kind of honest heart inventory is part of becoming a child. It is a humbling of your attitude. It is getting real with God and having the emotional integrity to let your feelings match the truth. At the beginning of a session of facing your weakness and neediness, you may feel some very slight impulses of emotion. Don't ignore these. This is your heart beginning to let go. Emotions are not bad - they are normal indicators of heart experience. Allow the emotion of weakness and neediness to overcome you. It is not only okay to fall apart, but I highly recommend it. Stop trying to hold it all together. You have many false ideas tied to your false self.

The Spirit of God is constantly working both from within and without in order to unravel you. He sometimes arranges your life circumstances to help you break. He is working to strip you of your independence and confidence. He is working to make you feel small and not big. He is working to dismantle the attitudes of your false self who keeps it all together. He is working toward you having a broken dependency on your Father. He is doing all of this because He loves you. It is the dependent heart of a child that is a candidate to receive love and intimacy. He wants this for you more than you can imagine, not just because He loves you, but also because you need it. Go ahead and cooperate with Him.

It is a good thing to feel weak. It is also biblical (2 Cor. 12:9). The emotion of utter weakness is one of the primary emotions your flesh avoids feeling. Your flesh has fought its entire life to avoid the feeling of being undone. It fact, your flesh has spent its entire life building itself up so that it does not have to feel undone and weak. You have worked hard to create an environment for yourself that keeps you from having to feel weakness and dependency. You have equipped yourself with knowledge, education, status, money, provisions, retirement plans, and "know how" in order to not feel your true vulnerability. *God has been working in the opposite direction your entire life.* Many of the most negative circumstances that have happened to you in your life were specifically designed just for you in order to jerk the rug right out from under your feet. But your flesh has fought the undoing process. Your flesh has fought to stay feeling big, powerful, and in control. Weakness, vulnerability, and dependency on someone else is your flesh's worst nightmare.

Only the Blind Can See

> Mat 11:25 *"At that time Jesus said, "I praise You, Father, Lord of heaven and earth, that You have hidden these things from the wise and intelligent and have revealed them to infants."*

True spiritual revelation is only given to infants and babes. Sure, the self-confident and intelligent can formulate airtight theologies and weave intricate dogma, but this is not true knowledge. As you become who you really are in your spirit (a babe who is not wise and intelligent) and rid yourself of the false self who is confident, then you will begin to *see* and have true revelation from God.

Responsibility

Heart postures are attitudes and emotions we tend to stay in and live with, as opposed to attitudes and feelings that just come and go for a short time. A heart posture is describing an abiding position your heart tends to stay in. In actuality, a heart posture is a belief that you are holding to. A very common heart posture that is part of the false adult self is the posture of responsibility.

Children do not carry adult responsibilities. Instead, they trust their parents to accomplish things that are "too big" for them to carry. Children are not worried about health insurance plans, the car breaking down, or financial budgets. They are not concerned with the things adults worry about. This is because children are either unaware of such things or they simply trust their parents to take care of them, and rightly so because they are only small children.

As you *became* an adult in life (as you took on a false identity), you realized that your parents weren't going to be responsible to take care of you anymore. Therefore, you had to start doing it yourself. This was an unhealthy shift that contributed to the creation of your false self. The proper response to the needs and requirements of life as we age is to shift the responsibility from our earthly parents to our heavenly Parent. All parents should help facilitate this process in young adults. We should never have to *become* an adult in the sense that the requirements of life tempt us into a heart posture of worry, fear, and then self-reliance. We, therefore, become big in order to handle it all, cutting ourselves off from the life of God.

If we are to be children who do not carry the weight of responsibility, then how are we to relate to the necessities that life requires of us?

"You Feed Them"

In John 6:9, we see the account of Jesus feeding a multitude of people who are following Him. The disciples inform Jesus that the people are hungry and that they should be instructed to go into a nearby town to get food for themselves. Jesus responds by saying to the disciples, *"You feed them."* Next, a young lad volunteers his loaves and fish to feed this group of 5,000 people. Jesus takes the loaves and fish from the lad and multiplies it to feed the entire multitude.

As a functioning adult human being in society, you "have a multitude to feed." There are tremendous requirements on you. There are people all around you who need your time, your love, your resources, your attention, and your energy. You have to go to work. You have to perform to a certain level of expectation in many areas of your life. If you will face it, the needs that are required of you are all greater than your ability. Yet, you have a multitude of people standing right in front of you that are hungry. Do you see them? They are looking to you to do something for them. More than that, Jesus Himself is requiring you to feed them! But you are only a child. How can you possible stay as a child in your heart yet take care of all of your adult responsibilities and feed the multitudes that Jesus is requiring you to feed?

What does the picture in John 6 teach us? Although Jesus told the disciples that they have to feed the multitude, *a lad* offered up his five loaves and his two fish.

A lad is a child. All the lad had was a few loaves and a couple of fish to feed 5,000 people. How ridiculous and silly it was for him to offer such a small amount of food to feed five thousand people. But to the heart of a child, this is not ridiculous at all. This is what children do. A child is eager to contribute what he has to give - without crunching the numbers to see if it will work. If the lad had observed the five thousand people then looked at his five pitiful loaves of bread and then did the math, he would have been like every other adult who was present. Instead, the lad remained a lad while he eagerly raised his hand to offer what he had to contribute. He gave his smallness to Jesus because Jesus said to feed them - then Jesus multiplied it.

As a child, all that you have to give is insignificant compared to the needs that are weighing on you. As you remain the little child that you are, you do not have the resources, the wisdom, or the power to fulfill all of what daily life is requiring of you. Nor do you have the ability to fulfill what God is requiring of you. All you can do is offer what you have to Jesus. He will multiply the little that you have to take care of all the requirements. But you have to eagerly give it to Jesus with all your heart and say, "I've got some loaves! I've got some fish!"

The lad didn't become a man. He didn't look at the need and then try to become big and wise - someone he was not. He remained a lad, and he eagerly gave what he had and nothing more. If you try to become big in order to feed the five thousand (that Jesus is telling you to feed), then the power of God will not be available to flow through you to take care of the need. In fact, it is not so much that God even needed the lad's loaves and fish. He could have created food from nothing. God took the lad's faith and used it to multiply the food. The smallest amount of childlike faith yields basketfuls of fruit for God's Kingdom.

> *2 Cor. 12:9 "And He has said to me, "My grace is sufficient for you, for power is perfected in weakness." Most gladly, therefore, I will rather boast about my weaknesses, so that the power of Christ may dwell in me."*

> *Ps. 131:1 "O Lord, my heart is not proud, nor my eyes haughty; Nor do I involve myself in great matters, Or in things too difficult for me."*

When you have bills to pay and not enough money to cover them, stay small and childlike. Don't rise to the occasion and take on an adult persona of strength and being capable. If you do, you will quench the Spirit in your life. Offer to God with a joyful heart what you do have and trust Him to multiply it in some way. You don't know how He does it, but He does. He might give you more money. He might give you a better paying job. He might lead you to work more hours. He might give you a plan. Or, your lights might get turned off and He may allow you to suffer for a while. But whatever He does, it will be Him doing it and not you. You *get* to stay small while trusting Him in His arms of love. You never again have to be someone you are not. You have a strong and wise Father who will take care of everything in your life as He sees fit.

On a personal note, I have tremendous responsibilities on myself as well. I have a wife, four kids, a job, a house, cars, bills, and continual work to do in the

Kingdom with the church and the families with whom I share life. No one has any idea just how really small I am inside. They would be shocked at the great gap between how small I feel and how much I give and speak with authority. What people see on the outside may be an active man who often has answers for people, songs to play on the guitar, and encouraging messages for the church. Little do they all know that I secretly put all of that responsibility on my Father. I *feel* clueless. I choose to feel clueless because it is a reality that I really am clueless. I choose to stay in the truth that I am small. Jesus tells me to do this. I get to stay a little guy inside, and it is nice.

I often show up to church meetings with a guitar in my hand with no song in my heart. I often open my Bible knowing the Lord is leading me to share something with the group, but I have absolutely no idea what I'm going to say, so I offer what I do have to God and He multiplies it. Somehow He shows up every time. To live childlike and free is sort of like flying by the seat of your pants. Some people would call it not living very responsibly. But the truth is that it is a life of trusting God. Spiritually speaking, it is a better and a more spiritual choice to give the responsibility to God so that He can use you in order for the five thousand to be fed. To become a responsible adult and quench the Spirit of God in your life because you are self-reliant is not being responsible at all. It is arrogance.

A man or a woman *of God* is entirely different than the world's idea of what a man or a woman should be. A man of God is a man who does accept the responsibilities of life, but then in his weakness and childlike vulnerability, he offers the smallness of what he has to God and gives the responsibility over to his Father to do the impossible and feed the five thousand. A man of God remains a humble child in his heart and says, "Yes Lord, I will feed them, but I don't have the power to do it. I will eagerly offer you the small bit I do have in order for you to multiply it."

Not So Fast

As you allow yourself to become childlike, you will start to feel very small and needy. Many times Christians go much too quickly to the strength they have in Christ, and they skip over their weakness in themselves. Yes, you can do all things through Christ who strengthens you. Yes, you are strong in Him. And, yes, you do have His wisdom and His power available to you. But without traveling through the death of the cross, there can be no resurrection.

Jhn 12:24 "Truly, truly, I say to you, unless a grain of wheat falls into the earth and dies, it remains alone; but if it dies, it bears much fruit."

If you allow yourself to confess too quickly the truths that you know in your head about the strengths that you have in Christ, you risk only being shallow in your confessions. It is necessary to go through the weakness and the unraveling of your flesh in order to find a true experience of Christ being your strength. He will catch you, but you have to fall off a cliff first.

Col 3:3 "For you have died and your life is hidden with Christ in God."

The strength that you have in the spirit is God's strength, not yours. Your spirit is meshed and made one with His Spirit, but you are the much smaller one in this relationship. The childlikeness that is true about you in your spirit speaks of you being so small that you are actually hidden in Him.

Notes:
[1] The desire for "holiness" in the flesh is really a desire for self-righteousness.

Questions for Understanding and Discussion

1. Why is it important to "become"?
2. List some characteristics of who you are in your spirit.
3. Why do you not always experience what is true in your spirit?
4. Describe the idea of aligning soul and spirit.
5. Why is humbling yourself becoming who you really are?
6. Describe the exhaustion of the flesh.
7. How can you remain humble and childlike and still function daily?

The False Self

Intelligent Space Suits

There has been a new technological discovery. Space scientists have recently developed a new kind of space suit. These new space suits have the ability to learn. Whenever the person inside the suit makes movements and performs tasks with his body, the suit learns his behavior. The suits are also wired into the brain in order to record thought. When the astronaut inside the suit repeatedly thinks about performing certain procedures, the suit learns his thoughts and can then anticipate future thinking.

Fred Snidely was a subpar astronaut. He broke all the rules, performed improper procedures, and did things his own way. Fred wore one of the new intelligent space suits during a recent mission. After the mission ended, Fred was tragically killed.

Mike White was a brand new astronaut with an impeccable record in the academy. He was the perfect astronaut. Recently, Mike was given Fred Snidely's old suit to wear during an important space mission. During the mission, Mike did many things right, but he also did many things completely wrong. He failed to follow proper procedures many times. He did not listen to his captain's orders during certain situations, and he acted completely independent from the rest of the space crew in some instances. When the mission was over, Mike was reprimanded for his behavior. Mike replied, "It wasn't me, it was the suit."

> *Rom. 7:17-23 "So now, no longer am I the one doing it, but sin which dwells in me. For I know that nothing good dwells in me, that is, in my flesh; for the willing is present in me, but the doing of the good is not. For the good that I want, I do not do, but I practice the very evil that I do not want. But if I am doing the very thing I do not want, I am no longer the one doing it, but sin which dwells in me. I find then the principle that evil is present in me, the one who wants to do good. For I joyfully concur with the law of God in the inner man, but I see a different law in the members of my body, waging war against the law of my mind and making me a prisoner of the law of sin which is in my members."*

The intelligent space suit in our analogy represents your body. The two men, Fred Snidely and Mike White, represent your spirit.

Before you were a Christian, you were dead in your sins and not born of God. The condition of your spirit was that it was darkened and unrighteous. Your spirit was dead. When we say that your spirit was dead, it was not dead in the sense of it being nonexistent or even dormant but that it was in a state of death due to its unrighteous nature (Gen. 2:17). The dead and rebellious spirit you had before coming to Christ is Fred Snidely. This is what scripture calls "the old man." The old man was then killed and done away with. This happened at the point of your conversion to Jesus Christ. Your unrighteous spirit was washed, joined to the Spirit of God, and made alive. Your spirit is now alive because of its condition of righteousness (Rom. 8:10). Fred Snidely died, and now Mike White is inside the space suit. Mike White is your new, cleansed, righteous spirit. He is the "new man." Mike White is now the driving force of the space suit which is your body.

While Fred Snidely inhabited the space suit, "the nature" of the space suit/astronaut combination was darkness and sin. Now that Mike White is the new man in the space suit, the new nature of the space suit/astronaut combination is righteousness. Whatever the nature of something is will also define its tendencies of behavior. The nature of a man is revealed by his innermost will. Mike White wanted to be a good astronaut. Fred Snidely did not. This is where the Apostle Paul says in Romans 7 that "the willing to do good is present within me."

So here is the question: If Mike White wants to do good, why doesn't he do good all of the time? If the nature of the man and suit is to obey, keep the rules, and do everything right, then why doesn't he do so in every situation? *It's because of the suit he is wearing.*

The suit was programmed by the old man, Fred Snidely. When Mike White "is after" or "according to" his true self (according to the Spirit), he performs perfectly. However, when he chooses to allow the suit to do whatever it wants, independently of his true self, the suit is not submitted to the inner man of the spirit. Without the direction of the inner spirit of Mike White, the suit will always act out of the learned behaviors of Fred Snidely.

Mike White certainly has power over his suit. He is in charge of it. When Fred Snidely was in the suit, he was the driving force behind it. Now that Mike White is in the suit, he is the driving force behind it. While Mike White is according to his true self, the suit is in subjection to him. The suit actually becomes a great tool to carry out what he wants to do. This is the same thing as your body being an instrument of righteousness when it is submitted to the spirit. When Mike White is not living according to his true self, the suit is not in a state of subjection to Mike White. In this condition, the suit goes into auto pilot mode, becomes independent, and thinks and does according to its old programming from Fed Snidely. In this condition, the body is referred to as "the flesh." Notice in Romans 7:18 that Paul says, "That is, in my flesh."

So then, the suit is programmed for error. When left in auto pilot mode, the suit can do nothing but error. However, the auto pilot of the suit can be overridden by the actual man inside.

As a side note, it is interesting that Paul called the flesh "the flesh." It makes sense if you think about it. If you are living according to who you really are in your spirit then life is great. But if you are not, you are living according to "your suit." The flesh is simply the body without the spirit governing it. In that independent condition, it is just blood, bone, muscle tissue, and the brain's gray matter – the flesh.

Mike White's suit can improve in some ways, but it can never be completely rehabilitated. As Mike White lives correctly in the suit, the suit learns new ways of thinking which do cooperate in better ways with Mike's intentions. This new way of thinking is similar to the Christian renewing his mind with truth. However, the basic tendency of the suit will always be to replicate what it learned from its original inhabitant. Eventually, the space suit will need to be destroyed because it cannot be redeemed. Mike White will have to get a new suit. Your decaying, outer man will be done away with, and you will receive a glorified body to match your new spirit man.[1]

Important Terminology

Eph. 2:3 "Among them we too all formerly lived in the lusts of our flesh, indulging the desires of the flesh and of the mind, and were **by nature** *children of wrath, even as the rest."*

2 Pet. 1:4 "For by these He has granted to us His precious and magnificent promises, so that by them you may become partakers of the **divine nature**, *having escaped the corruption that is in the world by lust."*

Terminology is important in this subject matter because it affects your identity. The first scripture listed above describes your nature before you were a Christian. The second verse above describes your nature after you became a Christian. As believers, we no longer have a sin nature.

It is also important to note that the old man is not the same thing as the flesh. It was the old man that had a sin nature. We could refer to it as the "old nature." The spirit that you had before you became a Christian wanted to sin. Your new spirit does not want to sin, but wants to obey God and does obey God. If you are born again, you do not have an old man anymore, nor do you have a sin nature.[2] The old man was killed when you were born again.

Rom. 6:6 "Knowing this, that our old man is crucified with him, that the body of sin might be destroyed, that henceforth we should not serve sin."

Although the old man (old nature, sin nature) is not present in the Christian, the Christian can still allow his body to act independent of his spirit. This is walking after the flesh. The Christian must remember however, that the flesh is powerless. It is only a bundle of old memories, learned behaviors, and preprogrammed responses. Before you were born of the Spirit of God, your old man (unrighteous spirit) was a powerful driving force for evil to be carried out through your body. This is not the case anymore. Now, in your innermost man (spirit), you want to do good and obey God which was not the case before you were saved. Yet, if you do walk after the flesh, you will do those things that are in your flesh to do but without the same power of darkness that drove it before. When a Christian walks according to the flesh, it is much like "going through the motions" of something that he really doesn't want to do.

Before we continue, there is one more clarifying point of terminology you must understand. You must also understand the differences between the phrases "in the flesh," "according to the flesh," "in the Spirit," and "according to the Spirit."

> *Rom. 8:9,10 "However, you are not in the flesh but in the Spirit, if indeed the Spirit of God dwells in you. But if anyone does not have the Spirit of Christ, he does not belong to Him. If Christ is in you, though the body is dead because of sin, yet the spirit is alive because of righteousness."*

Christians often use the term "in the Spirit" to refer to what Paul called being "according or after" the Spirit. There is a distinction. You are always in the Spirit if you are a Christian. But you are not always "according to" or "after" the Spirit. You are in the Spirit continually because Christ is in you. In other words, your human spirit (who you really are) *is in* Christ's Spirit. You are one with His Spirit whether you are walking after that Spirit or walking after the flesh (Col. 3:3, 1 Cor. 1:30, Jn. 17:23).

The Flesh is Not You

> *Eph. 4:24 "and put on the new self, which in the likeness of God has been created in righteousness and holiness of the truth."*

> *Col 3:9-10 "...since you laid aside the old self with its evil practices, and have put on the new self who is being renewed to a true knowledge according to the image of the One who created him."*

> *Rom 6:6 "knowing this, that our old self was crucified with Him, in order that our body of sin might be done away with, so that we would no longer be slaves to sin."*

The verses above directly address your identity. The word "self" deals with who you think you are. Who it is you think you are, feel you are, and believe you are, is your idea of "self". The *old self* is your identification with your flesh. The *new self* is your identification with your new spirit. The verses above are telling you to identify and think of yourself as being your new spirit. Notice that Ephesians 4:24 explains that your new self is righteous, holy, and in the likeness of God Himself. "To put on" the new self is not a fake or shallow acting like something that you are not. It is not saying that you should act right. The Greek word for "put on" actually means "to sink into a garment." These verses are telling you to go ahead and sink into who you really are in your spirit by identifying with your true self.

A major error of many Christians is that they still identify as being their old self, the flesh. This causes serious problems and dysfunction in a large majority of Christians, and here is why: the flesh will never measure up. It will always behave below God's standards. It will never live according to what the Christian knows to be right. Therefore, when a Christian identifies with the flesh as being "him", he continually feels as though *he* does not measure up. He feels as though *he* is below God's standards. He feels as though *he* needs improvement.

Identifying with the flesh as being you leads to an endless pursuit of "trying to do better".

This further results in an undercurrent of guilt that taints your confidence before God to boldly receive His love. You observe your behavior that falls short and you mistakenly think that it is *you* who is falling short.

> *Rom. 7:17* "*So now,* **no longer am I the one doing it,** *but sin which dwells in me.*"

> *Rom. 7:20* "*But if I am doing the very thing I do not want,* **I am no longer the one doing it***, but sin which dwells in me.*"

If you notice the two verses above, the apostle Paul realized that if he sinned, *he* was not the one who was sinning. This is because he realized that his real self was his spirit. Your spirit does not sin. It is the flesh that sins.

> *1Jo 3:9* "*Whosoever is born of God doth not commit sin; for his seed remaineth in him: and he cannot sin, because he is born of God.*"

The verse above is describing the truth about who you are in your spirit. Your spirit does not sin and it *cannot sin*. It is born of God, and God does not sin. This is explains why when you are walking after the spirit, you do not sin. As you recognize and identify your "self" as being your spirit, you will be able to say, "I am no longer the one doing it, but sin which dwells in me".

> *Rom 7:18* "*For I know that nothing good dwells in me, that is, in my flesh; for the willing is present in me, but the doing of the good is not.*"

It is very important to realize the place where sin dwells. Carefully read the verse above. The place where sin dwells is in your flesh. However, the flesh is not you, it is only the space suit. You are inside the space suit. You are the spirit inside the corrupt space suit. You must realize that you are not the flesh. If you do not realize this, you will live continually defeated. You will continually believe that you do not measure up, because the flesh does not measure up. You have falsely been identifying yourself as being a failed and corrupt outer garment (the body).

The vast majority of Christians today believe that who they are is the flesh. It is reflected in today's Christian music, books, and preaching. Christians are constantly trying to improve their failing "selves" and get it together, because they think that who they are is the flesh – and the flesh can only fail. The flesh will never get it together.

Who you really are is your spirit – the "new man" inside the space suit of your body. You are a delight to God. You are pleasing to Him. You are washed, cleansed, and 100% holy and blameless. You pray without ceasing. You have a continual, zealous love for God. You love scripture, you love to worship, and you crave holiness and righteousness.

Your spirit has been made perfect:

Heb. 12:23 "…the spirits of righteous men made perfect."

You have all of the righteousness of God:

Rom. 3:22 "even the righteousness of God through faith in Jesus Christ for all who believe."

2 Cor. 5:21 "…so that we might become the righteousness of God in Him."

You are perfect and complete in Him:

Col. 2:10 "and in Him you have been made complete."

You do not need to pray more, read the bible more, witness more, do more or be more. You can relax and rest because you are forever pleasing to God and one with God in your spirit.

Sin Consciousness

Therefore, we see another paradox:

1Jo 1:8 "If we say that we have no sin, we are deceiving ourselves and the truth is not in us."

1Jo 3:9 "Whosoever is born of God doth not commit sin; for his seed remaineth in him: and he cannot sin, because he is born of God."

It is true that who you are in your spirit (your true self) cannot sin. It is also true that a Christian can sin, and often does. How can this be?

If a Christian sins, it is because he is walking after his flesh. We are held accountable for the deeds done in the body (2 Cor. 5:10). If we choose to walk after the flesh, we are responsible for our poor choice. But it is not "you" who is sinning while after the flesh. It is the sin that is in your flesh (Rom. 7:20).

The point is this: It is imperative that you see yourself as God sees you. He does not see you as you being your flesh - sinful, guilty, and failing. He sees you as you are in your spirit – righteous, holy, loved, and blameless. God sees you as He sees His Son, Jesus. Again, you have become one with Jesus in your spirit (Jn. 17:23).

As a Christian, you are not to have what is called "sin consciousness". Sin consciousness is having a constant awareness of the fact that you have sinned, that you might sin, and that you probably will sin. Sin consciousness utterly destroys your intimacy with Christ. Sin consciousness keeps you from walking after the Spirit – the power to overcome sin.

Christians who have sin consciousness find themselves sinning constantly. Their constant battle with sin becomes their primary occupation. Their primary focus in their Christian walk is on not sinning. This leads to constant guilt over their continual sin. Their life becomes a life of defeat as they believe they are a perpetual disappointment to God.

> *Heb 10:1-4 "For the Law, since it has only a shadow of the good things to come and not the very form of things, can never, by the same sacrifices which they offer continually year by year, make perfect those who draw near. Otherwise, would they not have ceased to be offered, because the worshipers, having once been cleansed, would no longer have had consciousness of sins? But in those sacrifices there is a reminder of sins year by year. For it is impossible for the blood of bulls and goats to take away sins."*

In the passage above, we see that the old covenant sacrifices could not "make perfect" those who draw near (which is also saying that we are perfected now by the sacrifice of Jesus). Because the worshippers under the old covenant were not made perfect, they still had consciousness of sins. The old covenant sacrifices could not take away sins (as Jesus did).

> *Heb 9:9, 14 "...sacrifices are offered which cannot make the worshiper perfect in conscience, ... how much more will the blood of Christ, who through the eternal Spirit offered Himself without blemish to God, cleanse your conscience from dead works to serve the living God?"*

The verses above explain how the previous sacrifices could not make the worshipper perfect in conscious. But the blood of Jesus does make us perfect in our conscious.

> *Heb 10:22 "let us draw near with a sincere heart in full assurance of faith, having our hearts sprinkled clean from an evil conscience and our bodies washed with pure water."*

Correctly Viewing Fleshly Behavior

When you observe a discrepancy between your outward behavior and the truth that is in your spirit, it is important that you view it correctly. Although it is true that you are righteous and pleasing to God, your flesh is not. If you become according to your flesh and you sin, it is good to humble yourself and be honest with God. "Yes Lord, I chose to walk after the flesh and I sinned."

Sin is what the flesh does. This is not surprising. This is not some big and new revelation. If you walk after the flesh, you will sin. You should not try to go on a campaign in order to do better. You do not need to devise some strategy to not sin again. You do not need to create some great new plan to defeat sin in your life. You only need to return to your spirit - the place where you do not sin.

If you walk after the spirit, you will not sin. If you walk after the flesh, you will sin (Gal. 5:16). Do not try to "be good", in order to walk after the spirit. Being good and trying harder is of the flesh. This is not how you walk after your spirit. To walk after the spirit is to humble yourself, become the child that you are, believe the truth about who you are in your spirit, and find trust for Christ who is in you. You can *instantly* return to your spirit and resume fellowship with God at any time. You do not have to pay for walking after the flesh. The price has already been paid.

It doesn't "mean anything about you" if you walk after the flesh. Walking after the flesh does not "prove" that you are unworthy or bad. Nothing has changed concerning the condition of your spirit. Even while you were walking after the flesh, your spirit remained in fellowship with God – you were just not walking after it, therefore not experiencing the fellowship and joy of God.

Disarming the False Self

> Gal. 2:20 *"I am crucified with Christ: nevertheless I live; yet not I, but Christ liveth in me: and the life which I now live in the flesh I live by the faith of the Son of God, who loved me, and gave himself for me."*

Although the flesh generates feelings and thoughts in the soul and the heart that can seem very strong and powerful, it is critical that you realize that it is not you who is generating them. If a thought, a feeling, or a want is not coming from your spirit, then it is based on a false reality. Although it is real that you feel and experience them, they themselves are false. They are largely imaginations, projections, fears, and conclusions that are drawn from earthly logic and files in your brain attached to false emotions. Only the Spirit is in the truth with His perspectives, feelings, and thoughts on matters.

Who you were has died. More than likely, the identity that you currently have is a false one. Who you think you are is incorrect. You are basing your current thoughts of "self" on a bundle of memories and false feelings. Look at the amazing truth of Galatians 2:20 quoted above. I find this verse to be one of the most profound and powerful verses in the entire New Testament. This verse encapsulates much of the New Testament message and pinpoints the paradoxical condition of the Christian. You should spend quite a bit of time meditating and understanding Gal. 2:20. Who you think you are has actually died, yet you are alive. But it's not really you who is alive - it is Jesus Christ in you who is alive.

Through many empty philosophical gyrations, the famous French philosopher Rene Descartes came to a famous conclusion. In an attempt to prove the existence of self, Descartes declared, "I think, therefore I am." Nothing could be further from the truth for the Christian. The evidence of the Christian being alive is not that "I think, therefore I am." But rather, it is "Christ is in me, therefore I live." The point is this: You strengthen and reinforce the flesh as being your identity when you continually believe that your thoughts and feelings are coming from yourself. This is a *very* frequent error. It is very important that you grasp this, so please read on carefully.

Thinking is not evidence that you *are*. Thinking only reveals that your brain is able to recall and process information. Thinking, recalling, and processing information is what the organ of your brain is designed to do - just like the foot walks and the hand grabs. The thoughts that you have are not proof that they are coming from "you." The thoughts and feelings are coming from your body, specifically, the organ of the brain. Who you are is your spirit; thus, your spirit is your only true self.

If the thoughts you are having are originating from your brain, they are not coming from you. If they are originating from your spirit, then they are coming from you.[3] In the "Role of Knowledge" chapter, we discuss how the Spirit accesses the brain and uses it. Emotions that you feel are not evidence that they are you either. When the flesh is afraid, when it craves something, or when it experiences pain, various emotions will be felt and experienced. Again, if the emotions you feel are coming from your spirit, then they are coming from you. If they are not coming from your spirit, they are coming from your flesh which is not you.

Looking to the Spirit

I would like to invite you to do an exercise this very moment. If you just read the following exercise and observe it, but you don't actually do it, there will be no benefit to you. Right now, take a few seconds and consider your left foot. You probably were very unaware of your left foot until I pointed it out just now. Focus on it for a moment and become aware of how it feels. Is it tired from walking on it today? Is it comfortable in the shoe that it is wearing? Is the sock too tight? Is there any pain or discomfort? Does it itch at all, or does your left foot seem totally fine?

Now let's shift your focus to another part of your body - the stomach. Is your stomach empty? Is it calling out for food? Is your stomach full? Perhaps it is over full if you just ate a large meal. Is your stomach in any discomfort at all? Is your stomach feeling just fine right now?

The point of this silliness is not to actually get a gauge for how your foot or your stomach feels, but it is to teach you that you can *actually look* and focus on any particular part of your body. The very same is true for focusing on your spirit.

While you were focusing on your foot or your stomach, you were not so aware of the typical thoughts you tend to have which are generated from your brain. You were not problem solving for tomorrow's dilemmas. You were not obsessing about how someone offended you. You were not fearful about what might happen in a current situation you may be in, and you were not day dreaming about the past or the future. The reason is that you were not "listening" to your brain. Instead, you were "listening" for any signals that were coming from your foot and from your stomach.

You can listen to the Spirit just like you focused your attention on your foot or your stomach. You can focus your attention on the Spirit of God who lives inside you.

Take a few moments to focus on the Spirit of God who is in you. As soon as you do, you will have a shallow thought or some feeling come from your brain. Simply realize that this is not coming from you (your spirit), and turn your attention back to the Spirit of God within you. Just like you "listened" to your foot, listen to and sense the Spirit of God in you. Be still and pay attention only to Him.

Much of the time, He Himself is still and relaxed within you and He is only leading you to know and enjoy the deep fellowship of His love. At times what is in the Spirit is to pray for others in some way. He may tell you something for someone else in order to encourage them. He will reveal to you how He sees you. He will correct you and gently convict you of sin and poor attitudes. The Spirit speaks in scripture much of the time. He will whisper many secrets to you.

Let's look again at the verse in John 7:38, 39:

> *"He who believes in Me, as the Scripture said, 'From his innermost being will flow rivers of living water.' But this He spoke of the Spirit..."*

When you sense the thoughts and intentions of the Spirit, you are not sensing something that is "above the neck." God speaks to your heart. In order to help you separate what is above the neck and what is from your heart, it may be helpful to compare the mental act of reasoning with the passionate feeling of hatred.

Think of the last time you felt a deep hatred for someone or something. Hatred is not usually reasonable or rational. However, solving a math problem is very reasonable and very rational. Can you tell that these two activities are generated from different areas in your body? Solving a math problem or thinking through the solution to a rational dilemma is accomplished above your neck. However, love, lust, hatred, joy, and peace are all heart activities that are generated from a deeper place within you that is much below the neck. A feeling of violent hatred is an experience of passion that comes out of your heart. Thinking through how to get from point "A" to point "B" while examining a map requires rational thought from your brain - not passion from the heart.

As you practice listening only to Christ who is in your spirit, you will begin to yield and subject your flesh to the Spirit. You will not become "rattled" or overly concerned when your flesh obsesses, when it reacts, or when it screams loudly. You will not live your life listening to the constant generation of fleshly thoughts and emotions that your brain produces. Why? Because you will begin to learn that they are not you. The constant thoughts and emotions that you feel that do not come from your spirit are coming from the flesh, the false self.

As you begin to submit and subject your shallow, fleshly thoughts and feelings to the Spirit, you will begin to identify with your spirit as being the true you. As you look to the Spirit for what to think and what to feel, you will begin to quiet the impulses of the flesh.

As you begin to understand and experience what we have been discussing, it may become an overwhelmingly sad reality to realize that most of your life has been responding to, listening to, and reacting to the thoughts and feelings that are generated from your flesh. It is appropriate to grieve and repent before God.

More Description of Who You Actually Are

If your true self is not your typical and continual thoughts and feelings, then how can we better describe who "you" actually are? We know and have said many times already that who you are is your spirit. Yet, we know that your spirit has been joined, meshed, and intermingled with the Spirit of Jesus Christ. Let's revisit Colossians 3:3 and Galatians 2:20:

Gal. 2:20 "I am crucified with Christ: nevertheless I live; yet not I, but Christ liveth in me…"

Col. 3:3 "For you have died and your life is hidden with Christ in God."

When combining Colossians 3:3 with Galatians 2:20, we can see a very interesting thing: You are dead, yet you are alive. But it is actually Christ who is the One who alive in you. Your life is *hidden* in Christ.

I want to make a slight overstatement that must be qualified. The reason for the slight overstatement I am about to make is to push you far in the correct direction in order to drive home the point of these two verses. I will then pull you back just a bit to make the statement more accurate.

Here is the statement: There is no you. There is only Christ dwelling in your body. Ponder that for a few moments and see if you can identify with it.

Now, to make the statement more accurate, there is "a you," *but who you actually are, is not at all who you think you are.* Your actual, true identity is hidden, protected, and tucked deep away inside Jesus Christ, the Spirit who lives inside your body.

To illustrate this, imagine if a giant whale were to swallow a very tiny minnow. The minnow would be deep inside the whale and then assimilated into the whale's body. When you consider both the whale and the minnow, you could say that the minnow has its own identity separate from the whale, and that would be true to a degree. But you could also say that the whale is really all there is even though the minnow is now hidden within the whale. By no means have you become Christ, yet you are hidden in Him.

So how is it that who you really are is a small child and at the same time there is no you, and at the same time you are hidden in Christ?

The answer to this question reveals just how small and hidden away you truly are. The smallness of your true identity is extreme. In your spirit, you are a very, very small child in whom you find your identity in your Father. So again, yes, there is a "you," but you are so very small and hidden in Christ that Christ is actually the One in whom you find your identity. The flesh's idea of who you are, even the new and improved Christianized version of yourself, is a completely false identity.

The statement "There is no you" is helpful in going in the extreme right direction. It is actually a statement that should be made to your flesh. In the earlier exercise, you looked to a different place than where you are used to looking in order to see what you should think and feel. Looking to your spirit or the Spirit of Christ who is in you (you are one with Him) in order to see what to think and what to feel will seem very much to your flesh like "There is no you". The reason is that the "you" that you are used to listening to is a false you. It is only your flesh kicking out a continual parade of thoughts and feelings.

Self-Awareness

The old man or sinful nature is what programmed your flesh. It is only an intelligent space suit of learned behavior, old feelings, and thinking patterns. When you live from your false self and not from your spirit (your true self), you will hear and believe things that will cause you to respond with erroneous emotional responses and incorrect thinking. Often, you then assign meaning to what you are thinking and feeling based on your prior experiences which takes you further from the truth. Therefore, if you believe one lie, you will often build more lies on top of that one.

The nature of the Spirit is an awareness of Jesus Christ. The Spirit of God inside you is focused on the person of Jesus Christ. When you are according to the Spirit and you are identifying with your true self, your thoughts and the affections of your heart are very much directed toward Christ. The nature of the soul as you are according to the flesh is an awareness of itself. Your flesh is focused on yourself. If you are "after the flesh," you are very much "self-aware."

Although not a perfect example, little children can often give us a glimpse into what being according to the Spirit is like. Perhaps you have noticed that children at times can be very unaware of themselves. They can feel, say, and act without much self-consciousness.

The inner experience of the self-aware flesh is its own thoughts, feelings, and wants. They are readily available and easily accessed. In other words, if what you are experiencing is only your own thoughts and feelings, then you are experiencing your flesh. The thoughts and feelings of God are of a different realm. When they become your experience, it is very different (not only in content, but in their "flavor"). While living after the flesh, as thoughts about God enter into the mind, they remain just that – thoughts about God. When we move into a place of desperate trust and dependency in Jesus Christ, He becomes our world and our inner environment. Suddenly, we find ourselves extremely unaware of our own thoughts and feelings. Our primary experience becomes one of love, intense peace, and worship of Jesus Christ.

It may seem somewhat confusing that you have a new self, yet the new self is not self-aware. But this is exactly correct. *The new self that you are, the true "you" is not extremely aware of yourself or self-focused. But rather your true self is primarily aware and conscious of Jesus Christ.* Again, your true self is hidden inside Christ.

It is important that you spend time listening to and focusing only on the Spirit of Christ in you. If you have not had plenty of time basking in and experiencing the Spirit of God in you, you have very little true knowledge and experience of who you actually are. This lack of experiencing and "tasting" of the Spirit in you actually reinforces your false identity to your flesh.

Notes:

[1] Gen 2:16-17, Eph 2:1-3, Jhn 8:44, Rom 1:28-32, Tts 3:3-6, Eph 2:4-5, Jhn 3:1-8, 1Cr 6:17, 1Cr 15:22, Rom 3:22, 2Cr 5:21, Rom 3:28, Rom 5:1, Rom 8:9-10, Hbr 12:23.

[2] Only the NIV Bible translates "flesh" as "sin nature" in places. This is an incorrect use of the word and an unfortunate choice of translation.

[3] The Spirit accesses or uses the brain as a tool to give meaning to its thoughts. However, the brain can act independently of the Spirit which would be the flesh. Thinking and having thoughts are not bad or negative. You cannot stop thinking. The only question is: "Are your thoughts originating from within your spirit, or are they originating from the brain independent of the Spirit." (See "The Role of Knowledge" chapter).

Questions for Understanding and Discussion

1. What is the difference between the "old man" and the flesh?
2. Describe the dynamic of the programming in the brain being left over from the old man?
3. Is the flesh "you"? Why or why not?
4. Describe how you can look to and listen to the Spirit.
5. Describe the idea of self-awareness.

Who Is Grace?

Your heart was made to connect. You are made to connect with other people. To "connect" with others is to join. When we join with others in our hearts, we share and enjoy life together. For people to genuinely listen to you talk about the things that are most important to you and for them to care and be interested is an encouraging thing. Likewise, for you to do the same for others is uplifting and enjoyable as well. We are communal by nature. We are created to share, to connect, to enjoy one another, to be vulnerable, and to give and receive our deepest feelings and thoughts. When we consistently engage in this way with others, we become what scripture refers to as "knit together" (Col. 2:2, Col. 2:19).

God the Father and His Son Jesus Christ also have this kind of relationship. They love and enjoy one another in their fellowship of peace, joy, light, and life. You have been invited to join in this fellowship of sharing and enjoyment that the Father and the Son have together (1 Jn. 1:3). You are invited to join in the relationship of love that they have along with all of the other saints of God. What a wonderful thing! What a huge family we have available to us in order to share and enjoy the life of Jesus Christ.

The essence of this fellowship of sharing and enjoying one another is actually an exchange of life from each other. If you had some cake and you gave it to a friend, and in turn he gave you a piece of his pie – you would be sharing. When you give some of your heart away for others to enjoy and then receive who they are for yourself to enjoy, you are sharing and fellowshipping together.

When you connect with God, you are sharing who you are with God. He also shares who He is with you. Within Christian fellowship, we share a piece of ourselves and the life of God within ourselves with one another. When we receive one another, give ourselves to one another, and enjoy the life of God in one another, we are taking a piece of ourselves and giving it to God for Him to enjoy. He then takes a piece of Himself and gives it to us to enjoy. When you have a close relationship with someone you love and enjoy being with, it is doing the same thing. We are sharing the life of one another. We are sharing the life of God.

Christianity is not about memorizing a list of concepts and being able to explain and defend them. It is about sharing, receiving, enjoying, loving, and knowing the person of Jesus Christ directly and in one another.

Your heart cannot connect with a concept. Your mind can understand a concept, but your heart cannot connect with a concept. Your heart is made and created to connect with *another person*. When you share and receive the hearts of other people, and they in turn receive you, you are connecting in your heart with others.

1 + 1 = A Hippopotamus

Pretend just for a moment that you spent the afternoon shopping at different local banks in your home town for a new checking account. You will probably find that most checking accounts require that you have enough money in the checking account to cover any checks you may write. You might even find a checking account with a special "overdraft protection" feature. This means that if you mistakenly write a check while you don't have enough funds in the checking account to cover the check, the bank will pay the difference for you on a short term basis. However, while you are currently searching for a new checking account, you happen to find a very special kind of checking account at a certain bank.

This unique checking account has some amazing terms. The bank will actually pay you ten times the amount of any bad check you write. In other words, if you write a check for $10 and you only have $8 dollars in your account, the bank will automatically add $100 dollars to your account! While scratching your head and being totally baffled, you realize this doesn't make any sense. Why would any bank do this?

The grace of God is like this special checking account that you have found. If you mess up and sin, God doesn't give you the punishment and torment that you deserve, nor does He just ignore the fact that you sinned and bring you back to $0 in your account. If God were to bring you back to $0 in your account after "writing a hot check" (sinning), it would be the same thing as God "letting you slide" on your sin. When you can't seem to get it together, God doesn't just tolerate you. Rather, if you sin, God lavishes His love on you.

> *Lk. 15:20-24 "So he got up and came to his father. But while he was still a long way off, his father saw him and felt compassion for him, and ran and embraced him and kissed him. "And the son said to him, 'Father, I have sinned against heaven and in your sight; I am no longer worthy to be called your son.' "But the father said to his slaves, 'Quickly bring out the best robe and put it on him, and put a ring on his hand and sandals on his feet; and bring the fattened calf, kill it, and let us eat and celebrate; for this son of mine was dead and has come to life again; he was lost and has been found.' And they began to celebrate."*

You may now be asking the question, "So, if I sin, God will love me more?" No. He does not love you more or less if you sin or don't sin. His love for you is constant - apart from anything you do. However, if you sin, His *compassion* is very strong and heavy toward you. This is because you have been walking in death, and you have breached your intimate connection with your Father. He longs for your return. He does not have His arms folded, tapping His foot, waiting for you to return so He can punish you. However, His grace abounds toward you if you do sin.

If you really begin to understand the gospel, you will come to a very specific conclusion: If I blow it in some way with God, I actually get extra bonus money added to my checking account.

Rom. 6:1 "What shall we say then? Are we to continue in sin so that grace may increase?"

The apostle Paul understood the good news. He came to the conclusion that sounded something like this: "Well, if we get more compassion, grace, and mercy if we sin, then maybe we should just give ourselves to sin so we will get more grace." Paul answers his own question by concluding that we are not called to sin, but we are called to righteousness and fellowship with Christ.

Once you deepen your understanding of the gospel, you will soon realize an amazingly freeing thing - because God's grace and compassion is even more poured out toward you if you sin, you can't blow this in any way. God's grace, love, and mercy are strong toward you, no matter what. No matter how great you choose or how poorly you choose - you win.

Rom. 8:37 "But in all these things we overwhelmingly conquer through Him who loved us."

The true message of the gospel makes no sense at all. It's like a bank paying you ten times the amount for you making a bad mistake. You are loved before you do anything and loved with immense compassion after you blow it. The love of God toward you has *nothing* to do with your performance or how well you choose. The pressure is off. You are loved.

Rom. 3:28 "For we maintain that a man is justified by faith apart from works of the Law."

Rom. 4:6 "just as David also speaks of the blessing on the man to whom God credits righteousness apart from works."

In the flesh of every man, woman, and child, justice is at our core. The righteousness of God's law is written in our DNA. We know intrinsically that *"an eye for an eye and a tooth for a tooth"* is correct, right, and just (Exodus 21:24). We should all get exactly what we deserve. Nothing less and nothing more. However, Jesus Christ took your punishment and served justice. God poured His wrath out on His Son Jesus for the sins and wrongs that you ever have committed or ever will commit. Since justice has been served and the punishment has been dealt out - the love, acceptance and compassion of God are now lavished upon you.

According to the law and according to what is right and just, if you sin, you deserve death (Rom. 6:23). In other words, $1+1=2$. In man's fleshly understanding, the best way we can interpret the gospel is to say that 1+1= 0. This limited understanding of forgiveness says that if we sin, God decides to not count our sin against us, and He still tolerates us.

However, the gospel is more than this. The gospel is so illogical that it is like saying 1+1= a hippopotamus. A hippopotamus has nothing to do with 1+1. It is not even on the number scale.

> Gal. 6:15 *"For neither is circumcision anything, nor uncircumcision, but a new creation."*

What does being a new creation have to do with being circumcised or not being circumcised? Nothing. Paul is not specifically talking in this verse about the physical act of circumcision. Circumcision here represents keeping the rules of God. Paul is saying that keeping the rules or not keeping the rules is nothing. Instead, it is all about being a new creature in Christ.

Here is the point: The grace of God toward you has nothing to do with you doing it right or you doing it wrong. His grace and love have nothing to do with your performance. It is as though you were playing in a baseball game, trying very hard to hit the ball and trying very hard to not strike out. You are so busy trying to hit the ball and not strike out that it consumes you. You practice constantly how to hit the ball. You even read books on how to hit a baseball better. Your mind is obsessed with your performance on the baseball field. But God is not even playing baseball. He is into fishing.

The truth is you have failed at keeping God's rules. In fact, you have failed totally and completely at doing anything right.[1] But you are loved in your constant failing, and this is all that is important now. You are a "loved failure." Therefore, when you find yourself trying so hard to not strike out and do well at hitting the baseball, you should shift your goal to receiving a hug from God instead. *God is playing a different game than you are playing.* As you take your focus off doing it right and instead focus on receiving love, you will find yourself being used of God and doing many things right. In fact, this is the only way you can do anything right. Yet, doing it right cannot become your goal because you will cut yourself off from being able to receive love.

Grace is a Person

If you have been a Christian for very long, you know that you have been saved by grace (Eph. 2:8). You also know that we live by grace and not by rules (Eph. 2:9, Rom 4:4,5). We also are strengthened by grace (Heb. 13:9). And grace is how we live (Gal. 2:19-21).

> Tit. 2:11 *"For the grace of God has appeared, bringing salvation to all men,"*

The grace of God that we just discussed in the previous section is delivered to you in a person. To receive the grace of God is to receive the person of Jesus

Christ. This is the only way that grace is delivered to you. *Jesus is the grace of God.* When your heart is strengthened by the grace of God, your heart is being strengthened by Jesus Himself. When you receive and connect with Jesus, you are receiving more grace.

To remember only the fact that God has grace toward you is missing the point. Connecting with the person of Jesus Christ is to actually receive the grace of God. To get grace in your heart, you must connect with grace Himself. Now we can tie this back in to our discussion at the beginning of this chapter about your heart being made to connect with another person.

> *Jn. 1:17 "For the law was given by Moses, but grace and truth came by Jesus Christ."*

Knowing and relating to God as a person is an entirely different thing than only entertaining ideas "about" Him. Many Christians think they are supposed to think about God all day. How can anyone possibly do that? I couldn't think about one thing for more than 30 seconds. But I could "be with" someone all day. To be with someone all day lends itself to connecting with them, sharing with them, and enjoying them. This is much deeper than only thinking about Jesus. This is much more than only thinking about the things of God. You are both capable and are called to a continual connection in your heart with the person of Jesus Christ.

Often times the flesh wants to avoid relating to God as a person. If He becomes a real person that you have to relate to, then "What might He do? What might He say? What might He require of me?" The flesh is much more content to relate to God as a concept, a set of principles, or a set of rules to follow. This keeps God at a distance and allows us to remain independent and in control. God's Spirit is not a force or mystical smoke. He is a person.

When you begin to relate to God as the person of Jesus Christ, it moves you from your head and into your heart. The heart relates and connects with people, but the head keeps people at a distance and ponders concepts about them.

How do you come to Him as a person? Let me ask you this: How do you interact and connect with anyone else? When you meet a friend for lunch, do you close your eyes or stare off into space and think thoughts about your friend? Or do you look into his eyes, smile, say "hello," and engage with him? When you sit down to have a chat with a friend do you use your imagination and create mental images of what he looks like? I sure hope not. You are aware of your friend because he is sitting there right next to you.

Relating to your heavenly Father as a person is moving into the here and now. He is here with you right now as you are reading this book. He is not a concept. He is not an imagination. He is not a principle. He is not a list of rules to follow. He is not a lifestyle. He is not a church building. He is a person. If you will open your heart up wide to His presence both with you and within you during this very moment, you will begin to connect with Him. Believe His love for you. Don't just remember "that" He loves you; rather, be aware of the reality that He *is loving* you right now. His attitude toward you is an attitude of love right in this very moment. Take Him in. Let Him have you. Give Him total control over you. You can because He is kind and He is gentle toward you.

We read of the stories in the Bible of Jesus performing miracles, teaching the people, feeding the multitudes, rebuking the Pharisees, and living daily with His disciples. In many cases, however, they have become only stories to us. Although they are wonderful and amazing stories, they are much more than that. The stories in the Bible are actually historical facts. These things really happened with real people. Peter was a real man who lived on this Earth. Peter caught fish in the Sea of Galilee. He had dirty feet. He had body odor. He was impulsive. He had a wife. He laughed. He sinned. He loved Jesus.

It is historical fact that a few years back there was a real band of men who spent a lot of time together. They camped out. Many nights they had a fire. They often cooked fish over their fire. Jesus was one of these men. He would teach the other guys about things and talk to them a lot. Jesus and the guys who were with Him walked on dirt roads for many miles together. There were lots of other people around them, too. Real people approached Jesus and this band of men. They wanted to get healed, or they wanted to ask some questions.

Sometimes Jesus got tired. He would lie down and take a nap. Sometimes He would want to get away from it all so He would spend some time alone in prayer in the woods or try to find some spot where there were no people around. Jesus cried. He got hungry. He felt the cold during the winter, and sometimes He got stickers in his feet that hurt. That very same man who walked around all of those dirt roads a few years ago is actually here with you right now as you read. He is the same exact person.

The God you pray to is the same person, who as a little twelve year old boy, was left behind in the caravan. Have you ever asked Him what that felt like? The very same God who created the planet Mercury, the planet Neptune, the moons of Saturn, the quasars, pulsars, stars, and all the black holes in the galaxy is also the same person who was baptized by a man named John in the Jordan River. That same man is with you now, and He loves you. Have you ever asked Him about all the things He's done, seen, and felt? Or, are those only Bible stories? Are you on the path to knowing God? Or, are you on a path to only knowing things about Him?

Anything but the Person of Jesus

While coming to the Lord as a person is a simple thing in our hearts, we very easily take the simplicity of coming to Him and substitute it for many other things. The flesh does not want to encounter the person of Jesus Christ. To relate to Him as a person causes us to leave our world of concepts and imaginations – things the flesh can produce and still feel as though it were being spiritual. The flesh completely avoids coming to Jesus during the moments of our day. To do so would require humility and trust.

Our substitutions for coming to Him require no dying, yet they provide the illusion of being spiritual or religious. Our substitutions allow us to stay in control.

Various Forms of Legalism

We discussed legalism in an earlier chapter, and we will discuss it further here. Let's restate the definition of legalism again: Legalism is all and any form of *self-effort* (whatever it may be) that is an attempt to make one's self pleasing to God. Legalism becomes a substitute for coming to Jesus Christ as a person.

Only Jesus Christ is pleasing to God. He is the only one who is without sin. When the Spirit of Christ joined with your human spirit at the time of your conversion, you took on His nature and the righteousness of Jesus Christ. The true self of who you really are is pleasing to God because you now have the righteousness of Jesus Christ. Just like Jesus cannot become more acceptable to His Father because He is already completely and totally acceptable, there is nothing else you can do to make yourself more acceptable to God, for you are already completely and totally acceptable. There is nothing that you can do to make yourself more valuable to God. There is nothing that you can do to make yourself more loved by God. You are as loved, valuable, and acceptable as you will ever be - because of what Jesus has already done, not because of anything you can do. As I have stated, this truth is central to the gospel.

The grace of God is much more than God pardoning you of your sin. Rather, the grace of God is the person of Jesus Christ in you who is joined to your human spirit. Once you have received Jesus Christ, you have received the grace of God. When you relate to God as a person, you are experiencing and tasting grace.

Legalism ignores all of this. Legalism is putting confidence in your own self in some way, and not in the person of Christ.

Let me introduce you to Frank.

We All Know Frank

Frank was a sinner. He got drunk, he got high, he committed adultery, and he lied and cheated as often as he could get away with it.

One evening Frank was out with some friends having a few too many beers at the local pool hall. There was also a group of Christian guys shooting pool on the table next to Frank and his buddies. As the two groups of men shot pool together and had conversations throughout the evening, one of the Christian men began to explain the good news of Jesus Christ to Frank.

As Frank listened to the Christian man's testimony and the reality of Jesus Christ, Frank began to believe this man's words. The gospel suddenly all started making sense to Frank. Frank suddenly had a strong urge deep in his heart that he needed Jesus Christ. He had faith that Jesus died for his sins. He gave his life to the Lord and believed the good news. Frank became a Christian that very night.

Excited about his new life in Jesus, Frank found a church meeting to attend the very next Sunday. The preacher gave a message that Sunday morning entitled "How to Grow as a Christian." Frank heard the preacher explain to him that if anyone wanted to be a good Christian and get closer with God, they needed to do certain things. The preacher said that in order to grow, Christians should come to church regularly, pay 10% of all their earnings to the church organization, read their Bible every day, pray often, live a righteous life, be accountable to someone, and keep all of God's commandments. On top of all that, you shouldn't drink, smoke, chew, or associate with those who do. The preacher explained that doing all these good things and refraining from doing the bad things would ensure that the Christian was walking closely with God.

Frank left his first church meeting very excited about being a Christian! And now he knew exactly what he needed to do to be a good Christian and stay close with the Lord. He started right away.

As soon as Frank got home from the church meeting that Sunday morning, he studied his Bible. He loved it! He read all afternoon. After a while, when he got tired of reading, Frank remembered what the preacher said about doing good things for other people. Frank decided to try to find something good he could do for someone else. He decided that he would mow his neighbor's grass. After mowing the grass for his neighbor, Frank also decided that he would start eating more healthily. After his meal that evening, he read his Bible some more, said his prayers, and then went to bed.

As Frank lay in bed that Sunday night, he thought about how good he now felt about his life. Frank felt so pleasing to the Lord because of the good choices he was now making. After years of sin and displeasing God, he was finally doing the right thing. He was finally close with God. He enjoyed a peaceful sleep.

Over the next few days, Frank continued to read his Bible, eat healthily, and pray often. He also made it a point to find good things he could do for other people whenever he could.

After about three weeks went by on one particular day, Frank wasn't feeling quite as motivated to read his Bible as he had been. He wanted to read his Bible, and he was still excited about it, but he just wasn't quite as excited about it as he had been at first. He was also getting just a little tired of doing things for other people. He wanted to, but just not as much as he had wanted to previously. Frank wanted to take a little break.

Frank decided to go watch a baseball game one afternoon. He didn't read his Bible at all that day. He prayed some, but not as much as normal. That night when it was time to go to bed, Frank began to say his usual prayers. But something didn't seem quite right. He didn't feel the same about God as he had been. God seemed a little distant. Frank was feeling a little guilty.

Because Frank was feeling a little guilty for not doing all the things he knew he should have been doing, he felt like God was a little disappointed in him. For the first couple of weeks after Frank became saved, he felt very close to God, but now it was different. He felt like God was not as pleased with him as He had been a few weeks ago. God was now becoming more distant.

Self-Effort Replaces Trusting Christ as a Person
When we don't believe the truth of the good news in our heart (That the blood of Jesus makes us completely clean, right with God, and one with the person of Christ), we are susceptible to believing lies. The truth of the gospel is a simple and singular truth. If we are lacking in a daily heart belief of the gospel, then there are a variety of ways we can derail in error.

There is a lot of popular teaching today that gives us formulas for growth. Most are extremely rooted in self-effort and subtle legalism. In our story above, Frank believed the very common lies that are being preached today. In order to grow and be close to God, Frank believed he must do things. Frank felt closer to God when he was doing good things because he actually felt better about himself. However, the commandment of Jesus Christ is not that Frank do things, but rather that he believe:

> *Jn. 6:28-29 "Therefore they said to Him, "What shall we do, so that we may work the works of God?" Jesus answered and said to them, "This is the work of God, that you believe in Him whom He has sent."*

Believing God is our work. God doesn't want you doing things for Him. He wants to do it through you. But you cannot allow Him to do anything through you if you won't give up on doing things out of your own self-effort. Trusting God in your heart is what you are to do. Humbling yourself and becoming a child is what you are to do. This is really the only thing that you can do, for apart from Him, you can do nothing (Jn. 15:5).

Christian Growth
How do you grow in God? What is the ultimate secret to all Christian growth? It is receiving love, receiving grace, and humbling yourself to believe, trust, and receive the person of Jesus Christ during the moments of your day.

As you start to read the next passage, don't say to yourself, "I already know the point of this passage." There is always more depth and more understanding. Don't skip it either just because it is scripture and "You've already read the scriptures and know what they say." Read slowly and put your heart "under" the word of God as you read:

> *Lk. 10:38-42 "Now as they were traveling along, He entered a village; and a woman named Martha welcomed Him into her home. She had a sister called Mary, who was seated at the Lord's feet, listening to His word. But Martha was distracted with all*

her preparations; and she came up to Him and said, "Lord, do You not care that my sister has left me to do all the serving alone? Then tell her to help me." But the Lord answered and said to her, "Martha, Martha, you are worried and bothered about so many things; but only one thing is necessary, for Mary has chosen the good part, which shall not be taken away from her."

Letting go in your heart to who He is and what He has already done is the one thing that is necessary. The essence of what it means to "believe God" and trust Him is to cease from all of your self-effort. Stop focusing on doing things and relax your heart into Him. Let go to Him inside yourself. He will do what needs to be done. He will lead you. He will give you the thoughts you need to think. He will give you the words you need to say. He will give you the power, the desire, the clarity, and the unction to do mighty things- but it will all come from Him within you. You are to only be a trusting child who receives love. This is the only way to be used of God; otherwise, you are serving God in your flesh. You will only burn out, become exhausted, and develop hypocrisy in your life. It is the love of God filling your heart that grows you and matures you as a Christian. Doing good things for others, reading your Bible, and giving are all by-products.

The fleshly, legalistic Christian uses the instructions in scripture to love one another, to serve, and to do good works in order to feel closer to God and be more acceptable to Him. Doing things will never make you more pleasing to God. There are outward things we can do that are pleasing to God; however, doing outward things that are pleasing to God does not make *who we are* more pleasing to God. It is not the deeds you do that make you pleasing or not pleasing. It is only the blood of Jesus that makes you a righteous person. If who you are is righteous, then you will do righteous things. But doing righteous things does not make you righteous.

> *Isa 64:6 "For all of us have become like one who is unclean, And all our righteous deeds are like a filthy garment…"*

If you have children, you will be able to relate to this principle. If your children do things that are not pleasing to you, do you love them any less? No you do not. If they do things that are pleasing to you, do you love them more? No you do not. It is "who they are" that you love. Your love for who they are is not tied to what they do or don't do – at least it shouldn't be. Although you certainly want them to do the things that you want them to do, your love for them is not tied to their doing. Imagine if your children were constantly scurrying around the house trying to do things to get you to love them more and be pleased with who they are. Imagine if your children were constantly doing one chore after another just to see if you would love them more and see them as more valuable. When your children were not doing any chores to please you, they would then feel guilty and unloved as though you were distant and displeased with who they were as children.

As a parent, this would wear you out. It would also be frustrating because they were refusing to believe the truth that you loved them "no matter what" - apart from what they did or didn't do. You would want to say to your children, "Would you please relax? Stop all of that. I love you if you do things or if you don't do them. Will you stop all of your working and trying to get noticed and just trust that I love you?"

Self-effort is the number one characteristic of the flesh. The flesh is consumed with "itself." Many zealous Christians are very consumed with themselves, their efforts, and their spiritual ambitions. This is all of the flesh. The effort of the flesh is the direct opposite of trust. You may be familiar with terms such as "striving" or "self-righteousness" in order to describe the legalistic nature of the flesh. There are many very subtle varieties of self effort.

The Arrogant and Driven Self-Pleasing Flesh

The legalistic flesh will always judge faith alone in Christ as "easy believism." The flesh looks with condescension at the idea of grace. It judges the message of grace as follows:

>"Letting you off the hook."
>"An excuse for being passive."
>"The hippie gospel."
>"A freedom to sin message."

The flesh wants to work for God and do what God requires. The flesh wants to believe that it can make some contribution to righteousness and to God's acceptance. However, it is much *more difficult* to truly believe in the heart and receive grace than it is to do things for God.

>*Rom. 4:4-5* "*Now to the one who works, his wage is not credited as a favor, but as what is due. But to the one who does not work, but believes in Him who justifies the ungodly, his faith is credited as righteousness,*"

Doing good works for God requires no death of self. *It is much easier "to do" than it is "to die."* Believing God requires the total death of your flesh. Doing for God allows your flesh to stay active and alive.

Legalism allows you to feel good about yourself by doing certain things instead of having to go through the dying (cost of believing) that trust requires. Coming to Jesus as a person causes your heart to encounter Him as opposed to you working your own system of merit that allows you to stay in control. It causes you to see and admit that you can do nothing to increase your position in Him. To encounter Him causes you to release your own independence and reliance on yourself. To encounter the person of Jesus Christ calls to your heart to yield, to move over, and to trust Him.

Here is a brief list of just a few forms of legalism that replace a submitted encounter with the person of Jesus Christ:

- *A focus* on doing good things.
- *A focus* on living right before God.
- *A focus* on making good choices.
- *A focus* on avoiding what is evil or wrong.
- *A focus* on changing or improving yourself by either outward behaviors or inner attitudes.

Your focus is to only be on Christ Himself alone. As you are abiding in Him, allow Him to show you what behaviors to change or what inner attitudes to have – but only after you have come to Him. Allow God to initiate.

Even the many truths in this book are worthless unless Jesus Christ is addressing them in your heart. You must come to Him first and foremost at all times. If you take the truths in this book or any truth you hear from any source and use it as a methodology of self-effort, you will become defeated. Come to the person of grace and His love first, and let Him use the knowledge in your mind to lead you in what to do (Refer to "The Role of Knowledge" chapter).

As you are trusting the person of Christ in your heart and, therefore, walking after the Spirit, He will lead you to do good works. He will lead you and fill you with the power and desire for right living. He will be the source within you for a passionate love for God. He will pray through you continually. He will become the catalyst for you to make countless good choices. He will give you a strong repulsion to evil and what is unclean. You will only be along for the ride, "getting in" on His life. While abiding in Him, the right living and the good deeds you perform will never become your focus. You will never feel good about yourself for doing good works. Your heart will only care for Christ.

Your only job is to come to the King who is grace and yield your heart into a humble submission and a trusting belief that gives up all control and independence. Let's revisit the account of the Prodigal Son:

> *Lk. 15:17-20 "But when he came to his senses, he said, 'How many of my father's hired men have more than enough bread, but I am dying here with hunger! 'I will get up and **go to my father**, and will say to him, "Father, I have sinned against heaven, and in your sight; I am no longer worthy to be called your son; make me as one of your hired men. So he got up **and came to his father**. But while he was still a long way off, his father saw him and felt compassion for him, and ran and embraced him and kissed him."*

When the Prodigal Son came to his senses and realized that he had blown it, he didn't start trying to do good things. He didn't try to get his act together.

He just came to His father. Coming to your Father is the best thing you can do during the moments of your day. Allow Him to take you where you need to go and focus you on what you need to focus on - but only after you have come to Him.

The Obedience of Faith

To have a primary focus on your outward choices and try to please God through those choices can actually be disobedience. It is disobedience because you are focused on yourself. Trusting Him and believing Him from a heart of humility is your point of obedience.

> *Rom. 1:5 "through whom we have received grace and apostleship to bring about* **the obedience of faith** *among all the Gentiles for His name's sake,"*

> *Rom. 16:26 "but now is manifested, and by the Scriptures of the prophets, according to the commandment of the eternal God, has been made known to all the nations, leading to* **obedience of faith;"**

> *Rom. 6:17 "But thanks be to God that though you were slaves of sin, you became* **obedient from the heart** *to that form of teaching to which you were committed,"*

To obey God, you must first believe Him. You must believe Him when he says that you are righteous and clean. You must believe His love and receive Him as grace for your heart. To obey Him is to believe Him in your heart. As you believe the truth, you will find the place of rest and confidence that you are clean in His eyes apart from your works. Only as you enter into His rest, will you allow the life of Christ within you to express Himself. Your constant self efforts hinder Him from living through you. Your constant efforts at trying to please Him and do the right thing quenches the Spirit of God in your life. Your efforts and your own strength are not Christ Himself – they are your fear, your pride, your self-righteousness, and your fleshly, religious zeal. You are justified and made righteous solely by His blood.

> *Eph. 2:8 "For by grace you have been saved through faith; and that not of yourselves, it is the gift of God; not as a result of works, so that no one may boast."*

Although legalism and self-effort are unhealthy replacements for coming to Christ Himself and trusting Him, there is a danger in this area that must be pointed out. To realize the fact that we are justified and righteous in the inner man and then use that realization as an excuse to not live out that righteousness would be error. This error would lead to living in deception. Christ did not save us so that we could live ungodly lives. We are to allow the life of Christ within us to express Himself as He wills.

Gal. 5:13 "For you were called to freedom, brethren; only do not turn your freedom into an opportunity for the flesh, but through love serve one another."

Phl. 2:13 "For it is God which worketh in you both to will and to do of his good pleasure."

Past Spiritual Concepts

Spiritual concepts that you've seen in the past can also be a substitute for relating to God as a person. No matter how true they may be, past spiritual concepts are not Jesus Christ. Often we replay in our minds things He has shown us in the past or things we've seen about Him. When the revelation you had last month or last week was life-giving and helpful, you may feel as though focusing on it now will continue to bring you life. *Only the Lord Himself is life.* Past revelations are death. What He revealed to you yesterday was for yesterday. The Lord is new today, and He has daily bread for you. He is the bread that came down out of heaven (Jn. 6:51). Come to Him every day, and He will satisfy you.

Ex. 16:20 "But they did not listen to Moses, and some left part of it until morning, and it bred worms and became foul; and Moses was angry with them."

Yesterday's manna will soon breed worms and become foul. Perhaps you recently had a breakthrough experience from God. Relying on yesterday's breakthrough should not become a substitution for coming to the person of Christ today. We often try to bring life for today by working past spiritual breakthroughs into a current method.

Matt. 11:28 "Come to Me, all who are weary and heavy-laden, and I will give you rest."

Reproducing the Emotions of Music

Music can often become a substitution for the life of God. God will certainly put songs in your heart as you come to Him, both individually and corporately. However, it is a temptation to try to reproduce the life of God by singing certain songs that were prompted by the Spirit yesterday. Always come to Him first and then let Him put songs in your heart. Of course, the Spirit of God may put the same songs in your heart that you sang yesterday or last week, but the song will be coming out of His life instead of working backwards by trying to reproduce His life from a song.

Scripture and Truth

You can study scripture and not come to Jesus Christ as a person in your heart. Jesus separated Himself from the scriptures:

> *Jn. 5:39-40 "You search the Scriptures because you think that in them you have eternal life; it is these that testify about Me; and you are unwilling to come to Me so that you may have life."*

Jesus puts an exclamation point on the difference between coming to Him for life and searching the scriptures for life. Filling our thoughts and hearts with truth alone is not coming to Christ who is the source of life. You must purpose to meet with the Lord Himself as you read the scriptures. The Bible is not to be read as a book of rules or a code of behaviors. Jesus said, "the scriptures testify of Me." In other words, the Bible points us to the person of Jesus Christ. Faith is not the same as a concept; therefore, allow the concepts in scripture to lead you to faith in Christ as you read and study. Reading the Bible as a concept is not engaging your heart in faith. It is only engaging in a mental exercise.

> *Rom. 8:6,7 "For the mind set on the flesh is death, but the mind set on the Spirit is life and peace, because the mind set on the flesh is hostile toward God; for it does not subject itself to the law of God, for it is not even able to do so,"*

For years I thought this verse was saying "Think about spiritual or biblical things." However, "the Spirit" is not spiritual things – It is Jesus Christ Himself. Setting your thoughts and your focus on the Spirit is setting your mind on the person of Jesus Christ. This is life and peace.

Self-Production of Various Emotions
Reproducing certain feelings or emotions is not coming to Christ. Although love, joy, and peace are all heartfelt experiences, they are "fruit" or a by-product of the Spirit. Feelings are always a result of what is filling your heart. If the feelings themselves ever become your focus, you will miss the Lord Himself and never connect with Him. This can be a slippery slope at times, especially when you begin to encounter the Lord in a real way in your heart. When you begin to connect with God in a real way in your heart, you will often feel intense experiences of peace, love, and joy. These feelings can be highly addictive. It is imperative that you never try to reproduce those feelings. Your flesh will want to use the Lord as a means to feel wonderful feelings. If you do so, you will not connect with Him in your heart, and you will become frustrated. For the flesh, the good feelings are the goal. But when you are according to the Spirit, Jesus Christ Himself is the goal. The feelings are only the fruit of His life flowing through you. *You cannot want "to feel Christ" more than you want Jesus Christ Himself.*

God Changing Your Situation or Circumstance
It is tempting at times to focus on God changing your circumstance. If you do this for very long, you will set yourself up for a life of disappointment in God and ultimately a loss of your faith. We often add to the message of the gospel of what He promised. Our flesh subtly believes that "If He loves me,

then He will do this for me." This is not always so. *God never promised to change your circumstances.* He did promise that you would have His love, His comfort, the forgiveness of your sins, and eternal life. He also promises you suffering, persecution, and trials in this life (Matt. 13:21, Matt. 24:9). God is not your Santa Clause.

Lifestyle

Christians love to occupy their minds and hearts with Christian lifestyle ideas and feel justified in doing so. Gardening, living in community, living debt-free, end-time conspiracies, Bible prophecy, fixing your marriage, raising better kids, home schooling, etc. are all good "things," but they are not to become a substitute for coming to Christ Himself in the moments of your day. If you allow your heart to focus on these things, they will keep you from connecting with Jesus Christ Himself. Similar to biblical truth and concepts, these things appear to be noble pursuits, therefore we tend to not flag or check ourselves when they become a focus. Childlike submission to His Lordship in a connecting exchange of love is our primary heart posture. This can only be achieved through relating to the Lord as a real person.

When we are dealing with people (including the person of Christ), it tends to lead us out of our head and into our heart. True faith and heart belief is not a concept we adhere to but a person we are trusting in.

Faith is the Only Thing That Works

The flesh will use anything as a substitute for relating to God as a person and simply loving Him and receiving His love. All of the many truths you have learned and are learning are never to become a substitute for simply coming to your Father and just being with Him. The more you learn, the more you will be tempted to "work a system" or let those things replace Him. Truths such as "You have right standing with God," "It is no longer you that live but Him", etc. are only truths. Your heart cannot connect with a truth - only another person. *Every truth that you learn must become a distant second to relating to God as a person.* Once you have extended your faith to be aware of Him and His presence with you, then trust Him to remind you of certain truths (if and when He chooses to do so).

> Jn. 14:26 *"But the Helper, the Holy Spirit, whom the Father will send in My name, He will teach you all things, and bring to your remembrance all that I said to you."*

The New Testament Instructions

In this chapter we have covered many subjects that relate to knowing God as a person. We have also addressed how legalism and self-effort are common replacements for true faith. We will conclude this chapter by addressing a related issue.

As we have seen, the New Testament contains plenty of passages that encourage the Christian to engage in inner activities such as receiving grace, taking in love, and walking after the Spirit. The New Testament, however, is also full of instructions telling the Christian how to behave outwardly such as demonstrating patience, acting Godly, and doing good works. Because of these directives, some may ask the question, "If the primary things Christians are to give themselves to consist of inner activities such as humility, trust, and walking after the Spirit, then why is there so much instruction in the New Testament that addresses how Christians are to behave outwardly?"

Before Jesus came, the authors of the New Testament were Jews who were trying to follow the Old Testament law. When the Spirit of Jesus Christ began to dwell within these men and they began to experience Christ, a radical shift occurred in their experience of life. Because the New Testament writers *were writing the New Testament letters while according to the Spirit*, their letters reveal their new desires, conduct, and way of living while being after the Spirit.

On the contrary, the New Testament is often read by Christians while they are according to the flesh. As the flesh reads letters written by men who were experiencing Jesus Christ in their spirit while simultaneously writing scripture, a code of behavior is created in the flesh that the Christian tries to achieve using the outward instructions - but *without the inward experience.*

The outward instructions in the New Testament are largely describing *what it is like* to be according to the Spirit. Outward directives in the New Testament are not meant to be accomplished while living after the flesh.

For example, when an unbeliever observes the outward life of a Christian, it appears to the unbeliever that the life of a Christian is only about living under extreme rules and restrictions. The unbeliever does not understand that a Christian's desires are changed from within and therefore, produce in him a hunger and enjoyment for righteous living. The same is true for the many behavioral directions in the New Testament. These commands simply cannot be properly understood or even accomplished by the flesh of the Christian.

An analogy would be a skydiver who recorded skydiving instructions on a voice recorder while he was in the very act of skydiving: "Keep your head tucked! Spread your arms wide! Now, pull the chute!" If someone were to listen later to those recorded instructions while on the ground, many of the instructions would not make much sense. Some of the instructions would be impossible to replicate while on the ground. In spite of all that, many Christians try to fulfill spiritual New Testament instructions while in the flesh and not after the Spirit.

The instructions that address right living in the New Testament are easily accomplished when living according to the Spirit. Living from the Spirit of Christ in you is *the prerequisite* to daily Christian living. Living according to the Spirit is "the how" while the outward instructions are often "the what." If you try to fulfill specific behaviors without "the how" of the Spirit, you will become self-righteous, legalistic, hypocritical, and defeated. Multitudes of Christians try to accomplish New Testament instruction while after their flesh, but it was never designed to be this way.

As a result, zealous Christian men read the New Testament instructions without much understanding of living from the Spirit and the dynamics of the heart. They then become preachers and propagate their fleshly zeal from the pulpit causing a mass proliferation of self-effort and legalism throughout Christendom. Rarely is the complete message of the good news of grace and life in the Spirit preached without some form of legalism and self-effort attached to it.

Note:
[1] Jn. 15:5

Questions for Understanding and Discussion

1. What is connecting and why is it important?
2. Explain the illogical nature of grace.
3. Who is Grace and why is it important to realize this?
4. Describe various forms of legalism.
5. What is the obedience of faith?
6. How can spiritual concepts become dangerous?

Yielding the Heart

Scenario #1:

There once was a lady who had a terrible fall in a restaurant in which she broke her ribs. She was having trouble breathing and she was gasping for air. Afraid and panicked while she lay on the floor, she desperately called out for help. The manager of the restaurant came to her aid as a small crowd gathered around the lady to help her. The manager called out in a loud voice across the restaurant, "Is there a doctor here? This lady has fallen and she needs help!" A gentleman walked up to the injured lady who was lying on the ground struggling to breathe. "I can help you miss," the gentleman said. "Are you a doctor?" the lady blurted out in pain. "No, I am not, but I know exactly what to do," said the gentleman. "Somebody hold her head up," said the gentleman. He proceeded to work on the lady and perform specific procedures in order to stabilize her. The injured lady became even more panicked. This stranger, who was not a doctor, was working on her and performing medical procedures. She felt so afraid. "Careful!" she shouted. "What are you doing!" she yelled. "Oh my God, what are you doing now!" she screamed. Finally the man finished and the lady was completely stabilized until the ambulance arrived.

Scenario #2:

There once was a lady who had a terrible fall in a restaurant and broke her ribs. She was having trouble breathing and she was gasping for air. Afraid and panicked while she lay on the floor, she desperately called out for help. The manager of the restaurant came to her aid as a small crowd gathered around the lady to help her. The manager called out in a loud voice across the restaurant, "Is there a doctor here? This lady needs help!" A gentleman walked up to the lady who was lying on the ground struggling to breathe. "I can help you miss," the gentleman said. "Are you a doctor?" the lady blurted out in pain. "Yes, I am a doctor. I am the chief surgeon at the hospital right down the street." The doctor began to work on the lady and perform medical procedures to stabilize her. The lady was completely calm. She was at peace and at total rest. She knew that she was in the hands of a very skilled physician.

Scenarios Explained

Both the doctor and gentleman who was not a doctor performed the exact same procedure on the injured lady. There was no difference in what either of the men did. Yet, the first lady's experience was totally different than the experience of the second lady.

Why did lady number one have a different experience than lady number two? The second lady trusted in her heart, and the first lady did not.

Lady number one experienced fear and anxiety while the man who was not a doctor performed medical procedures on her. She was not at peace. Because of her fear, she was trying to control the situation.

However, lady number two experienced rest and peace. She knew in her heart that she was in good hands and that she would be just fine. She felt no need to correct the doctor. She felt no need to make sure he was doing it right, and she did not question him.

Lady number two yielded her heart to the doctor; lady number one did not yield her heart. When the doctor told lady number two that he was a doctor, she moved over and put herself "under him." She submitted herself to his authority and his expertise. Trust causes the heart to submit or "be under."

Recall from an earlier chapter that heart belief will always require something of you and cost you something. "Being under" is the cost of believing God. To trust someone else will cost you. It is the cost of belief. Why is "being under" a cost? - Because "to be under" someone else is very risky. The essence of trust is the act of *giving power to someone else*.

Protecting Yourself from God

> *Is. 6:1-5 "In the year of King Uzziah's death I saw the Lord sitting on a throne, lofty and exalted, with the train of His robe filling the temple. Seraphim stood above Him, each having six wings: with two he covered his face, and with two he covered his feet, and with two he flew. And one called out to another and said, 'Holy, Holy, Holy, is the Lord of hosts, The whole earth is full of His glory.' And the foundations of the thresholds trembled at the voice of him who called out, while the temple was filling with smoke. Then I said, "Woe is me, for I am ruined! Because I am a man of unclean lips, And I live among a people of unclean lips; For my eyes have seen the King, the Lord of hosts."*

How could we describe what it would be like to have a face- to -face encounter with the Almighty Creator of the universe? Overwhelming? Breathtaking? Astounding? Intense? There are no words that would adequately describe what it would be like.

How would you respond? Would you leap for joy? Would you dance with exhilaration? Would you cry? Would you bow before Him with your face flat on the ground in extreme, humble respect? Would you run toward Him as fast as you could and jump into His arms of love and hug Him? When His piercing eyes actually connected with your eyes and in the moment God looks directly into you and through you…what would you feel? Would you feel fear because He has known your every thought and every heart intent since the day you were born? Or, would you feel loved and completely safe?

None of us will know for sure how we will respond until it actually happens. We saw above how Isaiah responded. Let's look at another example.

> *Gen. 3:8 "They heard the sound of the Lord God walking in the garden in the cool of the day, and the man and his wife hid themselves from the presence of the Lord God among the trees of the garden."*

After Adam and Eve disobeyed God, their eyes were opened to know good and evil. They realized they were naked before God, and they hid themselves. Then Adam responds:

> *Gen. 3:10 "He (Adam) said, "I heard the sound of You in the garden, and I was afraid because I was naked; so I hid myself."*

When Adam gained the knowledge of good and evil, he suddenly became self-aware and self-conscious. When Adam told God that he was afraid and naked, God responded to Adam by saying, "Who told you that you were naked?" Of course, God knew the answer to the question. No one told Adam he was naked. Adam just became aware of the fact that he was naked after he ate of the fruit, and then he hid himself from God.

To be totally naked and exposed before God Almighty is a terrifying and fearful thing to our flesh. In the presence of God, our game playing is over. All of our self-deceptions and all of our agendas are exposed. Every dark deed and every wicked thought is before Him. Everything about us is laid completely bare in His presence.

> *Lk. 5:8 "But when Simon Peter saw that, he fell down at Jesus' feet, saying, "Go away from me Lord, for I am a sinful man!"*

To be totally exposed to our holy God can be a terrifying thing. God is much bigger than you. When you are near someone who is bigger and much more powerful than you are, it can be intimidating. What might they do? What might they say? They are in a position to really hurt you and cause you tremendous harm.

The Lord God Almighty is truly bigger than you. God is holy and perfectly righteous, and He requires righteousness from you as well. He is calling all the shots. He is in total control. He has the power to totally destroy you, annihilate you, and throw you into hell where you will be tortured forever. God is a consuming fire who will deal with His enemies with vengeance, wrath, and with fury. God is the ultimate authority figure who knows every thought and intent of your heart.

Unseen Walls in Your Heart

Perhaps you learned at an early age that your earthly father was not always safe and loving. Perhaps you realized that your dad can wound you and hurt you very deeply. Your dad can leave you and abandon you. Your father was the ultimate authority for you when you were a very little person – he was like God to you. Maybe your dad didn't physically leave you or move away, but if he neglected you emotionally, it was the same as him leaving you and not being present.

I knew a man once who personally described his father as being home often but never connecting with his children while he was at home. His dad would read the newspaper and he would watch TV, but he would never play with his children or engage with them.

When the five-year-old heart is longing to connect and engage with a dad who is not available, there is disappointment and hurt. When a dad is at home sitting in his chair preoccupied while reading his newspaper and ignoring his children, it feels like rejection to the five-year-old heart that is longing for connection.

So what does a little child do when dad rejects, abandons, or hurts him? Just like Adam and Eve, he protects himself from dad. You hide from him. You learn how to not need Him. You find other things to do and other things to fill your heart. You slowly become self-reliant and self-sufficient. You become independent.

You still have that little person heart of yours deep inside of you. As you grew up, you learned how to protect that tender heart of yours so that it is not so easily crushed. You have many fears inside of you that have caused you to build walls in order to fortify yourself. Your walls of fortification help you to not feel the fear. In many ways, you are still afraid of totally trusting dad.

There are a thousand different scenarios we could describe of abuse, neglect, abandonment, and hurt that we all received at tender ages. It is not even necessary for you to see them all or know what they all are. As you give yourself to vulnerability with the Lord, He will show you what you need to know, and He will address any specifics about the walls in your heart - all in His timing.

You may not agree that you have walls in your heart that protect you from God. However, it is very difficult to see your own walls of self-protection. Many walls have been there so long you don't even know they are there. Walls in your heart become like eyeglasses that have been permanently attached over your eyes since you were a baby. You see everything through them. You relate to people while wearing them, and you view yourself through those same glasses as well. You are so used to the walls in your heart, and they are so much a part of your everyday experience, that you become accustomed to them. You actually think that life's reality is viewed from your walls. But it is not. You actually think that your walls are "you." But they are not.

Walls of self-protection have horrible consequences for your life. You don't get to live who you really are. It is like settling for a jail cell of safety instead of the freedom of vulnerability. Walls of self-protection sacrifice your freedom in order for you to feel security which is an illusion. What's worse is that self-protecting walls do just that – they "wall up" your heart and then shut you down. Therefore, those around you don't get to taste who you really are. Those around you only get a shallow version of you or a part of you from time to time. Depending on how you've coped, people around you may experience "a witty you," or a "know it all you", or a "nobody is home you", an "entertaining you", or a "hopeless, discouraged, negative and depressed you."

Whatever false "you" you have predominately chosen, one thing is for certain: In the long-run, the false you is not very enjoyable to other people. Many times the false "you" is off-putting and unpleasant to others. Whether or not your false you "clicks" with others will depend on what person or group of people you are around, and on the false personas they themselves have. Another way to say this would be, "Does your flesh like their flesh?" Similar versions of flesh or "false-personas" will seek each other out for camaraderie and a joining together in things of the flesh. Fleshly relationships (which most are), are shallow, unfulfilling, and usually end poorly. Fleshly relationships can only go so deep because both parties are terrified of true intimacy and vulnerability.

Only your true self, without your walls of self-protection, is life- giving to others, enjoyable to be around on a long-term basis, and edifying. As a Christian, the childlike, unprotected you produces the fruit of the Spirit of God and genuinely loves others from humility and a place of contrition.

The extreme irony is that you originally put up your walls of self-protection because you didn't feel safe, loved, or enjoyed for who you really were. Therefore, you created a self-protecting wall. This wall, in turn, causes you to portray an unenjoyable false "you" to other people. This in turn provides you with even more feedback that you are not enjoyable or loved. The flesh always sabotages itself as you end up self-fulfilling your own prophecy.

Giving yourself to becoming the humble child that you already are in your spirit allows you to walk in the capacity for the Spirit you currently have. Moreover, your vulnerability while in this true state of humility allows the Lord to dismantle your constructs of false walls which insulate you and provide you with self-protection.

The Source of Control

As mentioned in the "The Anatomy of Man" chapter, the number one objective of all living creatures is survival. To put yourself under someone who is bigger and more powerful than you and to trust Him completely goes against the very grain of your flesh. Even the concept of trusting is directly opposed to the primary goal of the flesh. In any given moment, the death of the flesh is certain if you move to a position of trust because the flesh will no longer be in control and, therefore, will not remain independent. This situation is exactly what must take place in order for you to yield your heart to trust the Lord who is bigger than you. When the body (including your brain and its thoughts) submits to God in trust via the heart, the body ceases to be the flesh and becomes a tool in God's hand for righteous deeds and thoughts. *Letting go of control is letting go to trust.* Letting go to trust is allowing someone else to have power over you.

If you've ever been a passenger in a car while someone else was driving, you've probably experienced the fear of not being in control. Especially if the weather was bad, the terrain was dangerous, or if you didn't have a lot of confidence in the driver's ability, fear may have gripped your heart. You may have blurted things out such as, "Look out! Would you mind slowing down? There is a dangerous curve ahead…"

We human beings are a frail species. Our bodies are weak. We get sick and injured easily. Our minds are weak. We become easily confused, and we can frequently feel lost. It can be hard for us to make decisions if we get overwhelmed or if we don't understand.

If we will face it, deep inside each human being there is a feeling of powerlessness. We live in a harsh and hostile environment called planet Earth. Earth is a fallen world. Earth is like a holding tank that is full of wicked, fearful, evil, and selfish people who are all trying to survive together.

Because of our weakness and frailties while living in such an unsafe environment, we are often afraid. We are afraid of losing our jobs and being without money. We are afraid of people hurting us and rejecting us. We are afraid of getting a horrible disease and afraid of suffering. We are afraid of being manipulated, deceived, and controlled by other people. We are afraid of looking foolish to others, afraid of being a failure, afraid of ridicule, and afraid of looking stupid. We are afraid that who we really are as a person is unlovable and undesirable. We are afraid of rejection by those we esteem the highest.

As a species, we are gripped with, controlled by, and are largely motivated by fear. The Lord compares us to sheep, a very fearful animal.

You may not see much fear in yourself or think of yourself as a fearful person. But everyone has fear. The way that you deal with your fear may cause you to not feel it as much. In many ways, you have compensated for fear. This allows you to function as an adult in society and not live feeling constant fear.

Much of the adjusting and compensating you have done in order to not live in your fear has actually shaped your personality. How you have chosen to deal with your fear has created many of your ongoing choices and many of the patterns you live out every day. Your patterns of fear and the compensations you make for them has largely developed the daily experience you have in your heart. It has affected and shaped how you view yourself and the world around you. It has created the particular set of glasses you wear through which you view the world and yourself.

Compensating or coping with fear is actually how you have taken inner steps to alleviate fear's crippling effects. Adam and Eve hid from God because they were ashamed and afraid. When you were much younger, you may have felt the fear of other children not liking you or loving you in the way that you wanted them to. You probably made up for it in some way. You either made those particular kids "not matter," or you propped yourself up on the inside to make yourself feel bigger and better about yourself in some way. You may have tried to be someone that you were not in order to impress your friends or fool them into thinking you were someone to be liked and loved. This has happened many times, in many different relationships, and in many different variations.

As you grew older, you began to feel the expectations of other people's standards weighing on you. There began to be expectations for you to make wise choices, to become an adult, to provide for yourself, and to be responsible. You were expected to be a functioning member of society. In order to deal with this pressure, you coped and compensated by taking it upon yourself to develop skills and education so that you could rely on yourself and not on anyone else. You could not remain a little child on the inside. You had to "grow up" and *become* an adult. This became your new persona and your idea of who you really are.

Many times (It is certainly not true in every case), the wealthier a person is, the deeper his insecurities may be. Sometimes a very strong drive for success is really a strong drive to put away fear. Money, education, and pouring one's life into a business can all be compensations for fear. Over time, the fear is not as easily seen because it becomes buried under layers of self-protection and illusions of security.

Very often, strong manifestations and extreme outward expressions reveal equally extreme inward feelings of lack, weakness, and fear. The man with multiple tattoos, body piercings, rugged clothing, and an oversized pick-up truck has sometimes made these outward choices in order to cope with and mask his intense insecurities. The bigger his truck, the deeper his fear may be. We bluff.

More than likely, you have made many unhealthy compensations. Much of your coping and compensation to avoid fear is totally on a subconscious level. Much of it was developed at a young age. Many of your patterns are so much a part of your identity that you don't even notice them anymore. They are habits that are ingrained in your flesh that are now a part of "you" (At least who you think you are).

Remember that coping and compensation are choices and responses we make in order to survive and deal with fear. The fear is still there, but it is now below the surface and masked with the particular coping that you chose in order to deal with it. As God reveals to you your unhealthy coping and compensations, your original fear will scream at you as you attempt to let go and trust God.

However, in some areas you didn't cope so well. You still have some gaping holes where you still feel your fear. In other areas, you did cope and compensate well. But even in the areas where you coped well - it is a mask so you don't have to feel crippled and afraid.

The injured lady who did not trust the man who was not a doctor felt fear. Her constant questioning of him and yelling out was an attempt to gain some sort of control over the situation. If you are a passenger in a car, and the driver is going too fast on the edge of a cliff, you may try to make sure the driver slows down in order to gain a sense of control.

Hardness of Heart

Over time we develop "heart postures" of control. In other words, being in control is the way we tend to stay. These heart postures become internal positions that we tend to maintain. We have ongoing stances of self-protective walls that we maintain and do not see. When these walls are in place, they surround the fragile and easily hurt childlike heart. They serve to protect, but the effect is that they dampen the senses. Thick prison walls may keep us safe from the outside world, but they are also isolating and restrictive. They hinder us from loving and receiving love.

To begin the process of dismantling the self-erected walls of protection is to begin the process of giving up control. This activity introduces us to a terrifying word: Risk.

To let go of your control, you will have to risk the very thing you fear–being out of control. To allow God, your mighty and powerful Father, to have full control over you, you will have to let down your walls of self-protection in His presence. To release your stance of control and independence will mean that you will become extremely vulnerable to Him. Intimacy is the result.

The Vulnerable Heart

The Lord God certainly has the power to destroy, and a day is coming when He will destroy. Perhaps you are well aware how tremendously risky it is to trust someone with your heart who is bigger than you. But God is not the same person as your earthly father or other authority figures in your life who were imperfect.

I have met many children who avoid eye contact with adults. If you look into their eyes, the children's eyes will look up, down, sideways, anyplace but into your eyes. Children (and often adults) who do this are avoiding intimacy and any kind of vulnerability. We often have the same problem with our heavenly Father. We will look anywhere but directly into His eyes. However, this is the very thing we need to do most.

As powerful and as terrible as the Lord is, He is equally as gentle, kind, and tenderhearted. He will deal with His enemies with fire and fury, but He saves His tenderness for you who believe. He is full of love and tender mercy to those who fear Him and break under His holy power and authority. He is a strong Father. He is a good Father. His heart is toward His children. He loves you and wants intimate fellowship with you.

In order to let go of your control and need for safety apart from Him, you must realize that it is safe to do so. God is love. Therefore God is safe. He is not like a man or an earthly father who is imperfect, selfish, or hurtful.

In God you are perfectly safe. In fact, He is the only place that is truly safe. The self-made walls of protection that you have built to deal with your fear only provide a false feeling of safety. Your walls have not worked for you. They have only imprisoned you inside the death of your own lifeless soul. They have distanced you from others.

Instead of hiding in your walls, you can now hide in God who truly loves you and who will truly keep you safe. There is complete security in God and His mighty love. He will protect you, and He will fight for you like no other.

You are a delight to God. If you become your true self who is like a little child, you will be like an unprotected baby with the Lord (not protecting yourself, but protected by Him). Give yourself to becoming even more unprotected and vulnerable than you could ever imagine. When you find a heart of vulnerability toward the Lord, allow yourself to become even more vulnerable and unprotected. Let Him be your Father. Let Him inside the most intimate places within you. Open yourself up to Him completely and in every way. Let Him explore the depths of your heart. He is gentle, He is good, and He is kind. The Spirit Himself will help you in this. He is most definitely helping you to become the vulnerable child that you are in your spirit.

Many times you may find a flood of emotions come up in you when you move toward childlike vulnerability and intimacy. Most of your "false self" or your "adult identity" is a person of walls and self-protection. More than likely, you have lived a false self for many years. Your adult, false self is not vulnerable. There is no need for this false, protected self anymore. You may intensely feel a great need for protection. But "self" protection is not the answer. The Lord is your protection. No one can destroy you in Him. No one can get to you while you are in Him. Though your body can be destroyed, nothing can kill "you" (the inner, spiritual you) because you are in Him. You are eternal because you are in Him, and He is eternal. You will never die. You may feel hurt or feel grieved at times, but you can never be destroyed.

> *2 Cor. 4:8 "we are afflicted in every way, but not crushed; perplexed, but not despairing; persecuted, but not forsaken; struck down, but not destroyed;"*

Not Trusting "For" or "That"

Becoming childlike and vulnerable with the Lord, letting down your walls of self-protection, and giving up control are all postures within the heart. These heart postures are not necessarily focused on any specific thing. It is just how you are on the inside. In other words, when you move over to trust the Lord in your heart, you are not focused on trusting Him "for" any particular thing. Nor are you are trusting Him "that" a certain thing will happen.

Although it is good to ask for specifics and then release them to God (1 Pet. 5:7), it is never to be *your focus* that He will do something for you or change some situation. Your focus is on Him and who He is, not that He would change something for you. It is common for Christians to only trust the Lord "for" something or only trust Him "that" this or that will happen. This is a common error.

The only exception to this would be if perhaps the Lord were to speak to you in some particular way or give you specific wisdom concerning a situation. If this were the case, then it would be good to trust Him "for" what He has said. But for you to choose what you want to trust Him for, when He has not addressed it, would be amiss.

For example, perhaps you wanted enough money to purchase a new car so that you don't have to drive the old car you have now. For you to choose to trust the Lord for money for a new car would not be a good thing. He has never promised you a new car.

The Lord promises you Himself and His love. He promises you eternal life. He promises to give you wisdom if you ask for it. He promises forgiveness of sins if you trust in Jesus. But to trust in Him for what you decide that you want to trust Him for attempts to turn God into a tooth fairy. Your flesh will try to manipulate God, but He is not playing.

> *Matt. 6:32 "For the Gentiles eagerly seek all these things; for your heavenly Father knows that you need all these things."*

Many Christians have become disappointed in the Lord, and some have become shipwrecked in their faith because their trust in Him has been set on specifics and has not been "general" in nature. We are to trust Him in a general way inside of our hearts. Trust Him that He loves you. Trust Him that He is good. Trust Him that He is with you and leading you. Trust Him that He knows. He knows and is aware that you have physical needs such as a worn out car. You can certainly ask Him for a new car. It is good to ask Him for all things that you need. But to trust in the specific that He will actually give you a new car would set you up for failure if He hasn't spoken it to you.

Moving Toward Trust

The very essence of moving from the flesh to the spirit *is trust in the heart*. There are many other subjects that surround this core action: the character of God and who He really is, the nature of our true self in the spirit, the action of humbling yourself and becoming childlike, etc. These are all important subjects, and some are prerequisites to trust. But they are separate from the singular action of trusting in the heart. The core and most essential issue will always hinge on whether or not you are trusting Jesus Christ in your heart.

The essence of trust is giving up the control you have in your heart and then giving control over to God. When you know He is love and you have become very small like a child, giving control to God is more easily accomplished. Another way to describe giving control to the Lord would be to say that you are giving Him total power over you. You must be aware of Him as a person when you do this action in your heart. Otherwise, He will only be a distant concept in your head. To give control in your heart to the person of Jesus Christ is giving Him control and power over your mind, your will, your emotions, and your body. All that you are is to yield under His authority.

Trusting is More Than Humble Vulnerability

Letting go of your control and giving control to Him is a trusting heart posture. Humble, childlike heart postures with no walls of self-protection are a prerequisite to trust and letting go of control. You can become childlike and vulnerable but not move fully over into trusting. Trusting is giving Him "the steering wheel" of control inside of yourself. When you move into trust, you are giving the power to God to determine your worth, the power to examine you, the power to lead you, and the power to determine your value.

You can choose to yield your heart to your new Father. He is good. He won't destroy you even though He could. In fact, He has wanted to be with you this whole time. He has been waiting for you to come to Him and trust Him with your heart.

To yield your heart in total trust is to "give yourself" to Him. To trust Him is to place yourself under Him and His mighty authority and fully let go. Let Him have you - all of you. Surrender your will. Surrender your entire self under Him. He is a very skilled physician. He created you and He loves you. He loves you with an everlasting love. His heart is amazingly kind and tender toward you. God is for you, and is not against you (Rom. 8:31).

A Golden Key to Trust

Childlike Humility ⟹ **Knowing He is Love** ⟹ Exposed Vulnerability ⟹

⟹ Trust/Dependency ⟹ Intimacy ⟹ Love, Ministry, and Service

You have to know you are safe before you can become vulnerable and move toward total trust. The gospel makes us safe to be vulnerable. To have your sins forgiven is much more than just God letting you off the hook.

God is actually pleased with who you are. Because you now have His same righteousness, God is pleased with who you are as much as He is in His Son Jesus Christ (2 Cor. 5:21). There is no need to hide from God anymore like Adam and Eve did after they sinned. You can open to Him and expose yourself completely to His loving eyes. For your heart to fully know that you are pleasing to Him, loved by Him, wanted, and desired by Him is *a key to trusting God*. I cannot stress this enough.

In the diagram above, we see a progression within the heart from humbling yourself to intimacy with God which then results in love, ministry, and service. Humbling yourself before God is a characteristic of having the fear of the Lord. We can have the fear of the Lord without knowing that He is love. We can humble ourselves in childlike smallness before our Creator because He is God the Almighty. In order to take the next steps and move over into vulnerability, heart submission and trust, we must know that it is safe to do so. We must know that He is love, and that we are wanted and desired.

I have four children. When I think of each one of them, each one is my favorite. I mean that. Each is my favorite in his or her own special way. My son Samuel is the best son that anyone has ever had. I really feel that way about him. I tell him, "You are the best boy in the world." I love my son. He is my favorite of all my kids. But when I think of my oldest daughter Brittney, she is absolutely wonderful. She is so sweet and tenderhearted. To know her is to love her. I really love my Brittney Anne. She is my first born and my favorite child out of all four kids. But then I think of my Heidi. There is no one like my Heidi. She is the most wonderful delight a Dad could ever have. Her heart is so enjoyable, beautiful, eager and delightful. I promise that she is my favorite child of all. But then there is my Emily. I've never met anyone as wonderful as her. Emily has such a big heart and is so full of love and sweetness. I couldn't begin to describe my Emily Moriah. To know Emily is to love her. Yes, I know for a fact that she is definitely my favorite of all my kids.

So guess what? Your heavenly Father feels the same way toward you. You are, without a doubt, His favorite. You can trust Him because He is head over heels in love with you. He made you! There is no one like you to Him. He sees your heart like no one else does. He knows what you've been through, and not one of your tears has been lost. Every hair on your head is accounted for (Matt. 10:30).

It is important to fully understand the good news and all it implies. There is the fact that your sins are forgiven, but there is more to the gospel than just that fact. There is the *emotional import* of the gospel. Because your sins have been forgiven, God's heart is now toward you. You have His smile. You have His smile toward you completely apart from anything you do or don't do. Who you are has been changed apart from your deeds of righteousness or your deeds of unrighteousness. He loves you and His delight is toward you, and it is not based on what you do, but based on what He has done on the cross. You must understand God's heartfelt emotions of love and kindness toward you *before your emotions can connect with Him*. You must know that He wants and desires you.

To trust your powerful, loving Father is to open your heart to Him. Give Him full and total control over you. Right now and in this very moment you can do this. He wants to love on you. Will you let Him?

When you yield your heart to trust Him and let go of your control, it is much like falling. You are "letting go" on the inside and falling into Jesus. You are falling in love with Him. You are falling off a cliff into His arms. He will catch you. He has held you the whole time anyway while you have thought you were carrying yourself. Don't be afraid to let go. He is good and He is strong. He is worthy of trust and confidence.

Spend some time and ask the Lord to help you see how you are in control on the inside. Many times you are as tight as a drum in your heart. You may not see it, but often your heart posture is one of gripping and clenching. Let go and yield to the Spirit of God. Open wide to Him and give up all of your rights (2 Cor. 6:13).

Believing Truth in the Heart

Although it is true that only as the heart is filled with the Spirit are you able to experience the reality of spiritual things, there is sometimes resistance and blockages in the heart to *certain truths* in scripture. When resistance to biblical truth exists in the heart, it can quench or grieve the Spirit of God in your life, limiting your experience in certain areas. It is, therefore, important to be able to believe the truth of God's word in your heart while you are simultaneously allowing your heart to submit to the Spirit Himself. This is especially true in areas that God is specifically addressing with you.

For example, you may give yourself to yielding and trusting God with vulnerability in your heart, but as the Spirit reminds you or encourages you in a *specific* truth, you may resist because your heart has a conflicting belief in that particular area. Your heart must not only yield and trust in the person of Christ, but it must also be submitted to God's truth. In addition, we have seen that certain foundational truths must be believed in order to even begin the process of intimacy and vulnerability. Therefore, believing truth in the heart is important. Here is a good process for believing a specific truth in your heart:

1. Place yourself under the truth.
2. Address objections by reexamining your theology.
3. Release and rerelease current objections.

We will examine each of these in the following sections.

Placing Yourself Under the Truth

Let's look at an example of a truth that hopefully you already have clear in your head because you are a Christian: *You have the same righteousness as Jesus Christ*. This is a true statement according to 2 Cor. 5:21. Let's take it further and begin to believe it with your heart.

First, you must place yourself under the fact that you have the same righteousness as Jesus. In order to place yourself under this truth, you must realize that it is a true statement whether you are experiencing the reality of it or not. Truth exists apart from your perceptions. Just because you don't feel as righteous as Jesus Christ does not make it any less true (We are addressing the righteousness you have in your cleansed spirit, not necessarily the choices you make outwardly). Biblical truths are higher than your thoughts and your emotions (1 Jn. 3:20). God's facts are above you. You are below His facts and subject to them even if you are not fully experiencing them.

To realize that a fact is absolutely true even though you may not fully experience it or even understand it causes you *to be under* the authority of that truth. As you move in this humble direction in your heart, you may see some unwillingness on your part to let it be totally true that you have the exact same degree of righteousness as Christ. If you see unwillingness or hesitation, it could be a problem within your will that is masking itself. Let's look at a couple of possibilities.

Addressing Objections and the "Yeah But's"

We often have resistance and fight in our flesh to many biblical truths. The resistance is greater at certain times than at others depending on your circumstances and what you have been currently experiencing or going through in your life. Often, the resistance inside us is a mask so that we do not have to pay the price in order to "be under" a certain truth. In our intellect, we often don't disagree with certain facts until it is time to actually believe them and the cost is staring us in the face. When this happens, we will come up with logical arguments and excuses to avoid paying the price of changing what is currently in our hearts concerning the matter.

For example, when you press a non-Christian with the actual requirements of the gospel (such as repentance, humility, trust, etc.); he will often come up with many logical questions and rebuttals. A non-believer may say things like, "Yeah, but what about this?" or "Yeah, but what about that?" Many times these are only diversions. They may seem like sincere and legitimate questions and sometimes they are, but many times they are a mask for rebellion and a distraction in order to avoid paying the price of putting himself under biblical truth and ultimately God Himself.

If you will realize that many of the objections and "yeah buts" you have are often a smokescreen, it will help you to go to the root of the matter both with yourself and with others. The flesh does not want to be under anything unless it can create its own rules.

When logical questions are indeed a smokescreen, the person who has the questions could even feel very sincere about his questions. Many times, we actually create emotions that are real emotions and are strongly felt while our motives for creating them are actually hidden from our own selves. We do the same thing with rational questions. When dealing with other people, we must acknowledge what it is they are thinking and feeling but not be fooled in to thinking that these are always the root issues. Fear, pride, and control are some of the most common driving forces behind the flesh.

In our current example of believing that you have the same degree of righteousness as Jesus Christ, an objection may arise such as, "Yeah, but what about the fact that I sin?" This introduces the topic of your current understanding of theology (We are still in step two in our list above).

If your theology (the facts you've decided are true in your head) is a hindrance, then you will need to reexamine your theology. So with our example of "You have the same righteousness as Jesus Christ," if you have a "Yeah, but what if I sin?" or any other interference, then you will need to reexamine to see if you think it is a fact or not by comparing the objection with the authority of scripture. Does the scripture say this? I highly recommend that you always validate proposed truths with the objective facts of scripture before you give yourself to believing and trusting them with your heart.

The point is this: If you are having a problem with the facts in your head, then you must deal with your head first before you can really move on to yielding to them with your heart.

Once the "yeah but" is addressed with scripture (And in our example you should be able to address it very quickly because we know what scripture says about this subject), then you can proceed with giving yourself to believing the truth in your heart by placing yourself under it again.

Rereleasing Objections

Even though you have decided sometimes that the truth is indeed the truth, and you've addressed all of the "yeah but's" of your theology, you may still have the exact same "yeah but" come up in your heart and mind when you are giving yourself to believe a certain truth. This is often due to fear and deeply ingrained flesh patterns. When you have believed a lie long enough, and you've camped out there, so to speak (sometimes for years), in your heart, you will have many objections come up when you start to believe a new truth. This is no cause for alarm. Just remember that you have already decided in your mind what the truth is. As the objections and "yeah but's" come up over and over again, just remember the truth, release the objection yet again, and place yourself under the truth - as often as it takes. You may have to do this many times. Finding true heart belief can be work at times, but over time your objections will become less frequent.

Often when I am learning a new truth, I may have to let the same objection go forty or fifty times a day for a while. The reason is that I have believed something contrary for so long. You will see this phenomena happen a lot when lies are firmly lodged within your heart. A common example is attempting to forgive someone who has wounded you or trying to remove a judgment you have against someone. Just because you have forgiven them once - doesn't mean it will stick even for ten minutes. If your heart has held someone in unforgiveness and judgments for some time, the heart will tend to gravitate back to that place very easily. You will have to be diligent to continue to forgive and release the judgment many times a day, sometimes many times an hour.

You Have a Choice to Yield Your Heart

We mentioned earlier that you have the power to "choose your heart." Many people don't know this. Many people were never required as children to choose their heart attitudes nor have they been aware as adults that God is requiring this.

I certainly was not a perfect parent and I've made many mistakes, but I did have some degree of success. When my children were small, I disciplined them not only for outward disobedience but also for inner attitudes. I recommend you do the same with your children. Likewise, you should also require yourself to have good heart attitudes in order to cooperate with God's daily purpose for you. The attitudes of the heart are ultimately what matter most. Out of the heart behavior is manifested.

A good heart attitude is a heart that is humble, yielding, and trusting in the truth. When a person is not raised as a child to change his attitude, he is often not equipped with a skill set to do so. If this has never been required of a person, he may not even believe it is possible. Again, changing your attitude is the same as changing your heart.

Many are left with the opinion and experience that emotions "just come on you," or that you just have to wait for certain emotions to pass. Someone without the training or requirement to change his own heart and inner attitudes may say something like "I am just gloomy today or I feel depressed. I hope this passes soon." It would be common for him to react emotionally to everything in life. When negative things happen to him or people treat him poorly, he tends to feel like anger just came upon him or hurt feelings just happened to him. He does not realize that he is actually *choosing* to get mad or choosing to stay in his hurt.

You have control over your emotions. Remember that emotions are indicators of current heart beliefs. Those who are given to emotional reactions or who feel like the circumstances of life dictate what their emotions will be, have either not known or have not practiced the ability of choosing their heart beliefs.

"Only God Can Change Your Heart?"

This introduces a common idea amongst many Christians that says, "Only God can change my heart." This statement is somewhat paradoxical. But it is also often misguided.

As we see from many scriptures, God commands us to believe and trust Him in our hearts. *We choose* to believe God, and belief occurs in the heart. When the heart believes and trusts God, change occurs in the heart. Therefore, trusting Him and believing Him in our heart is the same thing as changing our heart. Because we have the choice and the power to yield to God and believe Him, we also have the choice and the power to change what is in our hearts.

While it is true that change in the heart is a work of the Spirit of God, we ultimately choose to cooperate with the process of change.

> *Rev 3:20 "Behold, I stand at the door and knock; if anyone hears My voice and opens the door, I will come in to him and will dine with him, and he with Me."*

This verse applies to both the unbeliever and the Christian. The Spirit of God knocks at the door of the heart in order to initiate change in the heart. Yet, a person must choose to open the door of his heart in order to let the Spirit of God in.

On a daily basis, as the believer yields to the Spirit and trusts Him, the heart is changed. This describes the Christian moving from being after the flesh to being after the Spirit. It is true in one sense that only God can change your heart, but only you can choose to trust and cooperate with Him changing you.

Many Christians have not received adequate teaching concerning the dynamics of the flesh, the Spirit, and trust within the heart. Therefore, they are left to flounder in their inner life. Many times this leads to the statement, "Only God can change my heart." This can be a true statement, but it depends on where you are coming from.

> *Eze 36:26 "Moreover, I will give you a new heart and put a new spirit within you; and I will remove the heart of stone from your flesh and give you a heart of flesh."*

> *Heb 3:12 "Take care, brethren, that there not be in any one of you an evil, unbelieving heart that falls away from the living God."*

We see in Ezekiel 36 that God is telling Israel He will give them a new heart and a new spirit. He will remove the hard heart of stone and give them a soft heart of flesh (not to be confused with the New Testament concept of "the flesh", as this verse is describing a tender and soft heart). God does give us a new spirit (His Spirit) and a new heart. Yet we see from many other scriptures that the heart must cooperate and yield to the Spirit in order for the heart to be filled with the Spirit. Prior to our conversion to Christianity, God does not force us to receive His Spirit. He also does not force the Christian to open his heart to the Spirit for daily living.

Hebrews 3:12 quoted above warns the Christian ("take care brethren") to not have an unbelieving heart. Although the Christian has God's Spirit within him, the Christian is told to have a believing heart, not an unbelieving heart.

When my own children would have an inner attitude of anger, discontent, boredom, complaining, whining, etc., I would *require* them to change their hearts. I would first tell them that they were having a bad attitude. Then I would tell them what their attitude actually was - so they could begin to see their own hearts and identify it. Very gently and sincerely I would say, "You are complaining right now." Dad does not allow you to have a heart that complains. Notice that I told them that I don't allow them to have "a heart that complains." Complaining is not only outward, but also inward, too. A person can have a complaining heart but outwardly make good choices. I would use those specific words with my kids because I was training them to see and choose their inner heart attitudes.

Next, I would say, "Dad is going to give you just a minute to change your heart. I want you to let that complaining go in your heart and start being thankful instead." I would wait a few minutes and then ask them again. "Did you change your complaining heart to a thankful one? Tell me some things you are thankful for…" I would lead them and coach them into the attitude I wanted them to have by leading them into thinking about certain things and by having them view the situation in a different way. When their heart was changed I would say something like, "Can you see now that your heart has changed? You were complaining a few minutes ago but now you are thankful. Isn't it better to have a thankful heart than a complaining one?" This would help them observe the change that took place. Again, this was for the purposes of teaching them to see their inner attitudes and empowering them with the ability to choose their hearts as adults; which is critical for walking with God.

If my children were defiant and not really trying to change their heart after I had required them to do so, I would spank them thoroughly and then start the process all over again.

Of course, at times if it were proper and in order, I would allow them to be disappointed about certain things (for a little while) or experience hurt for a while if something hurt them. Normal emotional responses should not be squelched in our children or in ourselves. We must allow ourselves to have "emotional integrity." If something is hard, hurtful, disappointing, or painful, it is good and healthy to let that come up in us and for us to feel it. We should not suppress emotions. But after we've bled and hurt emotionally for a little while, it is time to move over to receive comfort and love. We should always move over in our hearts to believe the truth in every situation.

I would tell my children, "Yes I know that was hard for you, come here, and let Dad hold you and love you." Then I would hug them and comfort them and let them cry a little while. When it was time, I would begin to tell them the truth and require them to believe it and move over in their hearts. "I know that you wanted to go with those other kids to play and they didn't invite you. I know you felt left out. I'm so sorry that happened (and I meant it). But Dad is here to love you and take care of you, and I have some other things you and I can do together that are fun too. Let's let your disappointment go now and enjoy doing some other things. I want you to let it go and choose instead to be happy about the things you and Dad are going to do together."

Again, if they resisted very much or wanted to stay complaining, it would turn into a matter of disobedience. But usually they did not do this once they received love and comfort.

My encouragement to you the reader is to require your children to have good inner attitudes – all of the time. This not only teaches them how, but it also teaches them that they can. As human beings, we really don't have any power except for the power of choice God gives us. Our human tendency is to do only that which is required of us. As we require our children to change their hearts, it creates the capacity in them to choose to believe and trust the Lord.

Your heavenly Father is requiring the same thing of you. He is requiring that you believe Him. He loves you and has good things for you. He tells you to trust Him from your heart. Of course, you can cry with Him and share with Him your disappointments and hurts. He wants to listen. But He doesn't want you to camp out forever in your pain and disappointments. After a while, He will require you to move over in your heart to believe Him, trust His love, and to see the situation as He sees it.

Christ Dwelling in Your Heart Is Not Automatic

Jesus is always dwelling in your spirit. He is one with your spirit. This is automatic because you are a Christian. But the heart is the place of belief and deep experience. It can be filled with many different things from one moment to the next. It requires faith for Christ to become what you experience and taste moment by moment.

Eph. 3:17 "So that Christ may dwell in your hearts through faith..."

This verse does not describe an automatic occurrence; it describes a result. "So that" is the phrase that means "as a result." "If this happens, then the result will be..." If faith is occurring, then Christ will dwell in your heart, or He will become your experience. If the heart is not trusting, then Christ is not filling the heart, although He is one with your spirit.

Concluding Remarks Concerning Yielding the Heart

Oftentimes the heart is stuck in various unhealthy postures. Walls of self-protection result from coping and compensating in order to deal with fear. They allow the heart to stay in a posture of control. When we have been burned and hurt by past authority figures, we form judgments on God, the ultimate authority figure. These judgments are in place to protect us from a perceived negative experience of vulnerability and intimacy with God.

The scripture tells us "The heart is desperately wicked, who can know it" (Jer. 17:9). Ultimately, only God can know the real truth about what is in your heart or anyone else's heart for that matter. However, God wants to show you your heart so that you can let go of your lies and believe the truth. The scripture, therefore, also tells us to "Watch over our heart with all diligence, for out of it flow the issues of life" (Prov. 4:23). The Holy Spirit is our Helper. He is actively showing us our own hearts much of the time if we will listen and pay attention.

It is not typical that you would be able to see all of the ways in which you have compensated and built walls, especially not all at once. There are often deep layers of self-protection around our hearts that God is addressing and dismantling over time. This is a major part of our growth, and God is actively shepherding us in this process. As you are more aware now that these things are indeed issues to be dealt with, you will be more aware and more sensitive to the Spirit of God showing you what we have discussed.

Although God is active and faithful to often show you when your heart is in unbelieving postures, it is also not always necessary to see all of the ways in which you are stuck in order to get unstuck. Depending on the season of growth you are in, the issue at hand, and ultimately as God sees fit, often it is only necessary for you to give up the position of control that you have arrived at and yield your heart to believe and trust God. In other words, sometimes it is important for you to see how and where you "got off," and sometimes it is not. I find that the Lord is faithful to work with me concerning recurring patterns of unbelief. But also at times, I do not know how or when my heart moved to an unbelieving posture – I just turn back to trusting Him.

There are small ways in which we stop trusting God almost on a daily basis. But then there are ways in which we do not trust God that are more ingrained and permeating. Broad reaching canopies of self-reliance and control address a general range of erroneous heart postures of unbelief. Usually some form of fear is at the root. As you find yourself in moments when you can't connect with God and the fruit of the Spirit is not being experienced, ask God to show you what lie you may be believing. Ask God to show you in what way you are in fear or how you are controlling or grasping. Ask and depend on the Spirit of God to help you see how, when, and where you are clutching inside your heart. To relax on the inside and to trust with your heart is to "put yourself under" the Lord Himself and to let go to whatever He wants to do or say, whatever that may be.

As you begin to let go of small pieces of fear and control, give yourself to enjoying the freedom you are finding no matter how small it may be. Enjoying is a "letting go" heart posture. As you learn to enjoy your freedom and enjoy His love for you, you will find even more freedom, and you will taste more of His love.

Be encouraged that yielding the heart or trusting from the heart can be very difficult at times. It can take some time to learn, especially if you have not made this an issue in your life until now.

I encourage you to begin the journey to believe all of God's truths in your heart that are found in scripture. There are many. A few examples of things you can start believing on a heart level are, "You are a son or daughter of God," "God loves you unconditionally," "You have a valuable function in the body of Christ," and "You have eternal life."

Questions for Understanding and Discussion

1. Describe protecting yourself from God. Why would someone do this?

2. Explain how walls in the heart are formed.
3. What is frequently the source of control in the heart?
4. Describe how to move toward vulnerability.
5. Explain what it means to not trust God "for" or "that."
6. Explain the golden key to trust and why it is important.
7. Describe the process for believing truth in the heart.
8. How can you become better equipped to choose what is in your heart?

While We Look

Perhaps you have noticed that during times of corporate worship or during longer periods of prayer, you may experience being more connected to the Lord. During such times, you may experience an increase in faith, and you may taste of the Lord's life more than you do during regular parts of everyday life. Although it is possible to experience great faith and a connection with God apart from spiritual activities such as prayer or worship; usually most Christians experience a greater connection with God and greater faith when they have been participating in a longer, set aside time of prayer, a dedicated session for Bible study, or an intentional session of worship.

Before we discuss the dynamics of this spiritual reality, we need to discuss more of the nature of faith within the heart.

Seeing is Believing?

Correction. Actually, *believing is seeing*. When you believe from the heart, you see things that are not seen. If you were to focus on a particular object in the room right now, you could describe its color, its shape, and the various details about that object. While you are seeing and describing the object, you would not be using your memory to recall things that you have learned about the object in the past, rather, you would be describing things that you are actually seeing and experiencing right now. When you look at and describe an object that is right in front of you, you do not have to close your eyes and imagine what it might look like, nor do you have to regurgitate facts and concepts about it from a book you previously read in order to describe it. Because you actually see it in front of you, you have the ability to talk about the object with great detail and with great authority. Seeing the object provides you with evidence of its description.

Faith is the same way. To have faith is to actually see things but with the eyes of your heart. Faith is having evidence in this very moment that comes from actually seeing spiritual things that are unseen and invisible.

> Heb. 11:1 *"Now faith is the substance of things hoped for, the evidence of things not seen."*

When you begin to enter into a trusting position in your heart towards the Lord as a real person, you will begin to see things with your spiritual eyes. You will be in touch with *the reality* of spiritual things, therefore, you will not need to regurgitate facts about spiritual things. You will not need to rely on your memory to recite the things of God because you will know and see the things of God in this moment. Spiritual things are not seen with your physical eyes like you would see a physical object, but you are seeing them nonetheless. To see the spiritual with the eyes of your heart is somewhat similar to the experience we are about to describe.

When you are with a group of people in a room, you may notice that every person has a certain presence in the room. The presence of a person describes the fact that he is real, alive, and he is taking up space in the room. The next time you are with a group of people, perhaps there may be another person who is sitting or standing next to you. Try to close your eyes but still be aware of his or her presence while next to you. Just because you cannot see this person does not mean he or she is not there. You could also practice doing this with your spouse who is lying next to you in bed asleep. Close your eyes and become aware of your mate's presence next to you without you having to see him or her physically. You can actually focus on him or her while your eyes are closed and while you cannot see. If you do this exercise, do not try to imagine what your spouse looks like or create images in your mind about your spouse. That would be using your head to create a picture. There is no need to create mental pictures and images while you are aware of someone's presence. This would actually be a hindrance in being aware of the presence of your spouse next to you.

I am not saying that you should make this a common practice because there would be no point to it. We do not want to practice metaphysical exercises that are not focused on Jesus Christ. It is only an example that explains how we can focus or be aware of someone next to us while our eyes are closed. This is focusing and looking at another person in an intuitive way.

Although it is not a perfect illustration, the above exercise is similar to being aware of the Lord's presence. You cannot see the Spirit of God with your physical eyes. But just because you cannot see Him does not mean that He is not here as a real person. God is a real person who is with you right now and who has presence. Using the eyes of your heart, you can train yourself to begin to know Him in this way.

> *Eph. 1:18 "I pray that the eyes of your heart may be enlightened, so that you will know what is the hope of His calling, what are the riches of the glory of His inheritance in the saints,"*

Relating to the Lord this way is not strange or mystical. Just like people are near you, so is Jesus Christ. He is also in you. His presence is just as much a reality as other people's presence is a reality. Other people happen to be confined to a physical body, but the Lord's presence is not. There is an unseen spiritual world all around you. You are not only a physical being but also a spiritual being. You were made to be able to know God who is spirit and commune with Him in unseen places.

Words Are Not Always Helpful

> *Ecc. 5:2 "Do not be hasty in word or impulsive in thought to bring up a matter in the presence of God. For God is in heaven and you are on the earth; therefore let your words be few."*

Although there is nothing wrong with using words to express communication to the Lord, words can often get in the way. Your brain is busy with words. Communication with God does not need many words. Being with the Spirit of God only requires an engaging of the heart. Have you ever experienced a lengthy car ride with someone you enjoy? You don't have to talk to someone constantly in order to be with them and enjoy them. In fact, too many words at times can become a hindrance to connecting.

> *1Th. 5:17 "pray without ceasing."*

Praying without ceasing is not talking constantly without interruption. To pray continually is to maintain a connection with God in your heart.

> *Rom. 8:26-27 "In the same way the Spirit also helps our weakness; for we do not know how to pray as we should, but the Spirit Himself intercedes for us with groanings too deep for words; and He who searches the hearts knows what the mind of the Spirit is, because He intercedes for the saints according to the will of God."*

Praying only with your head while rattling off fast and busy prayers is much different than praying with your spirit. Learn to slow down and wait. Wait and then watch the Spirit inside you move. When He gives you a prayer, then pray. If He does not, then be quiet and just be with Him.

> *Jn 3:3 "Jesus answered and said to him, "Truly, truly, I say to you, unless one is born again he cannot see the kingdom of God."*

Notice here that Jesus tells us that unless we are born again, we cannot *see* the Kingdom. Seeing the kingdom of God with the eyes of our hearts is now possible because our human spirits have been made alive to God when we became born again.

Spiritual Authority

We mentioned earlier that when you see a physical object with your physical eyes, you can describe it in great detail and with authority. Let's say that your Aunt Betty calls you on the phone from a distant state one afternoon. Aunt Betty heard that your wife recently purchased a new piece of furniture from an antique shop (My wife would never do this). Aunt Betty is calling to find out the details about the new antique. Because you answered the phone, Aunt Betty wants you to describe the new antique to her while you are on the phone with her. As you look at the new piece of furniture, you tell Aunt Betty that the color of the antique is a light shade of blue. It also has some weathered looking wood on the edges toward the top. And it has a few small nail holes on the back side toward the middle. Aunt Betty questions you about the color saying, "Are you sure it's a light shade of blue?" Because you can see it right in front of you, you are able to respond with authority. "I am positive Aunt Betty. The antique is light blue."

> *Mk. 1:22 "They were amazed at His teaching; for He was teaching them as one having authority, and not as the scribes."*

When you move from having only concepts in your head to having real heart belief, you will enter into having *evidence* of things not seen. You will see things and know things that are true.[1] If you only have confidence in a list of decisions that you have determined are true in your head concerning the things of God, then your confidence is merely a shallow and fleshly confidence. This is a confidence in yourself and in your ideas as opposed to a spiritual authority that comes from actually seeing what is not seen. You may have what seems to you a clear understanding of theology in your mind, and that is not always a bad thing. But this is far different from actually seeing what is unseen in the spirit.

> *1Tim. 1:7 "wanting to be teachers of the Law, even though they do not understand either what they are saying or the matters about which they make confident assertions."*

Many people who have plenty of Bible knowledge but have little spiritual experience often feel extremely threatened when you challenge their "beliefs." The reason for this is that their security is in their mental understanding of scripture and doctrine which is shallow and easily shaken. To challenge or question their understanding of scripture is threatening to their security. The challenging of doctrine is threatening to this type of Christians because his beliefs are not secure. They are only shallow constructs in the mind bolstered by a willful self-confidence (that usually emphatically states, "They are adhering to scripture").

Do you think after Moses saw God in the burning bush that he would have felt threatened if someone were to say to him, "There is no such thing as God and burning bushes?" On the contrary, Moses would not feel threatened at all by such a statement because he had just seen God in a burning bush! When you see, you have evidence. Faith is evidence of unseen things. Mental constructs based on ideas and opinions are a house of cards that are held up only by the pride and fear of the flesh.

Only when you become humble are you truly able to see. It is only when you "become blind" that you are able to see the Kingdom of God with the eyes of your heart and gain a confidence that comes only from true and real experience.

> *Jn. 9:41 "Jesus said to them, "If you were blind, you would have no sin; but since you say, 'We see,' your sin remains."*

For example, who you are in your spirit is totally clean before God. To take this from a concept to a heart belief, you must see the reality of it. Look inside at your spirit and see that you are clean and washed. Actually *see* the purity in your spirit (Your flesh is not pure, but your spirit has been washed). Explore other things that are already true in your spirit as well. See the childlike dependence you have deep inside. See the oneness you have with God. Don't just think about it and regurgitate it from memory but actually see it. If you begin to look at things like this with the eyes of your heart, you will start to get in touch with them and then believe them with a full assurance of faith. This is what true faith is all about.

> *2 Cor. 4:18 "…while we look not at the things which are seen, but at the things which are not seen; for the things which are seen are temporal, but the things which are not seen are eternal."*

Observing the Seen, While Seeing the Unseen

As you grow in your capacity to commune with God in the Spirit and see what is unseen with the eyes of your heart, you will want to maintain this posture in your heart while your physical eyes are open.

Again, stop and examine any item in the room you may currently be in. Focus on the item and look at it. Now, close your eyes and focus completely on the Lord. Pray and talk to Him, be with Him, and see Him with the eyes of your heart as best as you can. While staying in that same place in your heart, open your physical eyes - but don't leave the focus you had on the Lord while your eyes were closed. Stay focused and prayerfully looking at God while you now observe the physical room around you with your physical eyes. You may have to close your eyes again to refocus on the Lord. In order to do this effectively, you will have to see the objects in the room but not really look at them with your heart like you may be used to doing. Learn to live daily, keeping your inner heart focused on the Spirit of God while you observe from a distance the physical world around you.

Don't Confuse the Two

Do not make the mistake of confusing what is an unseen concept with what is spiritually unseen. Understanding biblical concepts mentally is very often confused with seeing the unseen, but they are not the same thing. The verse in 2 Cor. 4:18 quoted above is specifically addressing the spiritually unseen. A scientist is able to see concepts such as ideas, theories, models, and designs. But it does not require faith to see these things, although they are not seen.

The spiritual world is a real place that exists all around us. It is not a bundle of ideas. Faith is specifically seeing into the spiritual world with the eyes of the heart. It is not seeing a conceptual idea with the mind's eye, nor is seeing the spiritual the same thing as seeing an image in your imagination. Although concepts, ideas, and images are not seen with the physical eyes, they are generated from the brain. Christians frequently think that they are seeing the spiritual unseen when in fact they are only understanding concepts with their mind.

Many times the Spirit Himself will give revelations that involve truth. He will open your mind to understand the scriptures (Lk. 24:45). However, it is often a temptation to become more excited (and more addicted) to understanding than to be excited and addicted to the Giver of understanding. Seeing the unseen from your heart always has the fruit of the Spirit along with experience. There is heartfelt joy and a passionate love for Christ that burns from within when we connect with the Spirit of God in our hearts.

Seeing the Unseen is Seeing Jesus

> Col 3:1 *"...keep seeking the things above, where Christ is, seated at the right hand of God."*

> Heb. 12:2 *"...fixing our eyes on Jesus..."*

The two verses above tell us that our focus is to be on Jesus Christ. As God shows us new revelations of truth, we are never to fixate on those revelations. Rather, we are to keep our focus on Christ Himself. All revelation and truth are actually in the person of Christ (Eph. 4:21, Jn. 1:17, Jn. 14:6). As you are caught up with and seeing the person of Jesus Christ in your heart, you will see, observe, and know many things in the spirit. He will show you things about your own heart concerning areas of growth, He will reveal to you things about others that will edify and encourage them, and He will reveal to you great revelations in scripture and truths in the spirit. But none of these "things" are to become a preoccupation or your primary focus while looking at what is unseen.

It Can Take Some Time

Your heart is organic and not a mechanical device. Your heart is much like a flower that gently opens over a period of time. It is not a machine that you can make do something by pulling a lever or pushing a button. The heart has to be wooed and invited. It lets down slowly and relaxes into faith and trust.

Notice the words in 2 Cor. 4:18 quoted above, *"while we look."* At the beginning of this chapter, we talked about the phenomena of an increase of faith and connection with God being experienced more often during longer times of prayer, worship, and Bible study. Very often the reason for this is simple: During longer periods of a focused time of prayer and worship, you are spending plenty of time looking at the unseen, *allowing the heart to unfold.* Your flesh does not want to look at the unseen. The flesh is very content to focus on the physical realm or focus on the conceptual. As you spend enough time gazing and focusing on the unseen person of Christ, the flesh tends to give up and let go as the heart releases and relaxes into trust.

The longer you look at Him who is unseen, the clearer He becomes. In fact, *whatever you look at* for a long period of time is what fills your heart. The more you focus on money, the more it will fill your heart. The more you gaze at and focus on your past hurts, the more they will fill your heart. The more you meditate on fearful and stressful thoughts, the more gripped you become by them. Hours, days, and years of focusing on things that are not God Himself become strongholds in our lives. Our hearts latch on to other things and become easily filled with them. The same is true of seeing the spiritual and the unseen. As you spend time focusing only on the person of Christ, He will fill your heart.

While looking at Jesus in the spirit, very often it takes a considerable amount of time for your heart to let go and become empty of what is currently filling it (and then become filled with what you are currently looking at). This is why many people are able to connect with the Lord through scripture memory and rereading certain passages over and over. This activity is *continuing to look* at the things of God (James 1:25). Scripture should not only serve as a source of truth, but it should also serve as a diving board into the person of Jesus Christ Himself.

Because the nature of your heart is to be wooed and drawn out, the heart *falls* in love with the focus of its affections. Your heart will open slowly like a flower and then gently move through the process of letting go of what you have been loving, and then it falls in love with your new object of focus.

Therefore, it takes time. *"While we look"* is a phrase having length of time built into it. A good, lengthy dose of prayer, Bible study, or worship – all with the intent and purpose of falling in love and connecting with the Lord Jesus Himself as a person is what is required.

In most cases, your fleshly heart will not easily let go in just a few minutes. If you have been after the flesh for very long at all, your soul can become tremendously dominant over your spirit. Your soul will soon permeate and color all that you think and feel. When this happens, it may take a very long period of time of keeping the heart in a submitted state in order to break through to the Spirit.

We must give our hearts some time to fall in love and fall into trust by gazing for several minutes at Him. Because this has been a practice in my life for some time, most days my heart will often trust and let go to Him pretty easily. But there are times when I become distracted or when something in my life is bothering me. At those times, it can take much longer. Some days, it will take me several hours of letting go to see Him before I actually do. If I am tired, busy, tempted, or distracted, it can take me half a day to "find the Lord" in my heart. The best remedy for this is to frequently reconnect and make sure I am filled with Him on a daily basis.

What are some good things to do in order to look at Christ and gaze at Him? Describe His characteristics, love Him, worship Him, see Him, know His presence, let go to Him, humble yourself, praise Him and trust Him – for long periods of time. You can even do this on the fly while you are at work - although it is more difficult. Maintain seeing the Lord and loving Him as your primary concern while you outwardly go through the motions of doing your job during the day. This is the purpose of your life and the very reason for your existence. All good works that are of the Spirit only come from Him filling your heart.

If you allow your heart to go too long without being filled with Christ Himself, you will quickly start to develop strongholds. Your heart will not want to let go of things very easily when you've allowed yourself to be filled with other things for very long. One day of not connecting with the Lord in a real way is much too long. In fact, I find it dangerous. If this happens, I strongly encourage you to stop life and connect with Him. There is nothing more important than this. Nothing. If you do not connect and experience the Lord in your heart, very soon you will start to experience some degree of insanity by the thoughts and the will of the flesh. If you continue walking after the flesh and do not break through to trust and being after the Spirit, you will start to manifest the deeds of the flesh pretty regularly. You will live a life of turmoil, emptiness, selfishness, and general misery - while maintaining your Christian concepts and rules. This is extremely dangerous and deceptive. The flesh is constantly gravitating towards anything but the person of Christ. Even dwelling on things "about" Christ is not Jesus Christ but only outward religion. It takes long periods of daily doses of gazing, seeing, and basking in the Spirit for your heart to stay filled with Him.

Col. 3:2 "Set your affection on things above, not on things on the earth."

A Heart Turn Away

Although it may seem somewhat contradictory to our current discussion, you are always only "a heart turn away" from connecting with God. To repeat, it can take some time to have a full experience of depth in seeing Him and knowing Him in the heart. Although your goal is to have your heart let go completely in total abandoned trust to Christ, this will often not be the case right away. However, to just turn your heart toward Him is a wonderful thing. When you do this, you are well on your way to being filled completely with God in your heart "as you continue to look."

2 Cor. 3:16 "...but whenever a person turns to the Lord, the veil is taken away."

If throughout the day your heart becomes filled with work and the concerns of daily life, it will take some time for your heart to become emptied of those things and then to become filled with the Lord Himself. Gaze at Him again and let go to His love.

How Much Reality Have You Gained?

The more true experience you gain of the Lord in your heart, the more you will begin to wake up and know reality in comparison to the world around you. The world we live in is one of deception and lies. When you are walking after your flesh, you are in harmony with the lies of the world.

Although as a Christian you have the Spirit of Christ in you, if you are walking after your flesh, His life in you is being suppressed. Although positionally you are saved and justified by God, if you are walking after the flesh, His life is not filling your heart. Thus, His life is not filling your speech, your thoughts, nor are you experiencing or exhibiting the fruit of the Spirit. A Christian walking after the flesh has the potential to be filled with God while an unsaved person does not. But there is not much of a difference in the inner experience of the two. Both the fleshly Christian and the unsaved are miserable inside. Many times the saved Christian who lives a shallow, cranial Christianity and walks after the flesh is more distasteful to others than the unsaved person. The saved, fleshly Christian is often legalistic, self-righteous, opinionated, and spiritually arrogant.

Lost people are like dead zombies. They seem alive, but they are dead. Christians walking after the flesh are religious, dead zombies. The more you allow Christ to fill your heart, the more alive you become. The more alive you become, the more alert you become to the death all around you. Whether it be the unsaved or a Christian walking after the flesh, dead people don't usually recognize others as being dead. *They all think they are alive.* But once you truly become alive, you begin to see just how dead everyone else is. Once you begin to have several breakthroughs of transitioning from walking after the flesh and then walking after the Spirit, you will see the extreme difference within yourself and your own experience between the flesh and the spirit.

Only in the Spirit of Christ is there sanity and reality. Everything else is a lie. As you become childlike, begin gazing at the Lord, encountering Him as a real person, and fall in love with Him by trusting Him completely in your heart – you will grow in sanity, clarity, revelation, and reality. You will wake up from the matrix that you have been living in and see the world as it truly is. You will become extremely alert to evil. You will detect the stench of the flesh more readily. You will begin to notice fleshly dynamics within groups and individuals. And as the Lord grants it, you will see fear, pride, and the fleshly agendas of men's hearts.

Note:
[1] Everything unseen that you see and know in the spirit must agree with scripture. If not, then you are having a fleshly experience.

Questions for Understanding and Discussion

1. What does it mean to say that faith in the heart is seeing?
2. How can you commune and fellowship with God without using words?
3. How does faith lend itself to spiritual authority?
4. What is the difference in an unseen concept and the spiritually unseen?
5. Why does it take time to see the unseen?
6. Why is important to experience reality?

Breaking Through

> *Lk. 5:39 "And no one, after drinking old wine wishes for new; for he says, 'The old is good enough.'"*

If you've made it this far in the book, you've probably realized that being according to the Spirit is a big deal. Actually, for the born-again Christian, it's the only deal.

As a Christian, you would never counsel an unbeliever that he should be focused on doing good works. You would never tell an unbeliever that he should become a better person with better morals or that he should display the fruit of the Spirit. You would not counsel a non-Christian that in order to be fulfilled and happy that he should get a better job. The only thing that matters concerning an unbeliever is that he become a believer.

Unless the unregenerate become regenerated in their spirit, morals and goodness are of no consequence. There is only one event that can change the life of non-Christians. There is only one crisis moment that should be the focus - surrendering all to the Lord Jesus Christ, putting their faith completely in His blood to save them, and receiving Christ as Lord of their lives. The unbelieving need the gospel. Nothing else matters at all.

A similar thing is true for the believing Christian. Getting a better job, living morally, having Christian thoughts, memorizing scripture, learning sound doctrine, spending time in prayer, Bible study, and attending church meetings are all moot if the Christian is according to his flesh. Although these activities are not bad, they are not the point. Telling an unbeliever to read his Bible or to go to church may be pointing him in the general right direction, but it is not telling him all that matters is that he is saved. For the Christian to engage in any Christian activity may point the believer in the right direction and may put him in a position to achieve the point, but it is not the point for the Christian. This is one reason why it is good to attend regular Christian meetings. Attending a meeting puts you in a perfect position to become according to the Spirit, for many Christians simply do not endeavor to encounter the Lord until they are actually in the Christian meeting. To many, the affairs of everyday life are more important than intimacy with Christ.

Walking after the Spirit is the first priority for the Christian. Because as has been stated before, only when the Christian's heart is filled with love, trust, and dependency on Christ is the believing Christian living according to his true and created condition. Unless the Christian is abiding in the vine of the love of Christ, he can do absolutely nothing (John 15). Not some things, but nothing. Abiding in the vine of the love of Christ is not the same thing as remembering that Christ loves you or even being aware of the concept that you are loved. True belief always shows up in our experience and is manifested in the emotions. The experience and emotions are never the goal, yet they are the manifestations.

I first believed on the Lord Jesus Christ in 1987 while driving home in my car after attending a church meeting. During those early months following my conversion, I encountered God in amazing ways. Others tell similar stories of their early days after their conversion. Many refer to this experience as "the honeymoon stage." Although I had deep and encouraging experiences with God at times, other times were very dry and miserable after I became a Christian. I needed to know and understand why this was the case.

Why was it that at times I felt so close to the Lord and at other times I did not? Sometimes I was experiencing His love to such a degree that I knew He was all around me. It was like He was hugging me tightly with His cheek next to mine while His liquid love was pouring into me. At other times I felt as though God was in outer space somewhere in some distant heaven concerned with more important things than me.

A large part of the answer I've come to is this: We become born again in a crisis moment when we give up all hope in ourselves and all self-reliance. When we've exhausted all of our efforts and become so hopeless in ourselves and in this present life, we come to Jesus and are born of His Spirit. To be born again is to exchange our damaged lives for His perfect life. We come to Him out of desperation. When we are at the end of our rope, and then we let go of the rope, we find God. This condition of heart is intended to continue and remain the same in the maturing believer, yet it often does not (Gal. 3:3).

At the beginning of your Christian walk, you were probably very broken, lost, and not trusting in yourself. Your heart was tender and supple. But after some time had passed after becoming a Christian, you started to become indoctrinated. You learned theology. You also took on the "Christian law" by trying to please God by your self-efforts. You took on a regimen of Bible study, prayer time, and church activities.

These Christian activities caused you to gain confidence again in your flesh, but now you had a confidence in your flesh that was couched and masked with spiritual things. You became less and less *undone* and desperate for Christ as you gained confidence in your new Christian identity and activity. Without contrition and brokenness, Christian activity will validate and strengthen the religious flesh.

Most pastors preach and encourage a system and methodology of strengthening religious self-confidence. Most of these systems fall into one of five categories: "Be good, pray, tithe, read your Bible, and witness to others." You feel better about yourself when you do these things because they are espoused as the right Christian things to do. There is a slow hardening of the heart by trying to be a good Christian. This is because the effort of trying to be good strengthens a cycle in you of self-righteousness and then guilt. This cycle causes you to leave desperation and trust.

Here is how it works: When you focus your energies on being a good Christian, guilt follows by not being able to keep all your rules consistently. Secondly, self-righteousness is also developed during the times you are able to keep your pet rules. In either case, your experience of God is squelched. You soon leave the early days of experiencing the love of God and walking in the freedom of the Spirit, and you begin to walk after your "self-confident, Christianized, religious flesh."

God doesn't want you to try to be good, He wants you to come to Him. *Christian activity is good only if it comes out of an intimacy with Christ that is born from desperation and need.*

If you are a born-again Christian, you have certainly experienced times of knowing the nearness of Christ. You've had times when you've experienced His love. There have been times when you've experienced being on the mountaintop with God. You could probably relate stories of "there was a time when I was on fire for God…" You would describe something real: an intimacy with God, a deep, heartfelt encounter with your Lord.

Those times when you have tasted and encountered the Lord in such a real way, when you have experienced His love and His Spirit – are times when you have been "according to the Spirit." Those special times of intimacy with God are what walking after the Spirit is like. Those kinds of experiences should not be rare, but you've settled for them to be exceptions and not the norm.

2 Cor. 6:12 "You are not restrained by us, but you are restrained in your own affections."

It is sometimes thought that intimate encounters with the Spirit of God are only experienced when God decides to pour out His Spirit during a Christian church meeting. There can be times in Christian meetings when the presence of God's Spirit in the room is evident and strong, and because of that, you experience His presence no matter what. However, most encounters with God during those moments is the result of humbling yourself and surrendering your will during the meeting. Oftentimes during Christian meetings, one believer is very touched by the Lord and another believer close by is unaffected.

We are called to maturity. Our Father wants us to walk daily in what He has given us. We are not to immaturely chase Christian meetings and hope "God will show up." If we are only experiencing intimate encounters with the Spirit when "the church meeting was good" or when our situation in life becomes desperate, then we are not mature.

Rom. 5:5 "…because the love of God is shed abroad in our hearts by the Holy Ghost which is given unto us."

Jesus Christ has already given you His Spirit and has poured out His love in you. He is loving you right now and embracing you. You can experience the fullness of the Spirit right now if you will allow yourself to believe, become utterly humble, and if you will receive.

If there is only one message you gain from reading this book, let it be that you learn what it means to be according to the Spirit, and you do whatever is necessary each day to be according to the Spirit.

We often settle for the normalcy of life without truly connecting with God. It becomes good enough for us to accomplish the tasks of each day while only maintaining Christian concepts. We become content with just the label of being a Christian while we live in control of our lives without walking in a heart posture of trust toward the Lord. This kind of living is that of experiencing the soul rather than the spirit. The soul, rather than the spirit becomes your life. You respond to the impulses of the soul rather than the impulses of the Spirit.

As we forsake such a mentality and we endeavor to do what is necessary to have true heart belief and pay the cost of believing God each day, we move from a life of living out of religious concepts to intimate relationship.

The experience of being according to the Spirit is nothing less than amazing. It is spiritual bliss. Paul called it "life" and "peace." The "life" of God is intensely satisfying. His peace is not the absence of outward turmoil and problems in our lives, but the spiritual satisfaction of inexpressible joy which remains no matter the circumstances.

However, all of this poses another problem. If you have ever found the reality of being according to the Spirit (which means you have tasted the life and the peace of God), the flesh will want to reproduce the experience.

The Necessity of Breaking Through

The flesh is purely animalistic and base. It wants control, it wants power, it wants various forms of pleasure, and it will take any kind of gratification it can get. It wants to avoid pain and the threat of painful relationships. Ultimately, the flesh doesn't care what it is pursuing or avoiding as long as it gets to stay in control and remain independent from God. The flesh enjoys trying to keep the rules in order to achieve. The flesh also loves rebelling against the rules. The flesh wants the experience of spiritual elation or the experience of a deep depression. Really there is only one thing the flesh does not want.

It does not want to submit to the Lord Jesus Christ and live dependent on Him. But the flesh is quite content to live with the concept that dependence on Christ is a good thing without living with the reality of dependence.

The flesh is completely resistant to submitting to the authority of Jesus Christ. It does not love God and it does not want God, although it believes it does. It is incapable of this. The religious flesh can have the idea that it loves and wants God, but when it comes down to choosing Him, deceptive games are played. The flesh will be satisfied with concepts about God, but it does not want God Himself and the authority He brings. The flesh's main objective (as with any animal species) is to stay alive. The flesh cannot remain king on the throne when Jesus Christ is King.

The very moment the flesh humbles itself and submits to the authority of Jesus Christ, it ceases to be "the flesh." At this moment, the body and the mind become a submitted instrument for God to use. It is no longer in control but submitted.

Because one of the desires of the flesh is "to experience," you must lay aside your desire to experience God. In order to find a humble heart of trusting God and to break through to His life flooding into your heart, you must give up on wanting all things – except Jesus Himself. This is very important to understand. The desire to experience Him is different from God Himself. You must separate your desire *to experience* Him from who He is. Experience is only a result. You cannot want this above Him. The desire to experience God is of the flesh. The desire for the person of Jesus Christ is of the Spirit. This is part of the maturing process of every believer.

The more you are broken of your animalistic, fleshly impulses, the more you will come to discern them for what they are. As you mature in love and submission to God and nothing else, you will realize more and more that the flesh is not "you"- It is only the body and brain independent of the Spirit. Its extremely subtle desires will only become more evident as you live more and more in the presence of God.

Fleshly impulses such as the desire to overthink, the indulgence of mental understanding and knowledge, the various securities of money, the lust for food (or the control from not eating food), the need to be noticed by others and esteemed in some way (no matter how), the security and good feelings we get from our physical environment being a certain way (a clean house, a certain kind of car, nice weather, the temperature outside, being happy when it is sunny and sad when it's cloudy), the satisfactions we get from accomplishments, and the myriads of other hidden fears and anxieties- all of these things the Christian community *does not typically recognize* as being from "the flesh."

In contrast, the flesh's more obvious wants are very recognizable according to Paul's list in Galatians. We typically only call the things on Paul's list "the flesh." But again, Paul concludes his list with "and things like these." For example, we will call an outburst of anger "the flesh," but micromanaging a project would be considered responsible. Micromanaging is usually from a root of fear, so it would be another manifestation of the flesh. The subtle desires of the flesh are truly intricate, complex, and endless. You simply cannot identify all of them because when you begin to deny the flesh in one area, it will often change and morph into something else.

The only answer to the insanity and complexity of the flesh is to frequently taste the quality of the Spirit of God. Only then will you notice the stench of the flesh in all of its ways. You must taste of the Spirit often because the flesh is so pervasive and so insidious that it will actually cause you to forget the truths and realities of the Spirit very quickly. The flesh is constantly trying to hide from you the things of God that will spell disaster for its goal of living and remaining in control. Things you know to be true are often later questioned (Gen. 3:1). Breakthroughs you have received from the Lord are soon forgotten (1 Kings 18, 19). Huge revelations that were once life changing, slowly have become minimalized and don't seem so great. Days of zealous love and passion are cooled down by daily distractions. The flesh is constantly pulling you toward an experience of emptiness, busyness, control, misery, fear, anxiety, problems, and defeat.

You must *break through* to experience the reality of Jesus Christ very often (without the actual experience being your goal, but only Him being your goal). At least a daily breakthrough is recommended. If you don't, the flesh will start to gain a foothold very quickly and you will slide hour by hour further and deeper back into an ingrained pattern of the flesh. It is urgent that you wholeheartedly trust Jesus Christ right now in the depths of your heart.

Ingrained flesh patterns soon solidify and become what we call "strongholds." Living after the flesh soon invites demonic influences in your life. If you are walking after the flesh for even a short period of time, you will either begin to hurt or neglect the people around you because you are incapable of loving while walking after the flesh. The flesh can have sentiment and very moving feelings of care, but it is incapable of holy, pure, unselfish love. If you are walking after the flesh, it will quickly tempt those around you to *respond to you* in their flesh. Then, a stronghold develops between the both of you of relating on a fleshly level. This "dance of death" that two or more people can do together invites more demonic activity and strongholds. In this case, unclean spirits are not only oppressing one person, but they are now invited to be in the midst of the relationship.

If you do not break through often to encounter the Lord Jesus in a real way by believing and trusting in the heart in total submission, you will develop many problems:

1. You will live with spiritual dryness.
2. You will remain predominately conceptual.
3. You will trust your fleshly emotions and feelings as though they were reality.
4. You will become outwardly focused by taking your cues of reality from the situations of life.
5. You will develop a focus on the outward – resulting in a false belief that what you are doing or abstaining from doing is determining how pleasing you are to the Lord.
6. You will develop an outward focus on "right living" but without the power inside to match it. There will be no true spiritual reality of experience and intimacy with Christ in your heart.
7. You may excuse your lack of a submitted heart as "freedom in the Lord." You may disguise your arrogant self-righteous living as "holiness."

8. Your flesh will develop strong habits and patterns that will become ingrained and solidified. Painful and difficult breaking of your will through life's outward circumstances will be required to humble you.

When I use the term "breaking through," I am referring to moving from the flesh to the Spirit. Hopefully, this will be a daily event for you. Specifically, the early part of each day is a good time to break through. The reason for this is that as the hours pass by in a day, the flesh becomes more distracted and more firm with its control. Early in the day is usually the easier time to break through to the Spirit because it becomes more difficult as the day goes by. You can trust the Lord at any time day or night, but it is often easier early in the morning before you get too distracted and off on your flesh's agenda for the day.

Acceptance of the Issue of Flesh vs. Spirit
The first step in breaking through is realizing that to break through in leaving the flesh and going to the Spirit is in fact *an issue*. You must realize and embrace that this dynamic is in place at all times (flesh or spirit), and you must believe the extreme importance of the issue. This is critical for the initial humbling of the flesh.

The flesh will vehemently resist and fight the entire idea of the flesh vs. the Spirit. If it can dismiss this entire subject, then the flesh gets to stay in control all the time. Many Christians I've met simply refuse to accept this and make this an important issue before God. Christians often respond with phrases such as "I am always with the Lord" or "It's no big deal if I am after the flesh," or "We are always according to the Spirit because we are Christians." I invite you to reexamine the scriptures concerning these issues. Briefly, we are always with the Lord, but He is not always filling our hearts. We are not always trusting Him, and we are not always humble. (Refer to the chapter "The False Self" for discussion on being "in vs. after" the spirit.)

If you wake up tomorrow morning with no awareness of the concept or idea of being after the flesh or being after the spirit, you will probably tend to stay in the condition you wake up in – which is usually the soulish condition of being after the flesh. Depending on what your variety of flesh's religious standards may be will determine how many spiritual concepts you entertain that day. But if you do not break through to trusting the Lord in your heart in a real and living way, then you are walking after the flesh.

The first step in breaking through to the Spirit each morning is to realize that you are probably after the flesh and have not broken through to the Spirit when you first wake up. Again, if your opinion is that "Everything is just fine," then you will live out your days walking mostly after the flesh, perhaps with religious concepts. Like most Christians, you will have experiences with the Lord from time to time particularly in church meetings; but this is a far cry from all that He has for you. Every time you encounter the Lord in a real way is a life giving and life changing experience. You can walk in the miracle of a changed life and an encounter with the living God on a daily basis. This is to be the norm for all believers, not the exception.

The flesh will cause you extreme discouragement in the area of breaking through to the Spirit. After much "trying" to trust God and believing Him from the heart, you won't be able to do it. You will be strongly tempted to give up. Usually, you will first experience discouragement. Next, you will tend to settle in for a life of living dry in your heart with only spiritual concepts and occasional drinks of spiritual water. Discouragement from failure is to be expected. It should not surprise you. However, discouragement in this area is only another temptation of the flesh, just like any other temptation. You should view it as part of the journey and as a part of the learning process. It does not mean anything about God's value of you.

Having said that, breaking through to trust God in a real way should become a standard for you, and you'll want to slowly move toward settling for nothing less even if it takes you half a life time to learn it. The Lord continually teaches me new things about my lack of trust and how I can love Him more deeply from the depths of my heart. I've gained more ground in this area than I had a year ago, and much more than I had 15 years ago. But even now, I do not walk after the Spirit all day every day. But this is my desire, and I will not settle for living only as "a mere man" (1 Cor. 3:3).

Your Imaginary World
Meet Anna, a 6 year- old little girl who lives with her mom and dad in a very nice upper-middle class home. She has her own room filled with new toys. She has a bike and a swing set in her backyard. Anna is a healthy, well fed, and well-dressed little girl. She is loved by both of her parents. There is nothing Anna lacks, and there is nothing for her to fear. Nothing is required of her on any given day. Anna's world is perfect. However, you wouldn't think this was the case from spending time with her.

Anna is a nervous little girl. She constantly busies herself with making sure all of her dolls are dressed and fed. If she forgets to meet the perceived needs of one of her dolls, she feels stress and she is bothered. All of her toy zoo animals have to be taken on imaginary walks, be fed often, and be given pretend baths. Anna obsesses over making sure that every toy she owns is properly attended to. If they aren't, Anna feels a sense of anxiety.

Anna is a child who has created an imaginary world of "have to's." There is nothing wrong with her imagining and pretending to take care of her toys. But her self-created tasks have become the energy she lives from. Instead of the love of her mom and dad filling her heart, and instead of the peace and enjoyment of her safe environment, Anna lives in a state of non-reality. It is all a self-created, task- oriented life that gives her purpose, yet when things don't run as smoothly as they should, she feels very anxious.

Most people's daily life experience is not much different than Anna's. They simply go from one project to the next. Let's look at an example.

When you wake up each morning, you begin working on the task of showering and getting dressed for the day. Job accomplished. Next, it is time to eat your breakfast or drink your coffee. Done. Now it is time to travel to work. Goal completed - arrived at destination. Now it is time to accomplish the multiple lists of projects that your work requires. Work day finished. Next, it is time to drive home from work. Done and completed. The next task at hand is to relax for a while until it is time to eat supper. Achieved. Now it is time to get ready for work starting again tomorrow. And so we live our lives going from one task to the next. As a Christian, you must also fit into your busy schedule of life the tasks of prayer, Bible study, and church attendance.

The daily tasks of life actually become your life. They become your purpose. And you assign importance to your daily tasks based upon your own arbitrary perceptions. Why *must* you do this or that today? Is it simply because you decided that you must? Do you feel pressure from someone else's expectations? Is it all so necessary because *you feel* it is all so necessary? Perhaps the job that you have and the various duties you accomplish daily do originate from a reasonable and legitimate need. Perhaps God is even leading you to do some of the things you do. However, the compulsion you have to accomplish and do all that you do can take on a life of its own. The flesh lives off of the energy of a task driven life - the energy to "have to do," the energy of accomplishment, and the energy of anxiety when those tasks are not accomplished. It does not care what energy it is feeling as long as it is not from submission to Christ.

This entire mindset of living a project oriented life of completing a continual series of tasks is driven by insanity. It is insanity because it is not based in reality. You must stop everything and find the truth.

Who are you? Where is God? How does He see you? What matters to Him in this moment? You must find Him and let all of the dust settle. Learn to just be and exist in your spirit with nothing else to do, nothing to accomplish, no place to go, and without a project or a task in view. The state of just being in your spirit, one with God, as the small, dependent, loved, child that you are - is the only thing that is actually real.

The world you've created of tasks, projects, work, errands, chores, duties to fulfill, and things to accomplish is an empty and shallow mirage. You have allowed *your heart* to be filled with shallow, external, and temporal activities that the body performs. When these things fill your heart, *they become your life*. Just because you strongly feel compulsions to do this or that does not validate them as legitimate or worthy of your heart.

Much of the flesh's imaginary world of "things to do" has been created to avoid emptiness. *The flesh would panic* if it had nothing to work on, no problem to solve, no place to be, and no cause to obsess over.

And what is the true reality? It is that you are being loved right now by your Father, and you are the apple of His eye. You are clean and pure before Him because of His blood, and you can take as long as you like to rest, to receive, and to be strengthened in His Spirit. You are complete in Him, and you don't have to be more or do more to improve yourself. In fact, you can't improve yourself because He has already made you complete. These realities are the food for your soul. These are the things that God is saying to you, and they are the sustenance of your life.

> *Matt. 4:4 "But He answered and said, "It is written, man does not live by bread alone, but man lives by everything that proceeds out of the mouth of the Lord."*

What has your daily food been? What have you fed yourself with? Where have you been deriving your energy from? Has your food been accomplishing the tasks of each day? Has your food been obsessing over a problem in your life? Has your food been trying to fix other people around you?

Set your face like flint to gaze and focus on the true realities in God mentioned above. Purpose nothing else in your life other than breaking through to the Spirit. This will allow the illusions of your flesh to become dismantled. You need to wake up from your stupor of lies and the foggy world of imaginations that your flesh has created.

When you go to sleep at night, you enter into a state of non-reality. You dream. And while you dream, you are unaware of the details of the room you are sleeping in and all of your physical surroundings. You may experience dreams of floating on clouds, fighting dragons, or falling from a cliff, yet none of these change the truth of reality that you are in your bedroom asleep in your bed. Although you dream and experience great things while asleep, you are still in your room and still in your house.

You must wake up from the daily dream of your flesh that you have while you are wide awake and find the reality of what is true in Christ.

As You Begin to Focus on Breaking Through

As you desire to move from your head to your heart, you are transitioning from your religious flesh and into the reality of the Spirit. There is a common and expected hindrance in doing this.

As we've previously mentioned, the desire to break through to the Spirit can actually become a hindrance to breaking through to the Spirit. You cannot want to break through more than you want the Lord Jesus Christ. We discussed this earlier concerning experiencing the Lord. Although experiencing the Lord and tasting of His amazing joy and peace is an important goal, you simply have to die to this goal in order to achieve it. You cannot want to experience the Lord more than you want the Lord Himself. Your desire to experience Him will keep you from experiencing Him. You will actually break through to the Spirit and experience Him only by focusing on the basic foundational truths that we've discussed such as:

- Becoming who you are in humility ("Becoming Who You Are" chapter)

- Believing you are clean and washed before God (mentioned in many chapters).
- Believing and receiving His love ("Yielding the Heart" chapter).
- Trusting the person of Jesus Christ by relinquishing control and giving power to Him over you in total submission. ("Yielding the Heart" chapter)
- Continuing to focus and gaze on the person of Jesus Christ ("While we Look" chapter).

Managing this can be difficult at times. At risk of becoming overly complex, embracing the need to break through to the Spirit and to truly experience God is part of the fear of God. It is a truth that is to be embraced in the vessel that you are. Your spirit does not need this motivation nor is your spirit motivated by the fear of God. The fear of God is for the flesh. You flesh must embrace the truth of the need to break through and experience the Spirit. But as your flesh begins to turn and humble itself, you can let go of the "need to experience and breakthrough to trust" by simply turning your focus to receive God's love.

A Chink in the Armor

During your sessions of giving your heart to being according to the Spirit, at some point you will notice that the flesh will begin to give up. Usually, it will give up only a slight bit at first. A good illustration to describe it would be as if your fist was tightly closed and only one finger in your fist began to relax a little. Your heart is like a fist when it is not yielded and not trusting. It is in a posture of clenching. When one "finger of your heart" begins to let go a little, a very slight bit of light will come to you. Go with it and continue to yield. Stay focused on giving up, seeing the Lord, becoming childlike, and releasing all control to Him. Your dependence will begin to shift from dependence on yourself to dependence on your Father. As your heart begins to trust a little, it will then trust a little more. Usually, you will very slowly relax your heart until you are fully believing God.

When your heart starts to venture toward letting go and giving up all control to your Father, the flesh will usually make its last stand.

The Parade of the Flesh – Fears, Wants, and Distractions

When you purpose to sit down and do nothing else but to break through to trusting God, a constant bombardment of distractions will usually come forth. I call this the "flesh parade." I am not addressing outward distractions such as being interrupted by a phone call or a door bell, but diversions in your mind that do not seem to ever stop. You suddenly can't stop thinking about anything and everything.

Part of the reason this happens is twofold. First, the flesh parade of your busy and distracted mind was present even before you sat down to spend time with the Lord. You just notice it more now as you attempt to become still.

Second, the flesh purposely creates distraction in an effort to avoid its imminent death.

Because control is a fleshly solution for fear, as you move toward trust, many irrational fears may begin to surface. Sometimes it will help you let go of your fears to realize that they are not real and are only a result of you moving toward trust.

Your flesh parade will consist of many good ideas and many impulses to do this or that immediately. You may suddenly have an unusually strong impulse to empty the dishwasher. You may feel a strong impulse to solve a particular problem at work. You will then feel guilty for not trusting God and for failing at breaking through to the Spirit. Ignore it all. This is simply your flesh wanting to live and busy itself.

The other reason I refer to it as "a parade" is because you can effectively defeat the endless distractions by just watching them go by like you would a parade. Do not become rattled, discouraged, or surprised that endless distractions are occurring. Just as easy as the distracting thoughts come in, gently let them go. Keep turning back to the Lord and yielding your heart to the truth. Keep submitting yourself entirely. Keep turning back to seeing only Him. Keep giving yourself to Him by giving Him power over you. Keep receiving His love for you. Keep trusting Him. Keep believing that you are completely cleansed and desired by God. The flesh will eventually give up and let go.

I know I've broken through to the Spirit when I no longer want to get up and do something else or think through a problem, but my only care and craving is to enjoy and love Jesus Christ.

The sweet fruit of the spirit in our soul (love, joy, peace, etc.) is also evidence that we have broken through and are according to the Spirit of God.

When I was first learning this, it would sometimes take more than an hour, sometimes two or more. At times, I would give up in discouragement and just throw in the towel. The Lord also used this as part of my journey to know Him. You must remember that because of the blood of Jesus, who you are is always pleasing to God even if your capacity to experience Him is very small.

Trying Doesn't Work

Although it may seem contrary to our previous discussions, it will never work to "try" to break through to be according to the Spirit and experience the Lord. Only faith works. Faith is always letting go. If you try to be childlike, try to know God as a person, try to trust - you will never break through to the spirit. Why? Because the more you try, the more you are exercising the self-effort of the flesh and the more you are in control. So what should you do?

Many people realize that all of their trying and all self-effort is counterproductive. This is a wonderful revelation. However, the common conclusion is to "do nothing" and just let God do it all. In a sense, this is partially true. But to leave the flesh to do as it pleases and not give yourself over to heart belief is not faith either. So how do you give yourself to something yet not "try" to do anything? Again, the answer lies within the definition of what faith really is. Faith is always a letting go to what *has already been accomplished*. You do in fact do something when engaging in faith. But the doing that you are giving yourself to is not the self-effort of trying, Rather, it is the trusting action of letting go to what is already true. Letting go is doing something, but it is not the same as trying.

You don't have to try to sit in the chair you may have been sitting in while reading this book. You just have to realize that you have been sitting in it the entire time. Sitting in the chair has already been accomplished before you realized it. You don't have to try to hear the small noises in the room. You've been hearing them all along, but you haven't noticed them until I pointed them out. The noises were happening even before you realized them. But as you realize the noises in the room by focusing on them, you begin to experience them.

Realizing that God is and has been loving you and realizing the truth of who you are in your spirit (and have been this whole time) in your spirit is faith. As you realize what God has already accomplished, who you are in your spirit, and how God sees you – you will begin to experience the reality of these things that have been true all along.

Let Go, Let Go, Let Go

Give yourself to humility and becoming a child (who you really are already) as much as you can. Extend your faith to know God is here as a person and that He loves you. But at some point you will have to shift to letting go of everything. You have to become dependent on Him to lead you for what is next. The Spirit will access all of the things you have learned (in your memory) to tell you what to do or what to give yourself to. He may show you to humble yourself more in a particular area. He may show you more about His love for you. He may show you that you need to let go of this or that. But the point will be that your hands are off the steering wheel. As you depend on Him for what is next, you will be letting go and releasing all control. You must climb into God's wheelbarrow and give Him power over you. Trust Him and find enjoyment in the trusting. You will be well on your way to yielding completely to the Spirit and finding the joy of His life.

A Sample Scenario

It may be helpful to go through some possible examples of what it may "look like" inside yourself during the breaking through process.

You can always start out by giving yourself to the primary foundational truths: humility, faith that He is, and trust in Him and His love. As you turn to the Lord you will initially give yourself to becoming the child that you really are. This is the humbling process. That process will lead you to extend your faith to believe that He is, that He is love, and that He is a person who is present with you and in you.

Next, you will begin to let go to Him as much as possible. At this point, you have done all you can do. If you do find that you have broken through to finding the love, peace and joy of His life, then wonderful! Go with it and enjoy His love and rest. But many times at this initial starting point, this will not be the case.

Therefore, simply sit before Him and wait on God. Look at who Christ is. Trust Him to lead your heart into whatever that may be. You may experience small, childlike inclinations in your heart such as wanting to know that He is your parent, wanting to be taken care of, and needing understanding. Allow those to come up while directing them toward your Father.

Continue to return to just sitting before Him, gazing at who He is. You may have more gentle directions from the Spirit. Perhaps He may show you that you are still in control of your heart in some way. When God shows you ways in which you need correction, He will usually give you not only the correction but also the revelation of how to let it go as well. Anytime God shows us something, He gives the grace and the will to do it; however, this only comes when He is the one who initiates it. If you are on a hunt to root out and change yourself, it will never work.

Questions for Understanding and Discussion

1. Why is it important for the Christian to break through to the Spirit?
2. Why is accepting the issue of flesh vs. spirit so important?
3. Why is a project orientation dangerous?
4. Describe the dynamic of wanting to break through versus only wanting Jesus Christ?

The Frequency of Repentance

Repentance is often viewed as a negative word. The word might make you picture an angry, holy man with long hair and a beard who points his accusing finger at you with fire in his eyes. He screams directly at you, "Repent, you worthless, no good, filthy sinner!"

The way we view the word *repent* causes us to think that if we need to repent, then we must have sinned, or we've been a bad person in some way. Although the word *repent* certainly includes turning away from sin, it is much broader than that.

To repent means "to change." As with anything spiritual, repentance occurs on the inside first. Repentance addresses a change in our inner attitudes and our thinking which results in a change of our outward behaviors.

If we believe repentance only applies to us if we sin, *then we will only repent when we sin*. But if we realize that repentance is necessary in a much broader spectrum that includes all attitudes and ways of thinking, then we will realize that repentance must be a way of life.

It is vitally necessary that we repent often. I recommend repentance many times an hour. At least that's how frequently I need to repent.

It is not negative to repent. It only means that you are turning from the flesh to yield to the Spirit (from the head to the heart). We must see the seriousness of not walking after the Spirit. We must make a conscious effort to humble ourselves and fall in love with our Lord again when the Spirit nudges us to let us know that we have gotten off track.

If we seek repentance only when we sin, we will find ourselves sinning a lot. Here's why: If you humble yourself and yield to the Spirit only after you have sinned, you will certainly walk after the flesh much of the time unchecked – which will eventually cause you to sin.

When leaving the Spirit and choosing the flesh, it sometimes instantly manifests as sin. But many times it does not. For example, sin may be instantly demonstrated if someone were to accuse you or attack you personally. You may react quickly with an outburst of anger, or you may return the attack of self-protection. If someone cuts you off in traffic, you might honk your horn and cuss them out. In the case of "a perfect storm" set of circumstances, you can be fully yielded to the Spirit in one moment and then flip over into the flesh instantaneously and manifest sin in the next moment. But this is not how it always happens.

The diagram below illustrates a progression in either direction from our initial turning point.

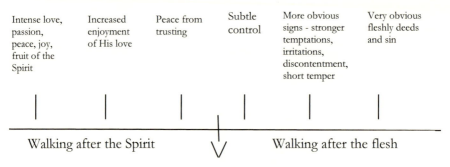

Point of Turning Your Heart

    The point at which you yield your heart to the Spirit or to the flesh is indicated by the center point on the line. At the moment you turn your heart to the Spirit, you may not instantly experience the depths of God. Usually, it takes some time for your heart to open fully and for you to experience a full degree of trust and a full expression of the fruit of the Spirit from your initial point of turning (while you look). Likewise, if you turn from the Spirit to the flesh, you may not see sin manifested right away. You may immediately experience the effects of your independence and your control, but you may not necessarily experience misery, dryness, or emptiness (and ultimately blatant sin) until your heart settles into a further condition of hardness or your life's circumstances provide opportunity to expose your fleshly heart.

    Depending on which side of the line your heart has been living on and to what degree will determine what your experience is. If for much of your day, you have been teetering around the turning point between the flesh and the Spirit, you may not notice huge differences in your experience. If you have been far off in the flesh for some time with a very hard heart, and you then turn to submit to the Spirit, you will probably experience a very cathartic change.

    Upon an initial yielding to the flesh, sin is not always manifested right away. Therefore, the progression of turning to the flesh and then ultimately manifesting sin may play out in the following fashion: You first subtly move over to the flesh by gaining some sort of control. A subtle irritation, a series of tempting thoughts that remain unchecked, or a reaction to a common stimulus are all commonplace. If you remain for very long in the fleshly place of independence from God and self-reliance, various temptations will grow stronger and you will begin to entertain such thoughts more readily. Your heart will become harder. The flesh will begin to enjoy its own feeling of control and power. Finally, the flesh will start to manifest the deeds of the flesh with overt sin.

    You may feel as though the current stimulus or temptation to sin is the root of your sin, but many times you manifest sin because *you have been walking after the flesh for some time*. It's usually the small things in life that contribute to you moving over to the flesh unnoticeably. Then, when the more noticeable trial comes, you are in no position to handle it, so you give in easily.

It is only possible to sin if you are after the flesh. Sin is a result or a by-product of walking after the flesh. Instead of maintaining a goal of not committing sin, the Christian should rather maintain the goal of not walking after the flesh. More precisely, your goal should be to walk after the Spirit, then you will not walk after the flesh.

Gal. 5:16 "But I say, walk by the Spirit, and you will not carry out the desire of the flesh."

The secret to not sinning is to walk after the Spirit. However, our Christian culture has taught us a backwards way of thinking about Gal. 5:16. We try to not carry out the deeds of the flesh in order to say that we are walking after Spirit. This is an incorrect and completely backwards approach. It also reveals a general lack of understanding in Christendom of what it means to walk after the Spirit. To focus on not sinning results in a suppression of outward behaviors while fleshly desires still remain deep in the heart. The result is legalism and hypocrisy. *A focus on not sinning actually produces more sin in your life.*

1 Cor. 15:56 "…the power of sin is the law"

A sure recipe to produce sin in your life is to give yourself to trying not to sin. The harder you try, the more you will strengthen the flesh. Trying is the self-effort and self-discipline of the flesh. Once you are walking in your own self-effort and your own self-discipline, you are then walking after the flesh. Once you are after the flesh, it does not matter what your goals may be - the deeds of the flesh will become manifest. You may have a natural capability to abstain from certain behaviors, but if you are abstaining out of your own self-effort, you will always walk in sin of a different type.

Instead of trying, you need to die. Dying to all flesh and moving to trust and love within your heart causes you to walk after the Spirit. Only the Spirit can overcome sin. Jesus Christ is the Spirit. He is the only man who has ever overcome sin (2 Cor. 3:17). Your only possible way to win over sin is to let Jesus Christ, the overcomer of sin, win the battle for you (Jn. 15:5).

Jesus taught that sin is not only outward, but sin is a heart issue as well. If you look at a woman with lust in your heart, you've committed adultery (Matt. 5:28). If you are angry with your brother, you are guilty of murder (1 Jn. 3:15). Because "not sinning" is the ultimate and commonly agreed upon goal of many Christians, dishonesty and hypocrisy run rampant in the church. All forms of legalism look for evidence of righteousness apart from faith alone. Most of the time, legalism has an outward focus. All legalism leads to dishonesty and hypocrisy. The reason for this is that no one can keep the whole law. Some varieties of flesh can keep *some rules* very well, but they secretly are failing in other areas. Some men may seek righteousness by not having televisions in their houses, but they quite possibly may yell at their family and belittle their own children. The legalist always holds others to high standards of righteousness on the points he himself is successful in. Yet the other ten thousand points of righteousness where he fails…somehow never becomes an issue. The legalistic flesh always has some degree of self-righteousness, the good feeling you get about yourself for doing it right- whatever "it" may be.

We must focus on the Spirit of God in order to walk after the Spirit instead of focusing on behaviors. Only then will the result be that we will not carry out the desires of the flesh.

Frequent repentance is necessary to walk after the Spirit. As mentioned, walking after the flesh usually begins with some sort of self-reliance or control in the heart. We leave listening to, focusing on, trusting in, and being in love with the person of Jesus Christ. We return to the familiarity of our own soul and flesh. We trade the weakness of trust for the strength of self-reliance.

Often, we feel the need to have solutions for inner dilemmas throughout the course of everyday life that flip us over into a heart position that is after the flesh. It could be as simple as how to solve a particular problem. It could be that you need to calculate dollar amounts at the grocery store while shopping. It could be that you feel pressure or expectations from your spouse, boss, or friends to do something or to be something. It could be as simple as you noticing that you have been speeding a little while driving your car. Your mind then drifts to your fear of getting a ticket. Next, you daydream of other related fears and anxieties. Pretty soon you've taken control in your heart to avoid feeling the fear. We resort back to trusting ourselves and relying on our own strength for our answers. Extremely small, subtle concerns, and unnoticed anxieties can lead to pressure and then to fear which cause us to leave a posture of trust.

>   Pro. 4:23 *"Watch over your heart with all diligence, For from it flow the springs of life."*

The Spirit of God inside you will always provide you with an inner witness when you are tempted to leave Him for the flesh. His voice is usually gentle and quiet. He does not yell at you to stay with Him. He invites you with tenderness. We are to remain in a childlike heart posture of trust and neediness while we slowly and gently ask God for His answer every moment of the day. We are to think through our daily situations in a prayerful manner with our Father. We have multiple opportunities to trust our Father every day.

>   Matt. 6:34 "…. Each day has enough trouble of its own."

I actually chronicled a few situations of a six-hour span of my recent activities during the time of this writing. This is a personal example from my life of real situations in which I either left the Spirit completely or I was distracted and tempted to leave the Spirit:

- I notice how I feel an urge to be sarcastic with someone while at work.
- While listening to a radio preacher, I experience a slight bit of irritation when he began asking for money at the end of his message.
- After I finish eating lunch, I have a fleshly desire to comfort myself with ice cream (not that eating ice cream or any certain foods is *always* wrong).
- While sitting in a parking lot in my car, I observe two ladies yelling at each other in the parking lot. I was overly curious instead of compassionate.
- I was noticeably bothered by someone because he sent me a text message.
- At the time I am typing this sentence, I am currently tempted with fear that the audience of readers might judge me because of the contents of this list.
- I experience a temptation of fear because of a possible negative surgery outcome for my son's hand injury.

The purpose of this is to show you just how subtle the flesh can be. During the timeframe of the above examples, I wasn't looking for signs of the flesh. I was looking at the Lord Jesus. But I noticed these as interruptions in our fellowship together. These interruptions wanted to pull my attention away from Him. I believe the Spirit of God pointed these various things out to me. It is the Spirit's job to convict of sin. It is not up to you to go on a constant hunt for the flesh. That activity, in and of itself, would be a fleshly activity.

Some of the items on my list did pull me away, and I gave in to the flesh. Whether I noticed the distraction, felt a strong temptation, or actually gave in and left the Spirit to entertain these – the solution was all the same. Repent back to a childlike, needy heart that is in love with my Lord. Find trust and give up my control. Then, simply be still in His presence and enjoy His love and His kindness.

The need for short accounts and very frequent repentance is critical. There are usually enough temptations, even in just one hour of a normal day of life, that require us to turn back to the Lord at least a few times. If we don't pay attention to the subtle corrections we receive from the Spirit, the flesh will gain a strong foothold, and you will stay in that heart posture of control in the flesh. Often times, you will not even become aware of your inward choice until you blatantly sin or your life begins to fall apart on some scale.

Another indicator and noticeable sign of walking after the flesh is a dry and empty heart. If this becomes a noticeable experience for you, it is an indication that you are not abiding in the Spirit of God.

Rom. 7:18 "For I know that nothing good dwells in me, that is, in my flesh; for the willing is present in me, but the doing of the good is not."

It does not matter how you arrive after the flesh - it will always produce death. The flesh is forever corrupt, through and through. You cannot change it, reason with it, or rehabilitate it. Even "nice flesh" is slippery and deceptive. "Moral flesh" is self-righteous and arrogant. "Loving and compassionate flesh" loves others because the act of giving to others feels so good – which is self-serving.

If you are according to the flesh, you will reason with yourself and survey every situation according to the master program of death that runs underneath your unconscious surface. Every "great solution" and every "wonderful answer" the flesh generates will ultimately produce spiritual loss and emptiness.

Rom. 14:23 "...and whatever is not from faith is sin."

Repentance is returning to faith. Faith is an active trust in the love and person of Jesus Christ. Repent and return to trust when you sin. Equally important, though, is to repent and return to trust when you have left your home base of childlike trust, love, and dependence on the person of Christ.

Living Distracted

Many Christians live the majority of their daily lives in a state of distraction. A shallow experience of God while in a state of distraction that is primarily focused on the daily situations of life is a hiding place for the flesh to live.

2 Tim. 2:4 "No soldier in active service entangles himself in the affairs of everyday life, so that he may please the one who enlisted him as a soldier."

Although who you are is pleasing to God because of the righteous condition of your spirit, the deeds that you do that are not of the Spirit are not pleasing to Him. Recall that there is always a separation between *what you do* and with *who you are*. Who you are is never defined by your deeds.

Living in a distracted state with your heart being filled with the affairs of everyday life is not what God intends for you. As you live according to the Spirit, your heart will be filled with love and worship toward the Lord Jesus Christ while you outwardly take care of the things the day requires. Have you ever been required to do a task when your heart was "somewhere else"?

Imagine for just a moment that a group of your best friends and family were all going to spend a wonderful evening together at a dinner party. However, you had to stay home alone and take care of household chores. While you outwardly performed your domestic duties at home, your heart would be meditating and longing for your friends and your family. You would be thinking constantly about what they possibly may be doing and saying each moment of the evening while you were cleaning, scrubbing, and washing at home.

It is quite possible for your heart to be focused in one place while your outward actions are currently engaged in another place altogether. If you are after the Spirit in your heart, you will be worshipping, loving, and enjoying your Lord while you perform your daily duties. However, if you are distracted from the Spirit, your heart will be filled with the duties you are performing while God will remain a distant thought in your mind. Anytime you are experiencing distraction, repentance is required.

Questions for Understanding and Discussion

1. What is repentance?
2. Why is repentance necessary often?
3. What kinds of things should the Christian repent from?
4. Why is it important to repent of subtleties?

A Tale of Two Cities

Leslie Evans lives in Houston, Texas. She works downtown in the business district. Her home is located on the northwest side of Houston which is a seventeen mile commute to work. The area of the city Leslie lives in happens to be one of the most traffic congested areas in the entire United States. It takes her an hour and fifteen minutes just to get to work every morning.

Houston also has one of the highest tax rates in the country. Leslie has to budget several hundred dollars every month just to pay her taxes. Dealing with pollution and high crime rates are also part of the daily experience of living in Houston.

Although Leslie enjoys her friends and relatives who live near her, the pressure and stress of big city life has begun to weigh heavily on her. She is tired of her job. She doesn't make enough money to pay her bills each month. Her morning commute to work each day is like going to war. And once she actually arrives at work, she has to do the job of two employees. She tries looking for another job when she has the time, but the job market is tough. Anytime a new job opens up in Houston, there are at least a hundred other people applying for the same job. But Leslie also has another problem.

Leslie Evans was diagnosed with a terminal illness just 2 years ago. Doctors told her that she may die within 3 years. There is a possibility that she could live longer, but it would depend on the progression of the disease in her body. The uncertainty weighs on her constantly.

Leslie finally decides to take a long-awaited vacation. She travels to a small island in the South Pacific called New Caledonia. The culture in New Caledonia is a mix of Melanesian and French. The people who live there are laid back, inviting, warm, and festive. When Leslie arrived, the very first thing she noticed were the amazing beaches. The beach scape villages in New Caledonia are absolutely breathtaking.

After arriving in New Caledonia, Leslie begins to experience the most relaxing, tranquil, and gorgeous atmosphere that she could have ever imagined. The air is so light and crisp. She can breathe. After only one week of her vacation, Leslie decides to move to New Caledonia permanently. She finds a job working at a local florist shop. Every day she rides her bicycle to work along a peaceful and beautiful beach shoreline. She enjoys making flower arrangements in the little hut where she works while the island breeze continually blows through the quiet little shop.

Leslie spends many of her evenings with close friends she has made while living in New Caledonia. It is so easy to make friends there because everyone knows each other and greets one another with warm smiles. After work, Leslie often strolls through the town square, or she relaxes at home in her quiet bungalow. Leslie is at total peace. She is completely relaxed. She is finally happy.

Even though Leslie Evans has relocated geographically, her problems are still not much different than they were in Houston. She still has very little money, and she still has a life threatening illness. But amazingly, those negative things don't affect her anymore. It is almost as though they no longer matter to her. Everything is very different now that she is living in a South Pacific culture. It isn't that her problems have changed so much. But the environment she is in *has changed her.*

Leslie's perspectives are very different now. She doesn't care that she is mostly broke financially. Life in New Caledonia is about relationships, not about making money, paying bills, or worrying about retirement. Everyone who lives there already lives a retired lifestyle. Leslie's illness was still a reality to her, but it was no longer a stressful thought. She so enjoys life now, every day has become an experience to be treasured. She has learned to savor every moment of everyday as she basks in New Caledonia's culture of simple pleasures.

The City of God

Heb. 11:10 "…for he was looking for the city which has foundations, whose architect and builder is God."

The Kingdom of God is a real place in the spirit. There are people there, angels, and created beings. God is there. The Kingdom of God has a specific culture and way of life just like any other city or country. It is a Kingdom – a country that is governed by a monarchy. Those who want to be a citizen of the Kingdom of God must become a subject of King Jesus.

Lk. 17:21 "Neither shall they say, Lo here! or, lo there! for, behold, the kingdom of God is within you."

The Kingdom of God is not just "heaven" – sometimes thought of as a far removed, ethereal place that we go to when we die. The Kingdom of God is now, and it is a real place. Jesus explained that the Kingdom of God is within you. It is a place that you can enter into and live in…from within.

Lk. 10:9 "…and heal those in it who are sick, and say to them, 'The kingdom of God has come near to you.'"

Mk. 12:34 "…you are not far from the Kingdom of God…"

Just like approaching the city limits of a town or the gates of an ancient city, the Kingdom of God is a place that we can come near, or that can come near to us. It is a place in the spirit.

Jesus Preached the Good News of the Kingdom of God

> *Matt. 4:23 "Jesus was going throughout all Galilee, teaching in their synagogues and proclaiming the gospel of the kingdom, and healing every kind of disease and every kind of sickness among the people."*

When we hear the phrase *the good news,* which is the same Greek word for the term "gospel", we immediately think of the death, burial and resurrection of Jesus Christ. The death, burial, and resurrection of Jesus is certainly the gospel. However, the scriptures record that Jesus preached the "good news of the Kingdom." The good news of the Kingdom is not the same thing as the death, burial, and resurrection of Jesus Christ for the forgiveness of sins. When Jesus was proclaiming the good news of the Kingdom, it is not recorded in scripture that He was going around preaching about His death, burial, and resurrection (although He did mention this, but not in terms of the Kingdom). When the scriptures record that Jesus proclaimed the good news of the Kingdom, what was it that Jesus was proclaiming?

Imagine that you lived in Israel during the days of Jesus. You would probably be poor. You would be heavily burdened and oppressed by the Roman government. You would be heavily taxed, not well fed, and not well clothed. Health care would be minimal or nonexistent. There is no opportunity to go to college and get a better job. The overall quality of life would be substandard. The possibility of anything very great happening during this life for you or your family would be slim. There would not be a lot of hope for you in this life of suffering and struggle.

In the middle of this depressing nowhere life of yours, Jesus Christ comes to your hometown. He does amazing wonders and miracles. He heals everyone who is sick. He feeds everyone with an abundance of wonderful tasting bread and fish. But most of all, He gives you hope for a better life. He doesn't say that He will change your circumstances, but He explains that there is a place you can live in your heart where peace, joy, love, and freedom are untouched by the sufferings of this present life. He explains to you some very good news about another Kingdom: a city, a country, a place in the spirit where you can dwell daily. You can know the King. You can be comforted, blessed, and loved.

The good news of the Kingdom of God that Jesus explained was the very news that there is a Kingdom, and that the humble and broken are all are invited to live in this new place of abundance. Jesus explained that access to the Kingdom of God was available to all. It was a new place to live for those who were weak, hurting, empty, and poor (Matt. 5:3-12). Jesus constantly taught about the Kingdom saying, "The Kingdom of God is like this…" or "The Kingdom shall be compared to that…" Jesus spoke of the Kingdom 119 times in the gospels. He proclaimed the good news of the Kingdom of God to a people who needed hope:

Matt. 10:7 "And as you go, preach, saying, 'The kingdom of heaven is at hand.'"

The Kingdom of heaven is a place that can be entered with an aggressive yielding of the heart.

Matt. 11:12 "From the days of John the Baptist until now the kingdom of heaven suffers violence, and violent men take it by force."

Where You Live Changes Your Perspective

Just like Leslie Evans from Houston, you are invited to relocate where you live. The Kingdom of God is a place of joy, life, love, and peace where King Jesus rules and reigns. The King is always available to every citizen in the Kingdom. If you ever need wisdom or just a hug, the King has plenty of time for you.

Just like Leslie from Houston, the problems and troubles you have on earth may or may not change, but as you live in a different city in your heart – you will change. Leslie's perspectives and emotions changed based on her surroundings and the culture of the new city she moved to. Your experience and view of your current problems will be totally different as you move from living in an earthly city to the heavenly one:

Ph. 3:20 "For our citizenship is in heaven, from which also we eagerly wait for a Savior, the Lord Jesus Christ;"

Heb. 12:22-23 "But you have come to Mount Zion and to the city of the living God, the heavenly Jerusalem, and to myriads of angels, to the general assembly and church of the firstborn who are enrolled in heaven, and to God, the Judge of all, and to the spirits of the righteous made perfect,"

Heb. 11:16 "But as it is, they desire a better country, that is, a heavenly one. Therefore God is not ashamed to be called their God; for He has prepared a city for them."

"Thy Kingdom Come On Earth"

When Jesus taught the disciples how to pray, He said, "Father, Your kingdom come, Your will be done on earth as it is in heaven" (Matt. 6:10). This not only addresses God establishing His physical kingdom on earth during a future time, but it also teaches the effect of the kingdom on Earth as we walk after the spirit.

When you are according to the Spirit, the kingdom of God is filling your heart, and you are living in a different place. You are actively participating in the heavenly city. When you speak, act, make choices, and respond according to that which is filling your heart which is of the kingdom, the kingdom of God comes on Earth, and the will of God is accomplished.

As born again Christians, we live in two places at one time. Our bodies are of Earth. But our spirits are of heaven.

2 Cor. 4:7 "But we have this treasure in earthen vessels, so that the surpassing greatness of the power will be of God and not from ourselves;"

Eph. 2:6 "and raised us up with Him, and seated us with Him in the heavenly places in Christ Jesus,"

If you are a believer, at this very moment, your spirit is in Christ, and you are seated at the right hand of the Father. This reality is not for some distant future, but it is true right now and in real time. At the same time you are in Christ seated in heavenly places, your physical feet are on the Earth. You are living within a temporal earthly body, while at the same time your spirit is in a spiritual place that is of a different realm. Within you, both the temporal and the eternal are true at the same time. Both heaven and Earth intersect within you.

This overlap between heaven and Earth allows for the Kingdom to come on Earth as it is in heaven and for God's will to be accomplished through us on the Earth. Whatever you hear and see the Father doing, you are able to do as well. He carries out his desires through you as your heart is living in the heavenly country. It is as though you are a stranger and an alien in this earthly land who has been sent out as an ambassador from the heavenly country (1 Pet.).

Questions for Understanding and Discussion

1. What is the kingdom of God?
2. How is the gospel of the kingdom different from the gospel of Jesus Christ?
3. What happens when you live in a different place in your heart?
4. What happens to your outward circumstances when your inward perspective changes?

The Role of Knowledge

Pro 3:5 "Trust in the LORD with all your heart and do not lean on your own understanding."

Mike was a recent graduate of a business management academy. He was proud of the fact that he finished the rigorous two-year program. Mike had learned tactical management techniques, organizational theory, strategic policy, and business management math. He felt equipped to handle the new assignment his company had given him. He could hardly wait to take on the new challenge of managing his own department.

When Mike arrived at his new job location, he immediately took charge and called a department meeting. "Hello everyone, my name is Mike Garner. I am your new department manager. I've been with the company for three years, and I just finished the company's management training program. We are going to start out by making a lot of changes."

The other employees were immediately skeptical of Mike. He didn't fully understand the dynamics of the department, yet he started implementing new policies and rules within the first week of his arrival. There were people under him that had been working in the department for over ten years who had plenty of experience with the various aspects of the department. Yet, Mike never bothered to ask them about their opinions or perspectives. Mike didn't really seem to care a whole lot about his employees personally. But worse than anything, he often pretended to know what he was talking about when he really didn't. Mike sometimes felt threatened while in front of his department employees, and this made him exert his authority all the more. Mike had plenty of management knowledge from attending management school, but he lacked a different kind of knowledge.

Col. 2:2 "...that their hearts may be encouraged, having been knit together in love, and attaining to all the wealth that comes from the full assurance of understanding, resulting in a true knowledge of God's mystery, that is, Christ Himself,"

2 Pet. 1:3 "seeing that His divine power has granted to us everything pertaining to life and godliness, through the true knowledge of Him who called us by His own glory and excellence."

2 Pet. 1:8 "For if these qualities are yours and are increasing, they render you neither useless nor unfruitful in the true knowledge of our Lord Jesus Christ."

All three of these verses above use the phrase "true knowledge." Notice in every verse above, true knowledge is directly linked with knowing the person of Jesus Christ. When the scripture speaks of true knowledge, it is not speaking of true knowledge as though it were the opposite of false knowledge. True knowledge is not the opposite of incorrect knowledge or erroneous doctrine. These verses are pointing out a specific kind of knowledge. True knowledge describes the knowledge which is the experiential knowledge of Jesus Christ.

The knowledge that is commonly sought after is *informational knowledge*. This knowledge is not true knowledge. When Mike graduated from the management school, he had learned plenty of informational knowledge. However, it was the ten-year veteran of the department who had a true knowledge of the department dynamics and the changes that needed to take place. Again, the verses mentioned above directly link true knowledge with knowing Christ Himself: *"True knowledge of our Lord Jesus Christ, true knowledge of Him, true knowledge of God's mystery, that is, Christ Himself."* True knowledge of God is the knowledge that only "an experience of Christ" can teach you.

When my wife was pregnant with our first child, we attended birth classes. We watched videos and read books along with three other couples about the labor and birth process. But nothing could have fully educated my wife about the experience of giving birth until she actually gave birth. As a man, I will never have a true knowledge of giving birth although I could tell anyone quite a bit about it after watching my wife give birth to four children.

Understanding a concept is not the same as experiencing the reality. *The Lord Jesus Christ is not a concept.* He is alive, and you can know and experience Him.

Suppose there was a book written about your spouse detailing his or her attributes and character traits. This book chronicled and described your spouse's thoughts, how he or she looks, particular likes and dislikes, etc. Suppose you were to wholeheartedly study and read this book for many years. Suppose that you were to memorize sentences in this book and even commit to memory very long passages. Although it might be helpful in getting to know your spouse, the fact that you know the book "about" your spouse would never be the same as actually spending time with your spouse. Knowledge is no substitute for experience. Experience is true knowledge.

> Jn. 5:39 *"You search the scriptures because you think that in them you have eternal life; it is these that testify about Me;"*

Jesus separated Himself from the scriptures. The scriptures are inspired of God, pure, wonderful, important, true, factual, and critically necessary. But we cannot substitute knowledge of the scriptures for the true knowledge of Jesus Christ Himself.

> *2 Tim. 3:7 "…always learning and never able to come to the knowledge of the truth."*

The danger of informational knowledge apart from true knowledge is that it can cause us to actually miss the Lord. The scribes and Pharisees knew everything about the coming Messiah, or so they thought. But a heart that is full of self-confidence cannot "see" the Lord when He actually does pass by. Western-minded Christianity has fulfilled the verse quoted above. We have volumes of books, teachings, study materials, and trainings. We are constantly learning without ever coming to true knowledge. The pursuit of informational knowledge has replaced the pursuit of true knowledge.

> *Eph. 3:19 "…and to know the love of Christ which surpasses knowledge, that you may be filled up to all the fullness of God."*

When we taste and experience the love of Christ, it actually surpasses knowledge. It is much better to know love than to have knowledge. Tasting of love fills us up to all the fullness of God. Many Christians experienced being filled up to all the fullness of God when they were new in their faith. All they knew was that God loved them and that they were saved. But as they began to "grow" (by following the popular teachings for what is erroneously believed to cause Christian growth), they gained more knowledge and a greater understanding of theology. They began to develop and fortify their positions on doctrines and grow in self-confidence in their Christianity. The less childlike we become, the less true knowledge we tend to walk in.

We've discussed at length how the knowledge of the scriptures can often become a substitute for a relationship with Christ. However, informational knowledge that is not true knowledge does have its role. Although true knowledge is essential, informational knowledge is also very valuable and helpful…if it is related to properly.

The Proper Place for Informational Knowledge

> *Pro. 1:7 "The fear of the Lord is the beginning of knowledge; Fools despise wisdom and instruction."*

> *Pro. 2:6 "For the Lord gives wisdom; From His mouth come knowledge and understanding."*

> *Rom. 15:14 "And concerning you, my brethren, I myself also am convinced that you yourselves are full of goodness, filled with all knowledge and able also to admonish one another."*

Most people seek informational knowledge in order to empower themselves. They perceive it as a weakness to not know things and to not be equipped with information. In order to avoid feelings of being stupid, lost, or ridiculed, people often seek knowledge to compensate for the lack they feel. Many people also feel a fear and a threat of being deceived or led astray by others. Therefore, they seek after knowledge in order to fortify their defenses. The flesh loves the illusion of strength that knowledge provides. But this is not how informational knowledge should be properly used or related to.

The information stored in your brain is there only in order to be *accessed* by the Spirit. In a way, therefore, we could say that we are to live from the Spirit first and the brain second. On the contrary, the flesh often lives from the brain first, taking its direction and lead from the independent thoughts within the mind that are not subject to the Spirit. However, when we are functioning in the proper order (Spirit first, mind second), the Spirit of God within us will first generate an impulse, a desire, or a thought, and then a file will be accessed from the brain to match the impulse which then brings understanding. If impulses from the Spirit were present without the knowledge in our minds to match it, we would have more difficulty in "hearing the Lord." In other words, the Spirit uses the informational knowledge we have gained in order for us to recognize what He is saying and doing.

Scripture tells us to renew our minds (Rom. 12:2). As you gain more truth and your mind is renewed, the old files in your brain that were created by the sinful nature become rewritten and updated with truth. The Spirit of God can access the new truth in your memory bank in order to bring clear direction and spiritual understanding. Yet, having only biblical truth in the mind without the Spirit accessing it is not spiritual understanding. It is only information.

It is often assumed that spiritual growth is the gaining of more informational knowledge. Your spirit doesn't grow. It does not need teaching, understanding, or revelation (Col. 2:10). Knowledge, teaching, and understanding are for the mind. As our minds are renewed, there is more truth for the Spirit to use and for you to recognize what the Spirit is saying and doing in any given situation (1 Jn. 2:27). Spiritual growth actually occurs as you embrace suffering and hardships in life that produce brokenness. As you live dependent on Christ during more and more moments of your day and in more areas of your life, you will grow spiritually.

Let's consider a simple example of the Spirit accessing the files you have in your mind. Sarah recently hears a teaching that God's primary desire for her life is that she sit at the feet of Christ, listen to Him, and enjoy His love for her during the moments of her day (Lk. 10:42). She has never heard this truth until now. Before hearing this new message, Sarah thought that God wanted her doing things for Him in order to be pleasing to Him. During the years while Sarah did not know this truth, God was leading her to sit at His feet and receive His love but she did not recognize His voice leading her to do so. The lie that she believed was louder than God's voice in her spirit. At times, God would prompt Sarah in her spirit, but the incorrect theology in her mind would override God's leadings. Now that her mind has been renewed with the truth, she can much more easily recognize His voice and the Spirit's promptings for her to rest and receive His love.

The mind and its knowledge base must remain submitted to the Spirit. From this place, the Lord can use your mind and access the knowledge you have gained. You must learn to allow the Spirit to access your mind and use it only as a tool. *The brain is a member of your body*, no different than a hand or a foot. It is to be used of the Spirit.

In a previous chapter, "The False Self," we discussed how you can actually focus on a particular body part which is somewhat similar to focusing on the Spirit of Christ who is in you. To continue with our silly illustration, let's pretend for a moment that you "lived only from your foot." Every feeling and desire that came from your foot would dictate your life and your choices. If your foot were too hot, you would only concern yourself with cooling it. If your foot were tired from walking, you would stop all walking for the day and rest your foot, no matter how important your other daily tasks would be. If your foot felt somewhat tight in its shoe, the only concern for the moment would be to make your foot feel less restrained. In essence, as you focused all day long only on your foot, then your foot would dictate your daily activities and your life.

Although this is a foolish example, it is not too far from the truth of how we live sometimes. If you have ever injured a certain part of your body, then perhaps the focus of your life was to nurture that injured part. In a similar way, some people only live from their stomach. Whatever their stomach desires, wants, and feels has become the governor of their daily life (Ph. 3:19). The love of food can dictate many daily choices and can actually become a focus.

Your brain is just like any other organ in your body. If you live *from* your brain for the moment by moment direction of your life, you will be controlled by your own self-created fears, your self-imposed rules, your self-created version of ideas, and your self-invented realities. Many people from developed, western cultures live this way continually. Human beings live by their own self-directed flesh according to whatever their minds tell them is the truth.

Whether you are living from the organ of the foot, the stomach, or the brain – that organ becomes the dictator for what your reality is and what your life is about. If your brain deduces that something is true, then you believe that it is true. Yet, your brain is fraught with error. Your mind (when it is not in a state that is submitted to Christ) is a broken machine that sometimes feels very strongly that it is right. How can you possibly know if you are right when you who are damaged are the one who is deciding when you are right and when you are wrong?

What if someone looks at you in a funny way during a social event? Does that mean that they have something against you? If the stock market plunges, are you in danger? If you don't pay a certain bill on time, are you going to suffer in some way? If the oil is not changed in your car at every 3,000 miles, will you experience a gnawing apprehension? When you seek validation by comparing yourself with other people, your comparisons are based on your own arbitrary standards that you have created (which may change from one day to the next). You probably have many incorrect views of yourself – such as thinking more highly of yourself in some areas and having self-contempt in other areas. You have created hundreds of unrealistic expectations of the people in your daily life that are impossible for anyone to fulfill. You obsess over your fears; you are self-absorbed in many situations; and when things don't go your way or you experience the slightest bit of stress in certain areas of life - you panic. During the summertime, you wish it were winter and in the wintertime you wish it were summer, yet you never face both of these at the same time.

Do you not see that you are insane? Of course not, because we rarely see ourselves as we truly are. Nor do we see the world around us as it truly is. We are not reliable judges of reality.

How many times have your perceptions of a situation been completely wrong? How many times have you been afraid for no reason? How many times have you been fully convinced that you were right, and you later found out that you were completely wrong? How many times did it seem that your world was falling apart around you, but now you look back at that same situation and smile, or you can't even remember it? Most of your perceptions, ideas, and your views of what reality truly is are altered in many ways.

Only the Spirit of God and the scriptures are the truth. Only His perspectives are sane. Only His opinions matter. Only the Spirit knows what is reality and what is not. Only as you spend time basking in His presence are you experiencing the truth. Trust only in the impulses that are from the Spirit, not your limited, fleshly mind whose ideas were formulated from an environment of fallen creation. Do not put your confidence in a mind whose memories and current realities are created from a broken childhood. Many of your current ideas of life are a result of fleshly parenting techniques that you received as a child. Many of your ideas, feelings, and perceptions of what you think reality actually is were all programmed from your old sinful nature before you came to Christ.

> *Rom. 8:26-27 "In the same way the Spirit also helps our weakness; for we do not know how to pray as we should, but the Spirit Himself intercedes for us with groanings too deep for words; and He who searches the hearts knows what the mind of the Spirit is, because He intercedes for the saints according to the will of God."*

This passage in Romans 8 explains that we do not know how to pray as we should. It is the Spirit within us that knows how we should pray. As we come from the Spirit *first*, allowing the Spirit to *access* our minds in order to express what the Spirit is saying, the knowledge we have becomes life-giving and fruitful. If you are living from your mind first, independent of the Spirit, then the knowledge you have is of little value.

> *1 Cor. 14:14-19 "For if I pray in a tongue, my spirit prays, but my mind is unfruitful. What is the outcome then? I will pray with the spirit and I will pray with the mind also; I will sing with the spirit and I will sing with the mind also. Otherwise if you bless in the spirit only, how will the one who fills the place of the ungifted say the "Amen" at your giving of thanks, since he does not know what you are saying? For you are giving thanks well enough, but the other person is not edified. I thank God, I speak in tongues more than you all; however, in the church I desire to speak five words with my mind so that I may instruct others also, rather than ten thousand words in a tongue."*

Here we see a distinction and a separation between the function of the mind and the Spirit. It is possible to come from the Spirit only in the activities of singing and prayer. However if we do this, it will not be edifying to those around us. In this passage, speaking in tongues is equated with praying in the Spirit only. Paul tells us that if you "pray in a tongue, your mind is unfruitful." Praying in tongues is very edifying for yourself. It is allowing the Spirit of God within you to express Himself verbally without having concepts in the brain to match it. To find a concept or knowledge in our minds that match what is being expressed in the Spirit can sometimes be a slower process. This is necessary, however, in order for others to be edified by what is occurring in our spirit. When the Spirit of God is stirring strongly within you, without words and concepts to match it, you may only groan or speak in tongues (Rom. 8:26, 1 Cor. 14:14). Especially when others are present, you should discipline yourself to allow the Spirit to search your knowledge base in order to find concepts and thoughts to match what is occurring in your spirit. In this way, others are edified. In other words, we should discern what the Spirit is saying with understanding so that we can edify others.

Do we always need specific knowledge in order to recognize God's voice? No, we do not, but it helps tremendously. God can tell us anything at any time. He can reveal things to us that we have never heard before and that we have no prior knowledge of. However, when we have a good knowledge base of truth (scripture), our minds are renewed and our files are updated. It then becomes much easier to recognize the promptings of the Spirit.

More often the problem is that we cling and grasp tightly to our theology and paradigms which hinder the Spirit's true promptings. As we sense the Spirit's nudge, our minds quickly dismiss it, and we return to what is familiar and more comfortable. Although not ideal, it is okay that our theology is not perfect and is a work in progress. However, it is often *the confidence* in our pet doctrines and views that causes us to totally miss the promptings of the Spirit. We should only cling to Christ while holding our doctrines loosely.

Scripture is very important. It is extremely beneficial to know what the Bible says. When the flesh wants to take you in a different direction away from the Spirit, if you have biblical knowledge, the Spirit has plenty of truth in your brain at His disposal to prompt you with and remind you of in order to check the flesh and bring you back in line to what is real.

The flesh is both cranial and sensual. It wants to think, ponder, and figure everything out, yet it also wants to experience and feel wonderful feelings. It doesn't care if its concepts are truly based in reality as long as it thinks they are reality. Nor does it care if what it is feeling is based in truth as long as it feels good and right.

Living from the impulses of the Spirit first and the mind second can seem like risky business. What if you "hear" something that isn't God? Again, it is vital to have a solid knowledge base of scripture. You must always check the subjective impulses of the Spirit with the objectivity of scripture. They will always agree if you are truly hearing the Spirit of God. Concerning this issue, there is also the very important safeguard of the body of Christ. It is very healthy to share what you hear from the Lord with those whom the Lord has knit your heart with. Very often the Lord will use the church to check your hearing and bring correction.

The Mind That Is Not Submitted

Knowledge and concepts can be dangerous and must be handled with maturity. Biblical knowledge is often toyed with, gazed upon, pondered, and researched- all without vulnerability to the person of Christ. It is often an independent activity. The knowledge gained is then used as artillery for pride and argument. Knowledge that is not submitted to the Spirit (each and every moment) can be used as a suit of armor to fortify and strengthen the "false self."

Knowledge also becomes a cloak of identity. Our only identity should be that we are our Father's child. We often think however, that "who we are" is defined by "what we believe." Our shallow, fleshly identity is defined by concepts as opposed to being defined by the person who gives us life. When reading the Old Testament, you can see that "who people were" was defined by "who their father was" (the son of …). Your Father defines who you are. You are not defined by what you know or by what you have done. Who you are is defined by your father because you are "of and from" your father. It is only your flesh that desires to build up its own self and find its identity in knowledge and accomplishments. In like manner, we as Christians are defined by who our spiritual Father is. Jesus is our identity.

Esteeming the Knowledge You Have

Total vulnerability and intimacy with Jesus Christ is your goal - not learning more information. We have stated that knowledge and information are good and usable if related to properly. An important element of relating to knowledge properly is seeing it for what it really is. Although informational knowledge is important and has its uses, when comparing informational knowledge to the true experiential knowledge of knowing Christ, informational knowledge must be thought of as crap. The word "crap" (or other forms of the word) is a biblical word that Paul specifically chooses to use when he communicates the very idea we are speaking of as shown here in the King James:

> *Ph. 3:3-8 "For we are the circumcision, which worship God in the spirit, and rejoice in Christ Jesus, and have no confidence in the flesh Though I might also have confidence in the flesh. If any other man thinketh that he hath whereof he might trust in the flesh, I more: Circumcised the eighth day, of the stock of Israel, of the tribe of Benjamin, an Hebrew of the Hebrews; as touching the law, a Pharisee; Concerning zeal, persecuting the church; touching the righteousness which is in the law, blameless. But what things were gain to me, those I counted loss for Christ. Yea doubtless, and I count all things but loss for the excellency of the knowledge of Christ Jesus my Lord: for whom I have suffered the loss of all things,* **and do count them but dung***, that I may win Christ"*

The word "dung" here means "excrement", that is, "crap." Paul gives his extensive resume and then tells us that "in order to gain Christ" he counted everything he gained as worthy of the toilet bowl. To state it more delicately, it is an important heart attitude to forsake all things that we have gained, including knowledge, in order for God to use those very things that we have gained. If you are esteeming anything higher than Jesus Himself, it is of no value.

> *1 Cor. 3:20 "The Lord knows the reasonings of the wise, that they are useless."*

> *1 Cor. 8:1 "...knowledge makes arrogant, but love edifies."*

Many Christians equate learning more things about the Lord with growth. We respect those who can memorize large amounts of scripture and who can quote Bible verses. Those who have a very thorough understanding of biblical theologies and who can explain and defend them are highly esteemed. PhD's of Bible colleges and seminaries are among those who are most respected and considered experts in the Christian faith. As we will see, the scriptures disagree with this view.

You Can Choose To Know Nothing

Paul begins the first Corinthian letter by addressing the divisions that existed among the Corinthians. One of Paul's major goals in writing the letter was to correct the division and fleshly relating that were found in the Corinthian church. Because of this, we can see that many of the verses in the first Corinthian letter tie in to this specific, original purpose of correcting the errors in Corinth. Paul explains that one of the causes of their divisions was their fleshly approach to the knowledge they had:

1 Cor. 1:19-20 "For it is written, "I will destroy the wisdom of the wise, and the cleverness of the clever I will set aside." Where is the wise man? Where is the scribe? Where is the debater of this age? Has not God made foolish the wisdom of the world?"

Next, Paul becomes an example to the fleshly, divided Corinthian church by telling them that he "purposed to know nothing, except Jesus and Him crucified":

1 Cor. 2:2 "For I determined to know nothing among you except Jesus Christ, and Him crucified."

Again, Paul was not just making a poetic statement. Nor was he trying to be falsely humble. He was telling the Corinthian church how to practically correct the error of division they were walking in. A major source of the problem for the divisions that existed among the Corinthians was the informational knowledge they had and how they were relating to it.

Paul, who wrote a large portion of the New Testament and knew many things, purposed and gave himself to not knowing anything except Jesus. Paul also goes on to say that "his preaching was not in persuasive words of wisdom, but in power" so that the Corinthian's faith would be founded on power and not on wisdom. Power is an encounter. Power is experiential.

Purposing *not to know* is having a heart of humility. It is humble to not know, because the truth is…you really *don't know*. If you are a Christian, you know the person of Christ. Your relationship with Him is really all that you have experientially that is real. This is the only sure thing that you have. All of the theologies, doctrines, and biblical understanding you currently possess are only a work in progress. Over time, your understanding of doctrine and theology will change as God gives you more light and revelation on every subject.

Let's look at a statement that would describe and serve as an example of having a teachable heart of learning and humility:

"This is my current understanding on the subject. Perhaps there is more revelation to be had on this issue."

This kind of attitude allows room for the Lord to speak and teach you more. No one has full knowledge on any subject- no matter how convinced he may be. All of God's truth has layers of understanding and levels of revelation. For example, when you are six months old in the Lord, you become aware that He loves you. When you are ten years old in the Lord, you are beginning to realize that He loves you. When you have been in the Lord for twenty- five years, you start to finally see and understand that He loves you.

1 Cor. 13:12 "For now we see in a mirror dimly, but then face to face; now I know in part, but then I will know fully just as I also have been fully known."

There is no end to the revelation contained in just one biblical truth. This is because Jesus Christ is the truth, and there is no truth apart from Him (Jn. 1:17, Eph. 4:21). *Truth is a person.* The truth is as vast and as deep as Christ Himself. We can certainly know the truth in a particular area, but usually more depth of understanding is available.

When others have opposing views that challenge your beliefs, it is only to the degree that you esteem your knowledge that you are offended and separated from your brother. In church life, we are to love others more than we love our own opinions. We are to hold on to Christ alone and allow our doctrinal views to just be our "current understanding." Paul's example to the fractured Corinthian church was an example of maturity that preserves the unity of the Spirit. Our unity is in the Spirit of Christ, not in the doctrines that we hold (Eph. 4:3). From time to time in the past, brothers have approached me desiring to have doctrinal discussions in order for us to have unity. Unity has little to do with agreeing together on the same concepts. It is always an issue of the heart. Unity is an attitude of how we see the other person - if we esteem him or not, or if we hold disdain or disrespect for him. Even the smallest degree of seeing another Christian in a negative light can be a temptation for a wedge of division. Although there are many brothers and sisters I walk with who do not see all things the same as I do (or with each other), they are not less than me, and we are not different from each other.

We are the same as those who believe differently than we do because we have the same Spirit within us. We have the same Father. We are brothers and sisters who happen to have different concepts, ideas, and understandings in our minds. You are one spirit with all Christians, no matter what they believe or walk in (1 Cor. 12:13, Eph. 4:4, Phil. 1:27). The one Spirit that we are all a part of joins us together with the deepest kind of unity there is (deeper than a blood relative). Unity of spirit is unity indeed because the spirit is the deepest part of a man. A person's concepts and ideas exist only in his more shallow parts – the soul. Although it is not bad or negative to agree with others' concepts, views, and ideas, this allows for only a shallow type of joining. Christians often view their unity with others only within the shallow plane of ideas and doctrines, and they are quite content to maintain a shallow unity while ignoring the realm of the spirit where true unity exists.

There is often a place to speak the truth to others. There is a time to correct and to refute incorrect doctrines, and sometimes it needs to be done sharply. But this is always to be done in a spirit of gentleness and humility. This can only be accomplished if we are coming from the Spirit first and allowing Him to access the knowledge we have. If we do this, we will discern the spirit of the man who is speaking error, and with wisdom we can restore him with spiritual correction.

How can you choose to not know something that you are fully convinced that you already know? The answer is to humble yourself. If you will face the truth, you will realize that there is no way you can possibly know everything about a subject. Even within the simplest of subjects, there is always more understanding to be gained. Many times when you gain more understanding about a subject, the new information you gain begins to alter the previous information you believed about it, thus initiating a shift in your overall paradigm.

Only God has complete knowledge. It is foolish and irresponsible to make confident assertions when there is always more light to be had. And there is always more light to be had. For me personally, I will identify with the apostle Paul's position. The only truth that I will absolutely never budge on is the person of Jesus Christ being Lord and that He was crucified for the forgiveness of sins and rose from the dead. This is not up for debate with me. However, every other doctrine, interpretation of scripture, etc., is open for discussion and more learning.

To discuss an issue and hear others' viewpoints does not mean that you will agree with them. Rarely do I agree with most doctrines I hear. But we are to have a heart of humility that genuinely listens to another viewpoint and then considers it. Otherwise, your pride will blind you into a narrow insanity. Overconfidence is a condition of non-reality. Only the humble stance of realizing that you could be wrong is a safe and sane condition of heart and mind.

Knowledge Does Not Connect Us To God

Knowledge can never connect you with God. It is faith that connects you to God. We cannot know God from our minds. We can only "know about God" from our minds. You can only truly know God from your spirit. God is spirit, and we commune with Him and know Him from within our spirits. To only live from your mind with thoughts about God is to be detached from intimacy with God and truly knowing Him.

You must release and submit the knowledge you have and then place your trust in the person of Christ. To the degree you trust in your knowledge, you trust in yourself.

> *Jn. 14:26 "But the Helper, the Holy Spirit, whom the Father will send in My name, He will teach you all things, and bring to your remembrance all that I said to you."*

Anything that you need to know, God will let you know. The Spirit will bring back to your memory messages, teachings, scriptures, and truths that you have learned and have heard in the past. In fact, you will find that if you let go of your trust in knowledge and understanding and begin to trust only in the person of Christ (right now), much more memory of scripture will come to your mind. As the Spirit prompts you and has control over your memory bank, scripture and truth will flow much more freely from within you.

Only come to Jesus in faith and forsake grasping after and holding onto your knowledge. Your flesh is an idol maker. It is in a perpetual state of carving some block of wood into a new idol. Even if you gain a new revelation that you have created an idol and then repent of your idol, the flesh immediately creates a brand new idol from a different block of wood. Stop trying so hard to understand…only trust and believe.

I strongly encourage you not to try to memorize spiritual messages and teachings you hear. Don't try to remember "breakthroughs" that you have gained, and don't try to recall truths that you heard in the past. Your strong focus on retaining information is often a mask for an unbelieving heart. Stop gripping so tightly and begin to relax inside. Forget and forsake all of your knowledge and let it go. Forget what you've read in this book. It is there in your brain's memory banks for the Spirit of God to access it as He sees fit. If the Spirit of God wants to use any information you have been exposed to, then He will bring it back to the forefront of your mind. Only believe, love, trust, and enjoy Him. Only then will you be free for the Spirit to move within your mind to access whatever files are necessary to help you in each moment. Having an anxious heart that tries to "make sure" you retain information will work against you. Only grasp and hold on to Christ. Let go in your mind and let go in your heart.

When you hear a good message, forget everything you heard and place your trust in Christ. When you read a good verse in scripture, forsake the knowledge of it but use the verse to receive the Lord in that moment. When a friend is speaking, listen to his heart, not so much the information he is communicating.

When you read a complex passage in scripture, believe exactly what it says instead of translating it to fit into your current theology. If you will believe what it says, then true spiritual understanding will usually follow. Don't make the mistake of having to understand with your mind before you will believe it. Believing is an act of the will, an act of submission, and an act of humility.

> *1 Cor. 2:14 "But a natural man does not accept the things of the Spirit of God, for they are foolishness to him; and he cannot understand them, because they are spiritually appraised."*

This verse has often been quoted as only pertaining to unbelievers. Although it does apply to the unbelieving, Paul also explained to the Corinthians that they were walking as fleshly, natural men (1 Cor. 3:3). Even Christians cannot understand the things of the Spirit of God if they are trying to understand them through their natural fleshly minds.

> *Eph. 2:3 "Among them we too all formerly lived in the lusts of our flesh, indulging the desires of the flesh and of the mind, and were by nature children of wrath, even as the rest."*

The spiritual person listens from the Spirit first and then allows the Spirit to give understanding in his mind secondly. On the contrary, the carnal person takes all direction from his own mind first and uses it as his guide.

> Eph. 1:17 "...that the God of our Lord Jesus Christ, the Father of glory, may give to you a spirit of wisdom and of revelation in the knowledge of Him."

Even with a thorough knowledge of the scripture, *without adequate experience of the Spirit* your fleshly mind will incorrectly handle the word of truth. Eph. 1:17 explains that we are to have a *spirit* of wisdom and of revelation in the knowledge of Christ. This verse does not say that we are to have a brain that understands. It is only with your spirit that you gain revelation, not the head. Once you gain a revelation in your spirit, then your mind can understand it. However, revelation always originates from within your spirit. Many times if you try to understand a spiritual idea with your mind first, you will either misapply it or only understand a shallow part of it. If you understand from your spirit, you see not only the deeper revelation, but also the true application.

We Use What Is Available

In this section, I will attempt to explain a complex subject as simply as possible. As you will see, the depth of this subject goes beyond the scope of the book.

If by chance your right hand were broken, you would have to use your left hand until the right hand healed. This is called compensation. Many people have tremendous pain in their hearts, and in order to compensate for the pain that is in their heart, they *avoid* their heart and live from their head. You could think of it as a water well that has been filled up with sand. If the well is not available, you have to use something else. A heart that is filled with pain or fear is often avoided because of the negativity that would be experienced if the heart were accessed. A person with this "hardness of heart," can only live and operate from his head.

As Christians, we are certainly new creations. However, it is in our spirit where we are made new creations. We will not receive a new body until the resurrection (1 Cor. 15:35-54). The memories that are stored in our brain are still a part of the body that has yet to be redeemed and glorified. Trauma and hurt from the past often goes unresolved and not dealt with. Painful emotional scars of the past certainly affect how we relate and how we process, which color the way we see our world today.

Many times when a person is in this condition, even the smallest amount of opening in his heart brings about a flood of painful emotion; even if the stimulus for opening the heart was unrelated to the pain that comes out. For example, if a person who has much pain bound up in his heart is treated with kindness or with love, it can sometimes feel painful to him. It is not that the kindness or love is negative, but these particular actions touch and move his heart – which is already full of pain. A wounded person like this can often avoid receiving anything on a heart level from anyone else because it is just too painful to take it in – not because of the act of kindness, but because of the residing pain within. Sometimes unresolved pain in the soul can cause a person to cry or weep for reasons he does not understand. Anger can reside just under the surface. Even the slightest, unrelated bump can bring forth violent rage. There are varying degrees of this dynamic in many people.

Heart Intimacy is Foreign

Negative emotions and pain are not the only reasons people avoid their hearts. Many times, the head is all that is available to live out of because the dynamic of intimacy is a foreign concept. The word *intimacy* may only have connotations of physical intimacy; however, there is an intimacy of heart that all people long for and desperately need. Heart intimacy is experienced when sharing occurs during a vulnerable exchange. The result is a deep connection. Our greatest need for intimacy is with Jesus Christ. However, women deeply long for heart intimacy with their husbands. Husbands also crave heart intimacy with their wives. In addition, both men and women desire and need heart intimacy with people of their same gender. Being an active participant within a tightly knit community of other believers where transparency, vulnerability, and intimate heart connections are practiced frequently is an extremely critical and vital factor in the health and well-being of all Christians. The results of continual heart intimacy with both a spouse and with others of the same gender dramatically increase the individual's well-being and contribute to the spiritual growth process both within the family unit and corporately. For an extensive look at church life dynamics, read my first book *"The Way Church Was Meant To Be."*

Those who have never had a capacity for heart intimacy created within them can find it extremely difficult to even relate to the idea. They long for it, but it eludes them. This can be the result of lacking a healthy connection with a mother as a young child. It can be the result of a distant father who was emotionally mechanical and shut down within his own heart. Those who had no father at all or who were abandoned in some manner often have little capacity for intimacy and vulnerability in their hearts. There is also the very pervasive occurrence of broken trust and betrayal. This occurs when a person's heart was open and trusting of a certain person at one time in his life only to discover that the vulnerable trust was broken. Tremendous pain is the result. When trust doesn't pay off, inner vows are erected that say "I will never" do that again. Many times these inner vows are hidden from sight and are buried deep with the soul. The list is endless of the possibilities of why someone's heart may be wounded and shut down, leaving only the mind to live from. The capacity for heart intimacy requires a large degree of emotional soundness and emotional health. A person who is a candidate for heart intimacy must know that he himself is desirable and lovable. He must be willing to risk rejection. And, he must have a desire to share the life of another because the other person is viewed as desirable as well.

Without going into too much detail, some form of forgiveness and the releasing of inner vows to never trust again often brings healing of unhealthy heart postures and dynamics in many people. It can, however, be difficult to see exactly where to apply the forgiveness and what the specific inner vows actually are. Christian counseling settings can be helpful, but this method is not preferable because it is an artificial replacement of a functioning group of believers. God's way of healing and restoration is within the context of deep relationships in the church.

The Lord Jesus Christ is restoring all of us, and we are all in the process of being healed. Again, we are already completely healed within our spirits, and as we walk after the Spirit we are able to live in freedom. However, the unresolved pain buried deep within our hearts and souls can often quench the Spirit in our daily walk with the Lord. This results in a certain degree of "shallowness" even while walking after the Spirit (Mt 13:8). When we are according to the Spirit, God fills the rooms in the house of our heart that have been unlocked and opened to Him. But the rooms within our hearts that remain nailed shut are unavailable for Him to enter and fill. In other words, as we walk after the Spirit, the Spirit will lead us into certain activities, either to think this or that, to feel this or that, or to do this or that. But often we will either refuse to venture into specific places within ourselves, or we will not hear His voice in some regard because it will take us into a place that is hardened, dark, painfully locked away, and has become a forgotten undiscovered territory. Rarely are we ever conscious of this.

As we live more and more of the moments of our day according to the Spirit and in vulnerable community with others, the Lord will address these hardened and painful areas of deception within us. Jesus will gently knock on doors that have been nailed shut or that have never been opened. As we come to the light and are healed and restored in these places, we experience "more room" as we walk after the Spirit than we did prior to the healing. This results in more room in our hearts and more capacity for experience.

Referring again to our water well analogy, when healing takes place, some of the sand in our well has been removed, and more water is able to fill the capacity of the well. We become deepened as we are healed. This results in a more intense and more intimate experience of the Lord within our hearts and souls, the place of experience.

Truth is in Jesus

2 Cor. 3:17 "Now the Lord is the Spirit..."

A large part of getting truth from your head and into your heart (into your real experience) is realizing that all truth is already in your spirit. Jesus Christ is the Spirit.

>*1 Cor. 6:17 "But the one who joins himself to the Lord is one spirit with Him."*

Because you are born again, the Spirit of Christ is now one with your human spirit.

>*Jn. 1:17 "For the Law was given through Moses; grace and truth were realized through Jesus Christ."*

>*Jn. 14:6 "Jesus said to him, "I am the way, and the truth, and the life…"*

>*Eph. 4:21 "…if indeed you have heard Him and have been taught in Him, just as truth is in Jesus."*

All truth is in Jesus Christ who is the Spirit and who is now one with your human spirit.

Notice Eph. 4:21: *"If you have heard Him and have been taught in Him."* You hear God from your spirit - where Christ is. You are also taught of God from your spirit where Christ is. Because truth is in Jesus and He is one with your spirit, you are taught all things from the spirit inside of you. Look at this amazing verse in 1 John 2:27:

>*1Jn. 2:27 "As for you, the anointing which you received from Him abides in you, and you have no need for anyone to teach you; but as His anointing teaches you about all things, and is true and is not a lie, and just as it has taught you, you abide in Him."*

When you hear truth with your physical ears and it goes into your brain, it is the Spirit of God inside you who illuminates it and says, "What you just heard is truth from God, and it is for you." As you hear and read truth, it is always the Spirit who teaches it to you.

Therefore, the many truths you have in your head are not realized as experiential reality until you see and understand them from within your spirit.

>*Jn. 6:63 "It is the Spirit who gives life; the flesh profits nothing; the words that I have spoken to you are spirit and are life."*

It profits you nothing to only hear and learn biblical information from your flesh and from your head. Your flesh knows plenty of biblical information but only the Spirit gives life. Working through faith, the Spirit breathes reality and experience into the words and concepts that are in your head.

When a biblical truth is only a concept in your head, it is crucial to find the reality of the truth in your spirit. If it is truth, it is there. All truth is in Jesus. Leaving your head as your primary place of context and seeing the truth from within your spirit will bring life, experiential reality, and true knowledge (Col. 2:2, Col. 3:10, 2 Pet. 1:3, 2 Pet. 1:8).

So how do you actually do this? How do you take a truth that is in your head and find the reality of that truth within your spirit? You must begin to discern your spirit from your mind ("Separating Soul from Spirit" chapter). As you learn to be in touch with your spirit, simply look to see the particular truth you are wanting to see. If you do not see it right away, then wait on God to reveal it to you. If it is a truth in scripture, then it is true in your spirit.

For example, we know from scripture that you are a child of God. But it doesn't do you a whole lot of good to know this fact only in your head. You want to *see* that you are a child of God in your spirit so that this can become an experiential reality to you. Looking at the truth in your spirit is much like looking at a picture hanging on a wall. There are many "truths" and elements contained in the picture all at the same time. In a picture hanging on a wall, there may be a tree, a house, a river, a bird, rays of sunshine, a road, and a fence. All of these elements are in the picture and exist at the same time. In order to focus on one element in the picture, you only have to locate, focus, and enjoy it. The same is true with the things of God. There are many things that are true in your spirit all at the same time (You are clean, you love God, you love righteousness, you are His child, you are one with God, etc.). If you are wanting to see experientially in your spirit that you are a child of God, simply look for it within your spirit. Look at the spirit inside of you. Did you look? Can you tell that you are His? Can you see in your spirit that you are His child? If you can't see it, then simply wait and keep looking and keep listening. It is true even if you don't see it – because it is in scripture. If you do see it, then you now have the experiential reality of being a child of God and not just an empty fact in your head with no life in it.

Questions for Understanding and Discussion

1. What is the difference between true knowledge and informational knowledge?
2. What role does knowledge play when you come from the spirit first?
3. How should you relate to the knowledge you've gained?
4. What does it mean to say that truth is in Jesus?

Milk and Meat

> *1 Cor. 3:2 "I gave you milk to drink, not solid food; for you were not yet able to receive it. Indeed, even now you are not yet able,"*

When you think about "the meat" of the word of God, what do you think of? Many Christians associate "getting into the meat of the word" with activities such as learning "strong doctrine," intricate Bible study, involved teaching, parsing out the complexities of scripture, or conducting deep biblical word studies in order to prove and understand theology. It is commonly thought that when we are doing these kinds of activities we are really getting into "the meat" of the word.

But is this really the solid food Paul was talking about?

> *Heb. 5:12, 14 "For though by this time you ought to be teachers, you have need again for someone to teach you the elementary principles of the oracles of God, and you have come to need milk and not solid food. ... But solid food is for the mature, who because of practice have their senses trained to discern good and evil."*

We see from this verse that solid food is for those who by practice have had their senses trained. *Your senses are not trained through head knowledge. Your senses are trained through sensing.* The more you practice engaging in sensing and experiencing God, the more your senses will be trained to discern good and evil.

Very often, the pursuit of love and the experience of God are despised by the arrogant and the intellectual kinds of flesh. This results in an opinion that things such as love, experiencing God, and walking after the Spirit are all equated with a spineless form of Christianity that lacks truth and meat. The pursuit of love has frequently become judged throughout Christendom as pursuing "feelings." Therefore, the healthy feelings of love have been removed, and love has been redefined as "a choice." Love is viewed as a weak commodity that lacks the truth - the truth of doctrine and the strong meat of the word.

It is a fact that the world's version of love lacks truth. The world's fleshly variety of love is a feel-good love that is gutless, cowardly, feeble, not safe, and not sane. The love of the world is blown to and fro by every wind of doctrine and by every whim of fleshly impulse. The love of the world says, "If you love me, you will cater to me, coddle me, and give me what I want." The love of the world does not embrace the suffering of the cross in the life of the believer. It bends over backwards and sacrifices the truth in order to demonstrate "tolerance." For example, truth is now becoming equated with "hate speech." If you declare the truth of God's word in certain situations, you are automatically considered to be a bully who is hateful.

Those who have bought in to the man-centered gospel only want to feel good and be blessed. They do not want to humble themselves and live in the brokenness of dependence and trust. However, the love that is from God allows for suffering, pain, and distress in the life of the believer. The love of God spanks children and breaks the will of the flesh. It does not give children a "time out." God does not discipline His children this way because it is not love (Heb. 12:7-11).

This type of fleshly judgment on God's love, joy, and peace keeps many from exploring it. It is very common to minimize love, experiencing God, and the practice of things that require us to use our senses. These sensing activities seem dangerous and not grounded in truth. However, anything that involves a human being has the potential for error. Only God's word is truth, and only Jesus Christ is truth. Clinging only to the cranial and conceptual understanding has just as much potential for error as clinging only to the experiential. We can have both incorrect theology and incorrect experiences.

We do not have to separate true experience from correct concepts. We can love *and* be in the truth. We can hold fast to the scripture *and* experience God. We can worship in Spirit and in truth (Jn. 4:24), and we must do so, for it is only the truth that leads us to love, and only love that leads us into all truth.

The love of God is the truth. Love and truth are both one and the same. Jesus Christ is love and Jesus Christ is truth (1 Jn. 4:8, Eph. 4:21). *If you only know the truth, you do not know God. And if you only know love, you do not know God.* God is both at the same time.

> *Mk. 12:28-31 "One of the scribes came..., and asked Him, "What commandment is the foremost of all?" Jesus answered, "The foremost is, 'Hear, O Israel! The Lord our God is one Lord; and you shall love the Lord your God with all your heart, and with all your soul, and with all your mind, and with all your strength.' "The second is this, 'You shall love your neighbor as yourself.' There is no other commandment greater than these."*

When asked the question of "What is the greatest commandment," Jesus did not respond by saying, "The greatest command is to get into the meat of the word by doing Bible study." The greatest thing you can do is *to love*.

> *1Tim. 1:5 "But the goal of our instruction is love from a pure heart and a good conscience and a sincere faith."*

Why did Paul and the other apostles write so much instruction for us in the New Testament? The goal of Paul's epistles and instruction is clear: it was love. Although it is extremely important, Bible study is not the ultimate goal. Love is the greatest and highest commodity because God is love (1 Jn. 4:8).

The love of God is the very definition of strength. It is as strong as death (Song of Songs 8:6). Only the love of God will endure fiery trials, go the second mile, lay down its life, turn the other cheek, bear all things, build up and edify, overcome sin, serve tirelessly, forgive seventy times seven, bear one another's burdens, and treasure and value others from the heart. Airtight theology will not help you much with these things.

It is often said that the greatest commandment of loving God with the mind is being fulfilling by a pursuit of intellectual study. This may be true for some. But the endless pursuit of knowledge is a common place for the flesh to hide while it spiritualizes and justifies its arrogant and selfish hobby of ideas.

Study to Show Thyself Approved?

What about the activity of studying scripture? Aren't we supposed to "study to show ourselves approved?" This very popular verse is used to support the idea of biblical study:

2 Tim. 2:15 "Study to shew thyself approved unto God, a workman that needeth not to be ashamed, rightly dividing the word of truth."

The King James translation is the only translation that translates the Greek verb spoudazō in this verse as "study." All other translations translate this verb as "being diligent." The King James translation of this word was not a bad translation during the 1600's in England, but the word "study" has come to mean something entirely different in modern times.

As we read the verse in another translation, it takes on a very different meaning:

2 Tim. 2:15 "Be diligent to present yourself approved to God as a workman who does not need to be ashamed, accurately handling the word of truth." (NASV).

The use of the word *study* in England during 1611 also was used as "to endeavor diligently." To prove this, look at how the King James also uses the word "study" in a different verse:

1Th. 4:11 "And that ye study to be quiet, and to do your own business, and to work with your own hands, as we commanded you"

The verse directly above is not telling us to study quietly (as if not to disturb others). This verse is instructing us to make sure or be diligent to live a quiet life. Every time other than the translation in 2 Tim. 2:15 ("study to be approved") the King James translates the word spoudazō *or* study *as being "diligent" or "endeavoring."*

The Actual Context and Meaning of 2 Timothy 2:15

Let's look at the verse in the context of the passage. Who you are as a Christian is already approved by God. But your actions and how you conduct yourself are to be pleasing and approved by Him as well.

The point of the verse is this: Paul was telling Timothy to "be a workman who handles accurately the word of truth." To handle accurately the word of truth is addressing *an attitude* and a quality of character, not one's ability to understand scripture. If you read the entire passage, you will notice that the context of the verse clearly indicates that Paul is encouraging Timothy to be a man who does not wrangle with words, to avoid empty chatter, and to refuse ignorant and foolish speculations that produce quarrels. Paul goes on to instruct Timothy that the Lord's servant should not be quarrelsome but rather be kind and patient when wronged. To be diligent in these things is "studying (endeavoring) to be approved by handling accurately the word of truth." Having this kind of heart attitude and quality of character is what it actually means to accurately handle the word of truth. We are to make sure that we have good character when it comes to God's word and not argue and fight with it. *This verse has nothing to do with studying the Bible.*

Those who have spent countless hours "studying the scripture to show themselves approved" but not spending time getting to know Christ Himself are often the very people who wind up in unprofitable arguments about doctrine. Therefore, these are the very ones who are not accurately handling the word of truth. The practices of wrangling about words, engaging in quarrels, and arguing about doctrine are mostly the result of a proud heart that has been puffed up by knowledge (1 Cor. 8:1). It is much better to learn to love - which actually edifies others.

The verse in 2 Tim. 2:15 is frequently used to justify an intellectual Christianity. A diligent mind can be a mask that excuses not having a diligent heart. We see that the actual point of the verse is not studying the Bible and defending doctrines (which can lead to engaging in the very activities the passage is warning against), but to be diligent to have a good heart in accurately handling the truth so as not to engage in fruitless quarrels, discussions, etc.

Bible study is an excellent and necessary activity, but it must be done in fellowship with the Spirit. Secondly, the knowledge we gain from study must be handled accurately- with love and patience. It is great to study scripture and to know it well. However, things that accompany love, which is the greatest commandment, is the solid food.

Questions for Understanding and Discussion

1. What is true meat?
2. How can you train your senses?
3. How is the word *study* used in the King James translation?
4. How can you handle accurately the word of truth?

Activities of the Heart

In order to help you further discern the difference between your head and your heart, we will discuss several heart activities in this chapter. The following activities lend themselves to utilizing the heart instead of only the head. It is extremely difficult to do these with the mind only.

Love and Hate with All of Your Heart

Love and hate are two very strong heart activities. When you are doing either one of these, you are operating out of your heart.

> *Matt. 6:24 "No one can serve two masters; for either he will hate the one and love the other, or he will be devoted to one and despise the other. You cannot serve God and wealth."*

In the verse above, we see that if we love God, we will hate all other masters (wealth in this case). *It is good for your heart to hate.* You are to hate and despise all things other than Jesus that would tempt you or call to your heart as a master or as a distraction from Him. At the very same time you are hating false masters, you are to love your true Master. It is a single heart action when you love your Master Jesus and hate all others. You cannot really love Christ unless you actively hate what is not of Him.

If you have ever gone on a boat ride, you are aware that you have to "shove off" from the pier. To hate what is not of God in your life is similar to shoving off. As you shove off and away from what is not Christ, you immediately cling tightly to your Master. Shoving off other loves is your inner attitude of pushing them away from you.

> *Lk. 14:26 "If anyone comes to Me, and does not hate his own father and mother and wife and children and brothers and sisters, yes, and even his own life, he cannot be My disciple."*

> *Phi.. 3:8 "More than that, I count all things to be loss in view of the surpassing value of knowing Christ Jesus my Lord, for whom I have suffered the loss of all things, and count them but rubbish so that I may gain Christ,"*

We have mentioned earlier that the apostle Paul counted everything that was gain to him as crap in order that he might gain Christ. The same principle applies here. It is *in order that* you may gain Christ that you are to count all things as excrement. If you don't, you cannot daily gain Christ. You cannot walk with the love of God filling your heart while you love other things, too. You are fooling yourself if you think you can. You will love one and despise the other. You cannot love and serve two different masters.

The tricky part about this dynamic is learning to hate the good things that God has given you and has shown you. Let's revisit Abraham and his son Isaac. God made a promise to Abraham to bless him and multiply his descendants. In order to fulfill God's promise to Abraham, he gave him a son in the most miraculous way. God did a miracle by allowing Sarah to conceive Isaac while Abraham was 100 years old and while Sarah was 90 years old, past the time she was able to have children (Gen. 16:1). Then, God told Abraham to kill Isaac – the miraculous gift God had given Abraham in fulfillment of the promise.

Isaac was a good thing that God gave to Abraham. God even gave Isaac to Abraham through a miracle. However, everything must be put on the altar to be killed, even the good things that God has given you. This is what Paul was talking about in Phil. 3:8. You must learn to hate all things and give them up in order to daily gain Christ.

After Abraham raised the knife to kill Isaac, God gave Isaac back to Abraham. Some things that you put to death will be given back to you by God. But all things must be slain. It is God's business to determine what will be given back to you and what will not.

Turning Your Cup Right Side Up

If a person from Australia were to ask you if you've ever tasted vegemite, you may not know what he was talking about. He could tell you just how delicious and tasty vegemite is, but unless you've eaten vegemite, you still wouldn't know exactly how it tasted. Vegemite is unique to Australia, and it has a very distinct flavor unlike anything else. Your Australian friend would probably describe to you the fact that vegemite is usually spread on toast or crackers. It is very dark in color, and it is thick in texture having a sort of salty tangy flavor that is made from brewer's yeast.

When someone describes to us something that we've never really experienced before, our typical response is to try to find something in our memory that matches closely with what we think we are hearing. We try to find a close match of the current description with previous experiences. We do this in order to understand and to identify with the new information. *This often leads to error on our part.*

The Australian says, "Vegemite is most delicious mate. It is very dark and flavorful, and you spread it on toast." You respond with, "I don't think I've ever had vegemite, but I know what you are talking about. I've had some really great thick jellies that were dark and rich. Yes, they are good, aren't they?"

You are not aware of it, but vegemite tastes nothing like jelly, not even close. But you so want to participate in the conversation and not be found completely in the dark with the topic that you find the closest association you can make and then try to identify with it. The problem is that you are wrong.

Asking Creates a New Grid

When a unique experience exists which has a very distinct set of characteristics to the experience – and you have never experienced it, I like to say that "you don't have a grid for it." Some people use a similar phrase for this by saying, "It is not on your radar." If you have never eaten vegemite, then you have no grid for it.

Our grid is sort of like boxes in our memories. Our boxes are all categorized according to subject. When you hear information that closely resembles one of your existing boxes, you try to relate it to the information in an existing box. When someone speaks of vegemite (which you've never tasted before), you try to find a related experience to compare it to.

When you don't have a grid for something, you either have no experience or so little experience with the subject matter that you have no place to put or assign the new information. Without a grid, if you try to apply new knowledge that you hear about a subject into an incorrect box, it will be misplaced within a wrong set of experiences, and you will totally "miss it." Vegemite is nothing like jelly, but you thought it was from the description you heard.

For example, if I began expounding on the phrase "the wave function of a total system," you may not know exactly what I am referring to. Instead of jumping into the conversation and adding to it with comments such as, "I've seen some pretty big waves, too. You must be a surfer also," a better response would be to simply listen and ask questions. Have the heart attitude of "I don't know, but will you teach me?"

There are many spiritual realities that you simply do not have a grid for (author included). There is no place to attach the new information you are hearing within your current understanding because you have limited experience if any.

I will venture to say that many readers (which probably includes you) have no grid concerning some of the things we've discussed so far in this book. Instead of misapplying these ideas, you need to begin to do a wonderful and amazing thing. This thing I am about to suggest that you do is a very rare activity among most people. Are you ready? *Learn to ask.*

We have spoken in many places in this book about the idea of being childlike before God. Instead of glossing over this idea or even doing a shallow little check of yourself by saying something such as "Yeah, I can be childlike, I got that one." Instead, *ask God* to begin to show you true childlikeness. You can always grow more in any area no matter what it is. Learn to make various truths current themes in your life. Give yourself to them, think about them, pray concerning them, try them on, and above all – ask God for more. Asking is a heart activity.

Asking allows you to *create a place* of experience and understanding in a subject when you have none. Asking actually begins to create a grid within you when you have none. I do not know how this works but it does. When you have no grid and no experience in an area, the very act of humbly asking God for it begins to create a new grid for experience to take place in that area. Asking creates a new box in you when you have none. With your new box, you are now ready to receive a new experience.

Having a grid for something is very important. If spiritual words are spoken to us when we have no grid for them, it is much like pouring water on to a cup that is turned upside down. The cup cannot catch and contain the water if it is not right-side-up. Asking turns your cup right side up.

> Lk. 11:10 *"For everyone who asks, receives; and he who seeks, finds; and to him who knocks, it will be opened."*

Asking is a heart activity that requires something of you. It requires vulnerability and humility to ask. At times, asking can be humbly painful. When you ask, it turns the cup of your heart in a position to receive. When something doesn't exist already (no grid is present), asking is the first step in establishing your grid. Asking opens you up to receive a new experience from God.

I see this happen all of the time when teaching students new concepts. A problem can be presented, but until they wrestle with the problem, realize they don't know how to do it, and then ask for help, they do not learn how to do it. Most people I have met in my lifetime do not ask questions when they desperately should be asking hundreds of them. The reason I have gained the things that I have in Christianity (and I have much more to gain) is that I have asked and sought. I honestly would wear out the older brothers who were around me when I was a young Christian in my twenties. I would find a man who knew more than me in a particular area - and I would blitz him. I would take him to lunch, ask him questions about "why this was the case, how this worked, and what was the reason behind this spiritual dynamic." God was very kind to me to bring people into my life who could help me early on. I also believe that if you have a seeking heart, God will bring people into your life to meet those needs when it is time.

You may be closed off to The Lord in ways you don't realize. Therefore, God is inhibited in giving you more because your cup is upside down. Many times you don't even know enough to know what you should be asking for. A good place to start is to begin asking God for what you should be seeking Him about. Perhaps some of the things we've covered in this book are good things to ask for as well.

I mentioned earlier that only the degree to which you've experienced the Spirit is the degree to which you can truly recognize truth. When you begin to experience the Spirit of God in your heart and leave your cranial Christianity, a new world will begin to open to you. You will begin to grow exponentially. And when you hear truth, you will have a place to put it that is from experience - not just from information that you've gathered and have pieced together.

True Asking is Craving

You may feel as though you have limited experience concerning the many subjects we covered so far in this book. I know that you "know" all about it, and you could probably preach a detailed sermon on the subject of moving from the head to the heart and walking after the Spirit. But how much have you actually experienced? Begin by asking God for more. Don't just ask Him because you know you should, but allow your heart to go to the place of craving and hungering. This is true asking.

When you long for and hunger for new things, you are cooperating with humility and with faith. God will use your faith to meet you. Usually the answer will begin in a small way. You might catch only a glimpse of reality in your heart. You may taste of something new in a small way. You might breakthrough for only a short moment of experience.

Zech. 4:10 "For who hath despised the day of small things?"

When even the smallest of reality is gained, do not despise it. If you employ it and use what you've been given, you'll be given more.

Matthew 25:29 "For to everyone who has, more shall be given, and he will have an abundance;"

Continuing to ask and then using the small amounts you gain allows you to increase. The more you actually taste of His love, the more you will taste of His love. The more you learn how to open your heart to the Spirit, the more you will open your heart to the Spirit.

Matt. 17:20 "And He said to them, "Because of the littleness of your faith; for truly I say to you, if you have faith the size of a mustard seed, you will say to this mountain, 'Move from here to there,' and it will move; and nothing will be impossible to you."

Our faith always seems small to us. You may compare "what you used to experience" or how close "you used to be with God in the good ole' days," or you may compare yourself to others' experience of God. However, if you *employ* the small mustard seed of faith you have, you will be "taking it and sowing it in your field" (as the verse says). It will seem smaller than anything, as though it were nothing. Yet it will increase if you do this and it will soon become big.

Thankfulness

Giving thanks is something we do with our hearts. If you are genuinely giving thanks, you leave the realm of the brain only, and your heart gets involved. Thankfulness is heartfelt gratitude. It is accompanied with humility and faith. To give thanks is to acknowledge that you've received something and have been benefitted by it. When you give thanks, you are taking into the heart what has been done for you.

Thankfulness is an easy activity to help you recognize an action of the heart, as opposed to the head. When you are thankful, you feel a deep appreciation.

You can become thankful when you are not already thankful. In other words, thankfulness is something you can give yourself to as with any heart activity. You can choose to be thankful for many things that God has given and done for you. This activity very quickly places you within the realm of the heart and of the Spirit. Very often as you give yourself to genuine thanksgiving, you become according to the Spirit.

Worship

Worship is a heart activity. Worship is love. It is nothing less than spilling your heart and expressing your passion for God. Worship of God is an appropriate response because we are the created and He is our Creator. He is great and we are small. We will all stand before Him in the great and terrible day of judgment, and He has been merciful to us to forgive us our sins.

> Ps 96:9 *"O worship the LORD in the beauty of holiness: fear before him, all the earth."*

Throughout the normal course of a day, because of various trials and distractions, we often leave our proper role of humility with the Lord. As we worship the Lord, we return to our proper place as we become small and under Him. We see Him as above us and over us. Worship allows you to practice this healthy posture in your heart.

> Ps. 2:11 *"Worship the LORD with reverence and rejoice with trembling."*

A heart of worship is a heart that is submitted to Christ. We worship Him when we realize His authority in our hearts. When we give ourselves to a true heart of worship, we find ourselves being according to the Spirit. Worship is more than just singing. It is expressing to God an attitude from your heart. You can worship in song, in prayer, in words, or in actions. As you worship, you see, you hear, you understand, and you turn because you have left the insanity of exalting yourself. Worship invites restoration and healing in your life.

Worship Deepens Our Capacity

As you have plenty of time in worship, your inner container stretches for more capacity and depth with the Lord. You get to practice good heart postures, fervency in the heart, and how to deal with distraction. Worship is one of the most intimate experiences you can have with Jesus.

> *Lk. 7:38 "...and standing behind Him at His feet, weeping, she began to wet His feet with her tears, and kept wiping them with the hair of her head, and kissing His feet and anointing them with the perfume."*

Again, our hearts are very much like water wells (refer to "The Anatomy of Man" illustrations). When we keep them filled with water, they stay open, clean, and large. If the well capacity is not filled with water, soil will naturally begin to cave in and decrease the overall capacity of the well to hold water. We are deepened as our hearts are filled with the Spirit of God in worship.

Speaking What is True

> *Matt. 15:18 "But the things that proceed out of the mouth come from the heart..."*

We can see from this verse in Matthew 15 that we speak from the things that fill our hearts. It is as though the mouth and the heart are connected in many ways.

If you have ever used a water pump to pump water from one place to another, you may have realized that at times you have to do what is called "priming the pump." Priming a water pump is placing water into the pump before it starts to pump any water. Because the mouth and the heart are connected, it is sometimes very helpful to speak truth in order to get that truth into your heart. If the truth is only in your head, not in your heart, speaking the truth with your mouth anyway can prime the pump of your heart and help you to believe what you are speaking out.

Praying the Scripture

Many times when we read scripture we read very fast as though it were a novel or an information handbook. The scripture is not only a source of objective truth for understanding, but it also serves as a diving board into an experiential relationship with Christ. In order for the reading of scripture to be more than a mental exercise, read slowly and prayerfully. Let's look at the following verse as an example:

> *2 Tim. 1:7 "For God has not given us a spirit of timidity, but of power and love and discipline."*

Instead of reading this verse very quickly, realizing that you understand it and agree with it, and then reading on to the next verse - let's try something a little different than what you may be used to.

Let's reread the verse - but in a different way.

"For God" – stop right there. Consider only those first two words. Prayerfully be aware of God. He is a person who is real. Get your heart ready because something is coming next in the verse that is about Him.

"...has not given us a spirit of timidity" – You may pray something such as, "God, you have not given me a spirit of timidity? The spirit you gave me is not fearful? Thank you Lord. When I am feeling fear, it must not be your Spirit inside me. It must be coming from my flesh."

"...but of power" – "I have a spirit of power. Father, you are so kind to have given me a spirit of power. I don't fully understand that, but I believe it is true. Reveal more to me about the power that is in me."

Now is a good time to stop using so many words and just reflect. Become aware that you actually have a spirit of power within you. Begin to enjoy this fact and give thanks to God.

"...of love" – "Jesus, thank you for your Spirit of love within me. I thank you that you gave me a Spirit of love." Enjoy this, believe it, and realize that it is true.

"...of discipline" – "Lord, your Spirit inside me is a Spirit of discipline. I am not very disciplined all of the time, but you are, and you have given me your Spirit of discipline…"

You get the idea. Do you realize just how full the scriptures are? To meditate and pray through one simple verse is very powerful and life changing. There is so much daily food in just a few verses. The point is not to feel like you have to read large amounts of scripture. The point of scripture is not only to provide objective truth and knowledge, but it also is there to connect you with Jesus, the source of life.

Questions for Understanding and Discussion

1. What does asking accomplish?
2. What are some examples of spiritual heart activities?
3. What does it mean to "prime your pump?"
4. How do you pray the scripture and why is this important?

The Lazy Heart

Lk. 24:25 "And He said to them, "O foolish men and slow of heart to believe…"

It is not typical to actively engage in believing God. It requires an inner effort to engage in faith. It is much easier just to think and feel - whatever we happen to think and feel in each moment. The idea of engaging the heart to believe and giving one's self to being "of faith" is very misunderstood.

Having faith is often thought of as only involving a mental acceptance of various doctrines. To the contrary, doctrines are only concepts. Deciding "what you believe" about any particular Bible truth has very little to do with faith in the heart. When faith is only thought of as one's stance on Bible doctrines and truths, it often becomes a false substitution for real faith. Therefore, the heart remains unengaged in true faith while the head is busily preoccupied with imaginations, models, theories, campaigns, and causes.

Although you may have come to a decision that Jesus Christ is Lord and that He has paid for your sins, if you are not employing your heart to engage in the purpose of His death, it remains only a conceptual file in your brain along with many others. His death and resurrection was more than a fact to agree with. His death and resurrection is a means to an end.

To many Christians, the death and resurrection of Jesus Christ remains primarily a distant event in history. At times you may be genuinely thankful that He suffered and died for you. At other times, you may try to muster up some emotion and passion about the event of His suffering and death for you. But you may not always be able to connect with the true import of the significance of Christ's death and resurrection.

When asked the question of "Why did Christ die for you?" many will reply, "He died for me so I could go to heaven." Or, "He died for my sins." But what good does this historical fact do for you on Tuesday afternoon at 2:35 p.m. when your kids are screaming and there are diapers to change?

It is much like having money in the bank that you never spend. The fact that you have money in some distant bank account somewhere can provide you with a feeling of security. But unless you get in your car, make a trip to the bank, access your cash, and spend it on something - you are not actually utilizing the money for its proper purpose. To leave your money in the bank and to not spend it or invest it leaves you only to enjoy *the idea* that you have it. If you are only resting in the fact that you are convinced of certain doctrinal truths yet you are not employing your heart with the intended purpose of those doctrinal truths, then you are not "spending" your faith. It is no more than an idea.

A Christian who is not employing his faith by engaging his heart to enter into real experiential belief is participating in some other method or ideology to live out his Christian walk. It may not always be a conscious effort, but if your heart is not filled with real faith that is encountering Christ, you are occupying yourself with other things. *The heart cannot be filled with nothing. It is either filled with the experience of Christ, or something else.*

As mentioned previously, it is common to rely on doctrinal positions as being sufficient. This mentality would say something like, "As long as I adhere to these correct beliefs (doctrines), then that is all God requires of me." Other common substitutions for an active daily faith are these:

- "God ultimately requires nothing of me daily because I prayed the sinner's prayer."
- "God requires that I read my Bible and study. As long as I am doing this, I am doing what is expected of me."
- "God requires that I abstain from sin and ungodly practices. As long as I am doing this, it is adequate."
- "As long as I am attending church meetings, I am doing what is required."
- "If I am witnessing and evangelizing I am doing what God expects of me."
- "God requires that I treat others kindly and do good deeds. As long as I am doing this, it is enough."

Many Christians have some variation of these, a combination of them, or all of the above. However, the beliefs on the list above are lies. What God requires is faith (Jn. 6:29). We are made right with God only by trusting in the blood of Christ and nothing else. All the Bible study, good behavior, church attendance, witnessing, and good deeds you could possibly muster would not make one iota of difference in your standing with God. Faith in His blood to cleanse you is what actually applies His cleansing blood to you. "God's requirement" is that you apply the benefit and purpose of the blood of Christ into your daily walk and experience. The purpose of the man Jesus Christ bleeding and dying was to cleanse you, and to cleanse you for a specific purpose.

God didn't cleanse you and wash your spirit as His final purpose. He didn't cleanse you and wash you of your sins "just because." He didn't cleanse you and wash you clean just so that you could fly away and go to heaven one day.

The purpose of His cleansing blood is to bring you into a daily experiential, intimate encounter with Christ. God's end goal is that He would know you and that you would know Him. Entering into heaven is only an extension of this intimate encounter that we are to be having while on Earth. Any other focus, no matter what it may be, falls short of the intended purpose of your salvation. [1]

> *Gal. 5:2 "Behold I, Paul, say to you that if you receive circumcision, Christ will be of no benefit to you."*

In the verse above, Paul writes to Christians in the region of Galatia telling them that Jesus will not benefit them if they are circumcised. Circumcision represents the keeping of the law. In other words, if a Christian tries to do outward things such as rule keeping, doing good works, and employing self-efforts, the fact of Jesus Christ dying on the cross for their sins is not benefiting them.

> *Gal. 3:2-3 "This is the only thing I want to find out from you: did you receive the Spirit by the works of the Law, or by hearing with faith? Are you so foolish? Having begun by the Spirit, are you now being perfected by the flesh?"*

The Christians in Galatia began their Christian walk by faith and by the Spirit. Yet, they wanted to continue their relationship with Christ and grow as Christians by keeping the rules of the law. *Rule keeping is a very common substitution for faith.*

It is not wrong to obey rules or do good works. But outward things should always flow out of the Spirit - a heart that is broken, dependent on God, and receiving from Him (faith). In short, as you truly give up on your own self-efforts, and instead give yourself to trust, you will discover that you are being used of God. This is another spiritual paradox. The only way we keep God's commandments is by giving up on ever doing anything right and by falling into His arms of love and forgiveness. Only then will we "find ourselves" keeping God's commandments. The way to keep God's commandments is to stop trying to keep them; instead, shift your focus to receiving love and knowing Him in intimacy. Only love can keep the commandments.

> *Jn. 14:15 "If you love Me, you will keep My commandments."*

Jesus says it plainly in John 14:15. We often miss the meaning of verses like these because we tend to read scripture through a legalistic, self-condemning lens. In the above verse, Jesus is not saying that you are to *prove* your love for Him by keeping His commandments. He is saying that if you love Him, *the result* will be that you will keep His commandments. You won't have to try to keep His commandments; you just will. Read the verse again with that understanding. He also goes on to explain later what His commandments actually are: forgiveness, loving one another, etc. Many Christians have erroneously read this verse as saying that you must keep the Old Testament law in order to show that you love God.

Often people will say that they are demonstrating their love for God by outwardly doing what is right even though their hearts may not be fully in it. This belief somehow excuses having an inner heart attitude that secretly does not want to do what is being forced outwardly. This is religious hypocrisy. The scriptures speak against this in many places (Matt. 23:28, Rom. 2:29, Jer. 9:8, Jer. 11:20, Ps 63:4, Matt. 7:15). God always wants our hearts first, and then our actions will naturally follow.

> *Matt. 23:25-26 "Woe to you, scribes and Pharisees, hypocrites! For you clean the outside of the cup and of the dish, but inside they are full of robbery and self-indulgence. You blind Pharisee, first clean the inside of the cup and of the dish, so that the outside of it may become clean also."*

Notice the phrase *so that* in the last sentence above. Outward rule keeping does not justify a heart that is begrudgingly keeping the rules. It is much easier on the flesh to work busily for God than it is to trust Him with dependency and brokenness. The lazy heart just wants to keep the rules. The lazy heart just wants to be told what to do and when to do it. Then it can outwardly try to meet the requirements yet remain inwardly unbroken and unyielding.

The traditional religious system often propagates such a practice. As long as you attend church meetings, pay tithes, read your Bible, and don't break the rules, you are a member in good standing. We think that if we are in good standing with a church, we are in good standing with God. Man's ideas of what is required seldom agree with what God actually does require. The next time you attend a church meeting, during the sermon perhaps try beating on your chest and screaming out loud "God have mercy on me, I am a sinner!" (Lk. 18:13). You may be escorted out of the sanctuary for interrupting the message.

Modern, traditional Christianity has many requirements of outward practices, but very little requirement of *inward condition*. As long as you show up consistently to the Sunday morning church services, everyone will think of you very positively. It does not matter if you inwardly rejected the message and are in rebellion in your heart. It does not matter if you were passively half asleep during the church meeting, and in your heart you only fixated on going to the cafeteria after the meeting. It does not matter if you are only a disengaged spectator during the church meeting as long as you show up looking good, smile often, and nod your head occasionally - you are doing what is expected (note taking yields bonus points). God requires *much more* of you than only these things during every meeting of the church you attend (1 Cor. 14:26), and His requirement stems from an inward experience of Christ.

Believing is a verb. It is a word of action that requires an inward activity of giving yourself to something.

> *Jn. 6:28-29 "Therefore they said to Him, "What shall we do, so that we may work the works of God?" Jesus answered and said to them, "This is the work of God, that you believe in Him whom He has sent."*

We are not saved by works – the outward doing of certain things or the abstaining of certain things (Eph. 2:9). Like the Galatians, we often forget that our daily walk is to be accomplished by the same manner in which it was begun. We begin with faith, we continue in faith, and we finish our race in faith. In the verse above, when people asked Jesus "What shall we do?" Jesus replied, "Believe." Remember that biblical believing is always more than mental concepts. It is an intense trusting with total abandonment that flows from the heart. The essence of Christianity is not in outward doing. The doing that you are called to do is an *inward doing*. And you are to be tremendously diligent.

Outward actions will always flow out of this inward doing, although the outward is never to be your focus. When the outward becomes your focus, you will automatically leave the inward, which is what you must give yourself to. The only way to produce outward fruit that is of God and of the Spirit is to only give attention to the inward things of the heart:

> *Heb. 4:11 "Therefore let us be diligent to enter that rest, so that no one will fall, through following the same example of disobedience."*

The inward doing that is required to believe from the heart and to engage in faith is exactly the opposite of outward trying. To engage in faith within the heart is to engage in an active *receiving and resting*. Here lies another paradox. Heb. 4:11 calls you to diligently rest. You must continually and diligently give yourself to *giving up*. You are commanded to actively die to all self-activity. You must always put forth effort to forsake all self-effort. Do you see the paradox?

However, the lazy heart does not want any part of this. The lazy heart of unbelief wants to remain passive and inwardly independent while exerting outward efforts. It is much easier to try to keep the law than to live broken and inwardly undone. The Christian who is busily focused on doing things for God is actually lazy. He is lazy of heart.

> *Heb. 4:10 "For the one who has entered His rest has himself also rested from his works, as God did from His."*

> *Rom. 4:5 "But to the one who does not work, but believes in Him who justifies the ungodly, his faith is credited as righteousness,"*

Ceasing from your own outward works is not always easy. Most Christians are addicted to activity and ambitions. God calls you to a walk of dependently receiving His love. He will take care of everything else. Receiving His love is extremely enjoyable and life-giving, but He does command that you do it.

> *Heb. 3:12 "Take care, brethren, that there not be in any one of you an evil, unbelieving heart that falls away from the living God."*

> *Rom. 11:22 "Behold then the kindness and severity of God; to those who fell, severity, but to you, God's kindness, if you continue in His kindness; otherwise you also will be cut off."*

God absolutely commands and requires that you receive His kindness. It is like being strictly told to enjoy a wonderful ice cream cone. Actively receiving from God is much like basking in the sunshine. Imagine just for a moment that you are reclining in your favorite easy chair on a warm, summer day. You tilt your head back, relax, and take in the comfort of the sunlight as it cloaks you like a warm blanket. You can savor this experience, or you can choose to just lay out in the sun and not be engaged in the activity.

Think about the last time you were hugged by someone. There is a difference between just accepting a hug from someone as a kind gesture and in actually "taking in the hug" into your heart. The next time someone who loves you gives you a hug, relax and receive the love. Take the hug in, all the way down to the bottom of your toes. There is a difference between what is happening in the heart when you actually take in a hug and receive the love, and when you just let someone hug you with no effect inside of you. This is what you are to do when you receive God's love toward you. God is hugging you right now, and all of the time (Rom. 5:5). You can receive His hug right now.

We could also compare receiving from God to eating a delicious meal. Every bite of a fabulous meal is meant to be relished. When you take in the aroma of the food, and you enjoy each wonderful and flavorful bite, you are doing something with your heart. You are engaging your heart in receiving.

Giving yourself to the enjoyment of God's love and His affection toward you requires that your heart become engaged. This is faith. The lazy heart does not want to receive or engage in faith.

> *Matt. 26:40-41 "And He came to the disciples and found them sleeping, and said to Peter, "So, you men could not keep watch with Me for one hour? Keep watching and praying that you may not enter into temptation; the spirit is willing, but the flesh is weak."*

Faith requires inward effort. But recall that faith is always an inward effort of receiving what has already been done for you. It is never an inward striving and straining to create something that is not. You are to have faith in what God has *already done or is currently doing*. Faith is letting go to what is.

Characteristics of the Lazy Heart

The lazy heart abides in its flesh patterns of escape and avoidance. When life gets too hard to deal with, the lazy heart runs from the pain instead of breaking and receiving comfort from God. The lazy, unbelieving heart is petrified of vulnerability and intimacy. The threat of being wounded again triumphs; therefore, trust is avoided. The lazy, unbelieving heart allows fear to remain. Therefore, it stays in control. This is not an acceptable place for the Christian to stay or walk in.

It is common for a woman's fear and thus her control to rule an entire household. Men often cower under a woman's panic and therefore abdicate their role as head of the household. Entire families are often controlled by and completely driven by the fear that resides in the heart of the woman of the house. The imaginations of fear, anxiety, and the avoidance of pain compel a multitude of decisions in many peoples' lives – and they are repeated countless times. It takes courage and inner effort to receive love that casts out fear. Only in God's love is there found true reality and the sanity of truth. You can change the patterns in your life because you can choose what you believe in your heart. You can change from not receiving love to receiving love. This choosing will require a new type of inner effort that you may not be used to exerting. It's okay to start small.

The entire requirement of the law is fulfilled by love and by walking after the Spirit:

> *Gal. 5:14 "For the whole Law is fulfilled in one word, in the statement, "You shall love your neighbor as yourself."*

> *Rom. 13:10 "Love does no wrong to a neighbor; therefore love is the fulfillment of the law."*

> *Rom. 8:4 "…so that the requirement of the Law might be fulfilled in us, who do not walk according to the flesh but according to the Spirit."*

> *Rom. 13:8 "Owe nothing to anyone except to love one another; for he who loves his neighbor has fulfilled the law."*

Capacity Must Be Created

A well does not dig itself. A block of wood cannot hold water unless the wood is carved into a cup that has capacity. The disciples were sleeping even during Jesus' darkest hour because they had not yet developed a deep, inner capacity for choosing well during hardship. Most people have developed *fleshly responses* for times of feeling pressure and stress. We tend to either rely on our own abilities to handle a situation, or we avoid it all together and run away.

Whether it is learning to jog long distances, working and laboring in the hot sun, learning to endure difficulties and hardships at work - all capacities must be developed and increased. Some capacities that you have now were developed from your childhood and are a result of how you were raised. Perhaps your father or mother required you to do your chores when you were young.

Therefore, by the time you were perhaps twelve-years old, you had a certain degree of capacity for overcoming the difficulties of work. When you became twenty-five years of age, your capacity for work had increased from what it was when you were only twelve.

It was the *requirement* placed upon you that caused you to develop the capacity you have for work. We tend to develop capacity only when we are required to do so. This is why creating capacity is painful and stretching. Wood must be *carved* to create a cup that holds water. Holes must be *dug* to create a space for a well. Within church dynamics, if you are used to a pastor bringing the message to each church meeting, and a professional worship leader always provides the music for you, you will tend to remain passive during church meetings in the areas of speaking and leading music. When nothing is required of you, you do not increase in capacity. If it were up to you to bring the message or the music for the church meetings you attend, you would wake up early, dig deep, and find what you needed in order to deliver.

Perhaps you feel very inadequate in engaging your heart in faith and receiving from God. It is time to put the point of the shovel in the soil and a knife into the block of wood. It is painfully stretching to engage in spiritual activities in which you have very little capacity. However, receiving even the smallest amounts of water will encourage you to keep on digging.

Notes:

[1] Good works, evangelism, loving others, etc. all come out of knowing Christ. It is only to the degree that you experience intimacy with Christ that the deeds you do are of Him. The church often teaches that you must be very busy working for God while skipping the most important element and source of power for Christian work. *A tree does not concern itself with producing fruit.* A tree is only concerned with finding water. Fruit is a natural result of the tree receiving water and sunshine. Good works (that are of the Spirit) are naturally occurring and produced as you focus only on knowing, trusting, receiving, and loving God.

Questions for Understanding and Discussion

1. What does it mean to spend your faith?
2. What are some examples and characteristics of having a lazy heart?
3. How can you create capacity in your heart?

How Does God Get To Your Heart?

During the time I attended college, I lived in a dormitory on the college campus. Butch, the janitor in my dorm, used to clean the hallways. Butch was not someone that most people would be drawn to by first impression. His hair was not usually combed, his speech was not always perfectly coherent, and he was a little socially awkward.

Butch would sing worship songs at the top of his lungs (no exaggeration) all day in the men's dormitory while he cleaned it. If you ever made eye contact with Janitor Butch, he would give you a big, goofy grin, a little too big of a grin for someone who really doesn't know you.

One day I was in the stairwell making my way up to the fourth floor of the dormitory. Butch was deafening me again with his singing as I started to walk past him. Curious about this man and even slightly annoyed by him, I finally engaged him in a conversation. "Hey Mr. Janitor, why do you sing so much?" Butch stopped mopping and smiled at me while he leaned on his mop. "Because I'm in love with the Savior," he said. The next thing that happened was totally unexpected. For no apparent reason, Butch immediately said, "Let me pray for you." He placed his mop against the wall, put both of his hands on my head, and started to pray fervently.

When Butch started praying for me, the Spirit of God instantly wrapped all around me. The physical and manifest presence of God was filling the room. I intensely felt God's power and love inside me and out.

That encounter with Butch began a friendship. As I got to know him, I learned that he had had a brain tumor removed a few years before I'd met him. During his battle with cancer, Butch suffered some degree of brain damage. Butch explained to me how his suffering with cancer had changed his life. Butch was one of sweetest and most humble men that I ever met even to this day. He seemed to always be filled with the Spirit of God. Butch was extremely kind and sweet to everyone.

Butch played football when he was in college. He was a running back for the Baylor football team in 1974. Butch said, "I used to be a very hard man before my brain tumor." He told me that he used to play football with no mercy and that he used to preach the same way. The Lord finally broke Butch's hard heart and stripped him of his ambition. God used the suffering of cancer to do it. I was blessed beyond measure in my short time with Butch. I feel very privileged to have been able to spend time with him during my early days of being a Christian. Forest "Butch" Reel died November 27, 2013.

Prem Pradhan was born in 1924 in Nepal. It is against the law in Nepal to change your religion, but Prem would constantly preach and lead Nepalese Hindus to Christ anyway. He was imprisoned for 10 years because of his faith.

Because of the Lord using Prem so mightily in Nepal, he was often referred to as "the apostle to Nepal." I had the privilege of spending some time with Prem in the early 1990's. Prem told me stories of when he was in prison. He told me one thing that I will never forget. One time Prem was locked up in a very small prison cell for days with rotting corpses all around him. This was a horrible experience for him. Prem also related many other instances when he was severely tortured for his faith. However, if you met him in person, most people would not be very impressed. Prem was just a quiet, small, unassuming man who smiled a lot. Prem died in 1998.

God's Breaking of Men's Hearts

Some of the godliest people I've known during my life have been people who have gone through tremendous and unimaginable sufferings. There is a depth and a stillness of the soul that only comes through pain, agony, and extreme distress. Our soul has ambition woven into its fabric. It has many dreams and plans that are well disguised as being noble, but they are saturated in selfishness. We all have a very deep self-reliance that permeates us.

Suffering brings us through a specific experience of despair within ourselves. Suffering produces an unraveling within us to such a degree that we give up and lose hope in ourselves. "Brokenness" is a word that is tossed around a lot in Christian circles, but the depth of this word's meaning is rarely understood.

Brokenness is not to be confused with being damaged. When there are dysfunctions in mind and heart (which we all have), we are damaged and in need of restoration. Brokenness, however, is a work of God that produces a degree of contrition and dependency that you could never choose on your own. The answer for the damaged soul is brokenness.

Pain and suffering move us from our heads and into our hearts. Suffering is the only thing that can touch the roots of our self-absorption in a way that no amount of teaching or head learning ever could. Suffering breaks the flesh and the independent soul-life and causes us to depend on someone else besides ourselves – because we have to.

We are in a very weakened state while we are suffering. When we forsake our own self-reliance and depend on Jesus Christ as our source, we easily move into the realities that are true in our spirits. In your spirit, you are utterly and totally dependent on Christ as your source for all things, yet this reality is not always found because of certain patterns in the flesh. We can certainly choose Christ during the moments of our day, but there are some flesh patterns that are so ingrained within us that we must be driven to Christ through pain, torment, and utter loss. There is no other way to ferret out our hidden independence. You walk in many flesh patterns and there is hardness within your heart that you are simply unaware of and simply cannot see until God touches it. When God touches these very deep places of self-reliance and self-focus within you, you initially fight. But when the heat is turned up enough and the pain is overwhelming, you give up and something in you dies. This is the point and purpose of many of the trials you find yourself in.

Christ is your source for wisdom, strength, direction, love, peace, and endurance. Suffering and pain break us from a reliance on self and propel us to seek help outside of ourselves. Haven't you noticed that when you are in pain, you simply want relief? When you have a crushing headache, you immediately want a pain reliever. When you are really sick, all you want is to just get it to stop. If you were in a horrible accident and were bleeding in pain, you would want to go a hospital right away. All of these things are you seeking help outside of yourself. God uses pain to teach you to seek Him who is outside of yourself. Suffering causes you to forsake the devices you have within yourself that you are so used to relying on.

All suffering, whether it be physical suffering or emotional suffering, is designed to break your soul of its self-reliance and bring you to a place of needing your Savior.

Personally speaking, I went through eight years of trauma and spiritual abuse while being mentored by a man during my early twenties. I moved my wife and children to a secluded area of the country on a dirt road to be discipled by a crippled man who lived in a mobile home nearby. The man who mentored me was heavily influenced by the shepherding movement of the late 1960's and 70's.

If you know anything of the shepherding movement, you know of its extreme "accountability" which is really spiritual abuse and control. I worked out of my home in those days, so my job required very little time away. For five or six days a week, six to eight hours a day, for eight years (this is no exaggeration) - I experienced a severe degree of torture mentally, emotionally, and physically - all "in the name of Jesus." At times, the anguish and torment were so unimaginable that I cannot begin to explain it, nor should I.

As a very zealous young Christian man in my early twenties, I believed that I was doing God's will and that I could not leave the discipleship program until I was officially "released" by my mentor. And so I gave myself to everything that was being required of me in order to obey the Lord. I had made a mistake.

But God has used it in my life in ways that are difficult to explain. A brother once said to me, "Look, you got away from that bad situation, you made it!" I replied, "No, I did not make it." Something died in me during that time in my twenties that can never be recovered.

Brokenness in the Life of the Believer

> *Ps. 51:16-17 "For You do not delight in sacrifice, otherwise I would give it; You are not pleased with burnt offering. The sacrifices of God are a broken spirit; A broken and a contrite heart, O God, You will not despise."*

How can we cooperate with the process of brokenness? We see several examples of brokenness in biblical accounts. The breaking of Moses is recorded in Acts 7:22-30. Moses was demoted from being a prince of Egypt to being a nobody as he became a shepherd in the wilderness. During his early days in Egypt, Moses was referred to as "strong in word," but afterwards, he was sent into the wilderness to tend sheep for forty years. Ironically, Moses told the Lord in the burning bush that he did not have the ability to speak properly in order to deliver Israel.

We see the example of God breaking the children of Israel in the wilderness that they might gain understanding (Deut. 8:2-3). We see a transformation in the life of Peter as he is taken from self-confidence to weeping bitterly (Lk. 22:62). We see the breaking of Saul who was previously a murderer of Christians and was later confronted in person by Christ Himself. Saul is blinded into helplessness and became the apostle Paul (Acts 8:1-9:9).

Ps. 34:18 "The Lord is near to the brokenhearted and saves those who are crushed in spirit."

Is. 66:2 "For My hand made all these things, thus all these things came into being," declares the Lord. "But to this one I will look, to him who is humble and contrite of spirit, and who trembles at My word. "

Matt. 5:3 "Blessed are the poor in spirit, for theirs is the kingdom of heaven."

The Hebrew word for *contrite* actually means to be stricken or smitten. Other definitions are "to rend violently, to wreck, to crush, or to rupture." The essence of brokenness is to face your own ugliness and utter incapability to accomplish anything. You then allow what you see to do a work in your heart that causes you to give up on your reliance and the love you have for yourself.

Do not mistake brokenness for self-hatred. Self-hatred still maintains a self-focus. Self-hatred is still rooted in self-love. Neither is brokenness feeling sorry for yourself. Self-pity also maintains self-love. Brokenness is often mistaken for these two counterfeits. True brokenness leads us to a comforting intimacy with Christ. Self-hatred and self-pity are fleshly replicas of brokenness which only leave us distant from God and alone in pain.

2 Cor. 7:10 "For the sorrow that is according to the will of God produces a repentance without regret, leading to salvation, but the sorrow of the world produces death."

We cannot compare one person's pain to another's pain and say that one is less or one is greater. Everyone's pain is his own pain. Christians often think that it is only missionaries in third world countries who are truly suffering for

Christ. However, Jesus tells us that there is plenty of opportunity to suffer on a daily basis.

> *Matt. 6:34 "Each day has enough trouble of its own."*

The daily requirements of your job, family responsibilities, domestic duties, financial limitations, and the minefield of relationships all provide for a variety of daily pain and stress in your life. A bodily injury or sickness can offer tremendous difficulties. How you handle and deal with daily stress and difficulty all affect your heart attitudes and heart postures.

You can allow pain and stress to break you in order for you to go deeper with Christ, or you can respond in your flesh which will further harden your heart.

Even some of the smallest stresses of daily life affect you. However, most people are so unaware of their hearts that they do not see life's daily impact upon the inner man. Your heart is extremely sensitive and is often unnoticeably troubled by many things. But a hard and desensitized heart is solidified as you relate to stress in your flesh. "Just dealing with it," complaining, venting irritation, or avoiding stress altogether by escaping to other gods and comforts are common, fleshly responses.

It's Quarry Time

> *1 Ki. 6:7 "The house, while it was being built, was built of stone prepared at the quarry, and there was neither hammer nor axe nor any iron tool heard in the house while it was being built."*

> *1 Pet. 2:5 "...you also, as living stones, are being built up as a spiritual house for a holy priesthood, to offer up spiritual sacrifices acceptable to God through Jesus Christ."*

When Solomon built the house of the Lord, all the shaping of the stones was completed at the quarry before they were brought to the building site. When the stones were ready, they were brought to the house of the Lord and fitted together. The house of God that Solomon built was a place of peace. All of the struggle and hard work was done outside of the house in a different place. In the same way, you are a living stone in God's temple that He is currently building. You are a living stone that is still in the quarry. Your rough edges are being made smooth, and your pieces that don't fit well with others are being chiseled away. It is painful to be a stone in the quarry; however, this is one of the major purposes of your suffering and for your time still on the Earth, the quarry for God's building.

God is using the circumstances of life to shape you - and it does not feel good.

1Pet. 4:1 "Therefore, since Christ has suffered in the flesh, arm yourselves also with the same purpose, because he who has suffered in the flesh has ceased from sin,"

Every moment that you deny the impulses of your flesh is a moment of suffering. If you are not sinning and you are staying engaged in faith from your heart, then you are suffering in some way. To maintain a constant view of unseen things in the spirit, while your flesh screams to focus on the physical world around you, requires suffering. To hold your heart still before God and listen under Him requires total death to your flesh. To let your words be few around others, to always choose kindness and love, to not react out of your own needs and desires - is all suffering in the flesh.

You must learn *to embrace* even the smallest amounts of suffering and find help and comfort from God. When you have failed, when there is pain, when there is stress, when you don't know the answer, when you are humiliated - you must learn to go to God for restoration and fellowship. Let's look at a couple of practical examples.

In this very moment while writing this paragraph, I can tell that I am tempted with frustration because of interruptions. I will choose to not go with the frustration. I will forgive others and then release my goal of getting a certain amount of writing accomplished today. It does not feel good to release my inner goal. I have to die to it. This currently brings me some degree of undesirable pain, almost like grieving a loss within me as I let it go. Jesus is my life and my source of joy. *Getting my daily goals accomplished is not what my life is about.*

I also just received a request from a brother who is in need of help and prayer. However, my wonderful daughter whom I love is coming over to spend the evening with me and my wife. I have a choice to make. I can tell that it is currently a source of stress for me. I will allow this dilemma to remain in the hand of God and not feel pressured to bring closure out of my flesh in this moment. We will see what God has as the day develops.

You must not avoid even the smallest amounts of pain or stress, but rather embrace them. Pain and stress will never go away; they will only change their form from day to day. Difficulties are a part of everyday life for all creatures. The Spirit of God is your help, your comfort, and your strength for all things. Living this way will cause a daily deepening of your heart.

Matt. 5:45 "so that you may be sons of your Father who is in heaven; for He causes His sun to rise on the evil and the good, and sends rain on the righteous and the unrighteous."

It Requires Courage

Having the courage to go through pain and not avoid it is an acquired discipline. It is a very good practice to learn the discipline of embracing pain in the small things so that you will respond the same way during great trials.

Heb. 12:11 "All discipline for the moment seems not to be joyful, but sorrowful; yet to those who have been trained by it, afterwards it yields the peaceful fruit of righteousness."

Brokenness Allows You to Love

The account of Mary sitting at the feet of Jesus is found in three of the gospels. If we look at them all at one time, we can get a more complete picture of what actually happened during this scene:

Mk. 14:3 "While He was in Bethany at the home of Simon the leper, and reclining at the table, there came a woman with an alabaster vial of very costly perfume of pure nard; and she broke the vial and poured it over His head."

Jn. 12:3 "Mary then took a pound of very costly perfume of pure nard, and anointed the feet of Jesus and wiped His feet with her hair; and the house was filled with the fragrance of the perfume."

Lk. 7:38, 47 "…and standing behind Him at His feet, weeping, she began to wet His feet with her tears, and kept wiping them with the hair of her head, and kissing His feet and anointing them with the perfume." For this reason I say to you, her sins, which are many, have been forgiven, for she loved much; but he who is forgiven little, loves little."

The beauty and fragrance of God are within your spirit. But hardness of heart keeps the fragrant aroma locked away. As your hard heart is broken as a vial, the sweet perfume of who you are in your spirit is released into the room. It is enjoyed by everyone around you including the Lord. The vial Mary broke represents our brokenness which results in anointing and blessing the Lord by the fragrance that comes forth.

When we are broken,

- We forsake our own self-reliance.
- We live dependent on Christ.
- We hunger after God.
- We enjoy His life and strength rather than our own.
- We leave our self-focused emptiness, depression, and the sickness that is within own souls.

Jn. 12:24 "Truly, truly, I say to you, unless a grain of wheat falls into the earth and dies, it remains alone; but if it dies, it bears much fruit."

The flesh avoids the feeling of being undone that brokenness brings. We avoid weakness. However, the Apostle Paul had a different view:

> *2 Cor. 12:11,12 "Therefore I am well content with weaknesses, with insults, with distresses, with persecutions, with difficulties, for Christ's sake; for when I am weak, then I am strong…"*

One of your flesh's primary missions is to avoid weakness and suffering. You have accumulated many things to make you feel clothed and equipped. Money, knowledge, careers, houses, possessions, and status are among the more obvious temptations to make you feel adequate and safe. *But the flesh also uses more subtle instruments that are hidden from view.* Various techniques you've acquired to avoid feeling embarrassed in social settings, equipping yourself with just enough knowledge in certain areas to be able to comment intelligently, falsely propping yourself up inside to not feel the effects of many fears that you tend to deal with – all of these are the kinds of things the Spirit of God will reveal to you as you go through the brokenness process.

Submit to Your Captivity

> *Jer. 24:3, 5, 8 "Then the Lord said to me, "What do you see, Jeremiah?" And I said, "Figs, the good figs, very good; and the bad figs, very bad, which cannot be eaten due to rottenness." Thus says the Lord God of Israel, 'Like these good figs, so I will regard as good the captives of Judah, whom I have sent out of this place into the land of the Chaldeans. 'But like the bad figs which cannot be eaten due to rottenness--indeed, thus says the Lord--so I will abandon Zedekiah king of Judah and his officials, and the remnant of Jerusalem who remain in this land and the ones who dwell in the land of Egypt."*

Due to Israel's refusal to listen to and obey, God allowed Israel to be taken into captivity by King Nebuchadnezzar of Babylon. God allowed this to happen in order to get Israel to return to Him with "their whole heart." Those who submitted to the captivity God called "good figs." Those who did not submit He called "bad figs."

The Lord is constantly designing the perfect captivity for your flesh. The current difficulties of circumstances you are experiencing in your life right now have been custom fit for you. They are a perfectly designed "mouse trap" for your flesh to die in and for you to learn what God has been trying to work in you. Give yourself to the captivity that you are in. Submit to the tightly formed box that surrounds you, and God will give you grace.

If you submit to your captivity, your circumstances may not change right away. Or, they may never change. However, as you submit to your captivity and the custom made box you are currently in, and as you humble yourself and depend on God - your heart will escape the prison walls that confine you. You will learn to live in a new place in your heart in the midst of turmoil and suffering. If you do not use your current difficulty to find God, you will be *recycled* and taken around the same mountain again and again until you learn the point of the lesson.

> *Is. 61:1 "The Spirit of the Lord God is upon me, Because the Lord has anointed me to bring good news to the afflicted; He has sent me to bind up the brokenhearted, to proclaim liberty to captives and freedom to prisoners;"*

God sets free those who are prisoners. But, you have to become a prisoner first to become a candidate for freedom. You must be afflicted to receive good news. You must be a damaged mess before you can be cared for and nurtured (Lk. 10:34). The goal of your flesh from day one has been to avoid pain, stress, difficulties, and the feelings of helplessness that come from these. Planet Earth is falling apart all around you, your body is decaying, and extreme weakness permeates this life. Because the ultimate goal of your flesh is to stay in control and escape the captivity of being imprisoned by the weakness of this life, it has endeavored to compensate and to escape the continual sufferings that are a part of daily life.

God is at work to box you in. The flesh is at work to escape the box. God desires to box you in so that you will give up and truly be free. The flesh's freedom and avoidance of the box only results in more bondage. The flesh's desire to be free and not submit to God only further strengthens the flesh and its strongholds. When we submit the flesh to captivity, the flesh gives up and dies. Then we are truly free.

> *Matt. 21:44 "And he who falls on this stone will be broken to pieces; but on whomever it falls, it will scatter him like dust."*

It is good to learn to fall on the Rock and to be broken to pieces. You must learn to do this now and during this life on Earth. If you don't learn to fall on the Rock now and be broken to pieces, at some point the Rock will fall on you, and you will be scattered like dust.

You ultimately cannot produce your own brokenness. It is a work of the Spirit. But He is constantly working. You can choose to cooperate with the process and give yourself to it. Each day you have an opportunity to break.

> *Jas 1:4 "And let endurance have its perfect result, so that you may be perfect and complete, lacking in nothing."*

In the verse above, we are instructed to *let* the trials of life have their perfect work so we may be perfect and complete, lacking in nothing. The work of life's trials is to break us. If we yield to this breaking, the trials will be profitable for us and have their perfect work. If we resist, the trials will only be pain, but without profit. Often, it is difficult to see a painful event as profitable. This is why James goes on in verse 5 to encourage us to ask for wisdom when we find ourselves in a trial. God promises to give us insight into the purpose of the trial and what it is working in our lives.

2 Cor. 1:8-10 "For we do not want you to be unaware, brethren, of our affliction which came to us in Asia, that we were burdened excessively, beyond our strength, so that we despaired even of life; indeed, we had the sentence of death within ourselves so that we would not trust in ourselves, but in God who raises the dead; who delivered us from so great a peril of death, and will deliver us, He on whom we have set our hope. And He will yet deliver us,"

Notice that Paul says in the above passage "so that we would not trust in ourselves." Paul and his companions were burdened so excessively that it was too great to bear within their own strength. It got so bad that they didn't want to live. But the purpose of this great suffering was so that they would stop trusting in themselves and begin to trust in God.

Brokenness Helps to Discerning the Difference

As mentioned previously, at times it may seem difficult to be able to discern the difference between your head and your heart. This may be especially true if you have been living primarily from your head. Impulses that originate from the heart may seem hidden or easily confused with concepts and logic. Brokenness is a tremendous help in discerning the difference between the head and the heart as we will see in the Parable of the Soils.

The Parable of the Soils

In three different accounts, we see the explanation Jesus gives of the parable of the soils (Lk. 8:11-15, Mt. 13:18-23, Mk. 4:14-20). The sower is sowing the word of God into four different kinds of hearts or qualities of soil. The first kind of heart where the seed fell was the soil along the roadside. The second kind of heart was called the "rocky soil." The third was the soil that yielded thorns, and the fourth kind of heart was called "the good soil."

Two of the soil types are more easily discerned, while two are harder to see. The good soil is easy to identify. A heart that is good soil receives the word of God, believes it, and then bears fruit. The soil that grew thorns is also easy to recognize. Various lusts, the cares of this life, worries, and the desire for other things choke out the fruitfulness of the word of God. It is usually easy to see when we want things that are not of God. Note that both the good soil and the soil that yielded thorns allowed things to grow in them easily and those things remained.

However, the rocky soil and the roadside soil are more difficult to recognize and to understand. Both of these soils had no depth. They were both shallow and hard. The soil that was by the roadside was hard and packed. The account says of the roadside soil that "the seed was sown in his heart" (Mk. 13:19), yet it was immediately snatched up by the evil one. The rocky soil had no depth of soil because of the rocks within it. The rocky soil also received the seed of the word, but unlike the seed by the roadside, the rocky soil received the seed "with great joy." Life sprang forth from the rocky soil immediately. Yet, because there was no depth of soil, the life of the plant could not be sustained. A root system could not be established to withstand the trials of life (the heat from the sun); therefore, the life of the plant was only temporary.

Why is it that the seed that fell along the roadside received the seed in the heart, yet it was quickly snatched away by the evil one? Why is it that the rocky soil received the word of God with joy and brought forth life, yet because there was no depth of soil, the sun caused the plant to wither?

Your heart is like soil that needs to be broken up and loosened. Those who have loose soil are tender hearted, soft, and malleable. Things grow in soft, fertile soil. Those who have allowed their hearts to be softened by the difficulties of life have chosen to allow the trials of life to humble them and break them.

Those who have very little brokenness are terrified of any kind of heart pain. They resist and avoid pain at all costs. They distract themselves. Therefore, their hearts are largely unavailable for the things of God.

When the heart is hard, there is not much soil *available*. There is no depth of heart with a hardened heart. A person who has a hard heart lives primarily out of his head and the thoughts that are in his mind. The person with a hard heart is shallow. He has no depth of soil in his heart.

It is often difficult for a shallow person who has hardened his heart to discern what is coming from his heart because he does not see much there. A shallow person without much soil might even say something like, "I can't really see my heart." All he tends to see is the thoughts he has in his mind.

On the contrary, a person who has plenty depth of heart is more obvious when it comes to things of the heart. A person with depth of soil gushes forth heart things all of the time. He cries, he craves things very deeply, he emotes often, he loves deeply, and he hates with passion. The things that are in his heart are more obvious both to himself and to others because of the depth of soil that he has.

A major contributing problem to not being able to discern the head from the heart is hardness in the heart. Hardness of heart is a result of not trusting God, not yielding to His Spirit, leaning to your own understanding, and living according to the flesh.

Living From Your Heart is Not Enough

Soil that yields thorns also has depth of heart and is able to grow things. However, it doesn't deny the lusts, wants, and distractions that are not of God. Just because you are living from your heart does not make it automatically righteous or spiritual. There are plenty of things that come out of the heart that are evil. People may say things such as, "I am going to do this because this is what is in my heart to do," or "This is what I am feeling in my heart." My reply is, "So what?" Just because a desire is "in your heart" does not automatically sanctify it or validate it. Although the heart is a sacred place (comparing it to the holy place of the tabernacle), it is not the most holy place (as the spirit is). The goal should never be to just live from your heart. For, the heart can be filled with either the flesh or the Spirit.

It is more important to discern soul (flesh) from spirit than to discern head from heart. As you are according to the Spirit, you will automatically live from your heart, for the Spirit of God fills the heart and not the head (Eph. 3:17). The Spirit only accesses the head to apply thoughts and understanding to the current spiritual leading.

Teaching Children to Break

> *Prov. 23:13-14 "Do not hold back discipline from the child, although you strike him with the rod, he will not die. You shall strike him with the rod and rescue his soul from Sheol."*

Previously, I briefly discussed a few issues related to child rearing because it was applicable to the subject. Obviously, the subject of child rearing is beyond the scope of this book. However, we will touch on it again because the subject is directly related to brokenness in adults. As adults, we are often only children in larger bodies. Hopefully, you will see the parallel of breaking a child to the breaking of an adult.

Spanking children breaks their wills (if you do it correctly). This is excellent training for the heart. It is imperative that you keep your children broken. You should require heart obedience in all things from your children. Simply put, all nagging, whining, manipulating, complaining, and trying to find a way around your instruction is evidence of an unbroken child. Unbroken children become unbroken adults. Unbroken adults raise more unbroken children. The tantrums and defiance we easily see in many children are the same attitudes that many adults have deep in their hearts towards God.

If you are a part of the small minority of parents, you may require thorough, outward obedience from your children. This small group of parents actually issue swift consequences for the noncompliant child. The larger majority of parenting requires little or nothing of children, and if certain behaviors are required, an inconsistent and ineffective pattern of discipline is administered that does little or nothing to break the will.

However, even within the small minority of parents who require a thorough, outward obedience from their children, many still allow children to whine and complain in their *heart attitudes* - even if they are outwardly obedient. Heart attitudes may seem insignificant or not important in raising children. But as an unbroken attitude in a child matures into an adult, his or her heart will continue in its defiance and rebellion toward the ultimate authority figure - God. If you don't break your children now, God will have to break them later, and you don't want that to happen.

Teenaged children who rebel often do so because they were never thoroughly broken as younger children. You should not *expect* your child to rebel at two years old and then again during the teen years. You will always get exactly what you expect in your children. If you expect them to rebel and defy you, then they will. If you do not expect defiance and you do not tolerate it, then your child will not tend to rebel.

Spank your children thoroughly. Sting the flesh hard enough and thoroughly to cause them to break and cry intensely. Remember, suffering is a part of life. It is biblical and right to allow or inflict suffering in order to break the hard heart. It is pure, unselfish love to aggressively drive out foolishness in the heart. When you spank your child, he should cry and be broken to such an extent that he wants love and intimacy with you. Otherwise, you should question if you really broke him. *Break the hard heart and comfort the broken heart.* God is doing the same thing with you as an adult if you will let Him have His work in you.

Do not bruise the flesh of a child but only sting it severely in order to break his hardened heart and his defiant will. I always used a thin wooden paddle that was age appropriate in order to not bruise my children. This method will train your children to break and then receive love. This is one of the most valuable gifts you can give to your child.

Questions for Understanding and Discussion

1. What is the difference in brokenness and being damaged?
2. Why is brokenness so important?
3. What happens in the heart during the breaking process?
4. What can you do to better cooperate with brokenness?
5. What does it mean to stay "in your box" or submit to your captivity?
6. How is brokenness an aid in helping you to discern the head from the heart?
7. Why is living from your heart not good enough?
8. How can children be a model for adults in learning about the importance of brokenness?

You'd Better or Else

We have discussed many ways that you can now cooperate with living out of your heart instead of only living from your head. We've covered in depth separating soul from spirit, not living out of decisions but rather learning to trust, issues related to brokenness, and moving away from a shallow life of walking after the flesh to the deep life of walking according to the Spirit.

To some, the ideas we've discussed in this book will be translated into a new form of legalism. "Now I feel like *I have to* walk after the Spirit."

> *Rom. 8:2 "For the law of the Spirit of life in Christ Jesus has set you free from the law of sin and of death."*

Walking after the Spirit of life *is* a law. It is a requirement of God. It is a New Testament commandment for the Christian.

You must always remember, however, that following a law, even the law of the Spirit, does not make *who you are* into a righteous person. Only the blood of Christ makes you righteous and justified before God.

> *Rom. 10:4 "For Christ is the end of the law for righteousness to everyone who believes."*

Let's say it this way. You are forever righteous in God's eyes because of what Jesus did for you apart from what you do or don't do. However, God does command you to walk after the Spirit which allows you to *live out* all of the righteousness He wants you to walk in and to receive the love and intimacy that He has for you.

The Law of the Spirit is the Summation of Every Law

God has made this all very simple for us. Under the old covenant, there were hundreds of rules to memorize and live by. Now, in the new covenant that we are in, living according to the Spirit is the only thing you have to do in order to fulfill every rule of the old covenant. In fact, the law of the Spirit sums up all of the laws of God:

> *Rom. 8:4 "so that the requirement of the Law might be fulfilled in us, who do not walk according to the flesh but according to the Spirit."*

So, Are You Under a Law?

Even though the law of the Spirit is the only thing you are to give yourself to, when you hear the words *law* or *rule*, it places you under a yoke that your flesh will rebel against and despise. However, as we've mentioned before, the law of the Spirit is like God commanding you to eat an ice cream cone (assuming you like ice cream).

> *Matt. 11:28-30 "Come to Me, all who are weary and heavy-laden, and I will give you rest. Take My yoke upon you and learn from Me, for I am gentle and humble in heart, and you will find rest for your souls. For My yoke is easy and My burden is light."*

There is indeed a yoke for you to take on, something to give yourself to, something to do. But it is not an outward doing like the Old Testament law; rather, it is an inward doing (actively believing from the heart and trusting). God's yoke of commandments under the old covenant was burdensome, and no one was able to bear it (Acts 15:10). However, the yoke of Christ under the new covenant is a yoke of love. There is a requirement, but it is a requirement to believe and to receive what God has already done for you.

Is it *a law* that you have to eat food? Yes it is. All laws have cause and effect. Certainly your body will die if you don't eat. But I've never met someone who didn't want to eat. Eating is enjoyable. People don't usually eat because they have to - they eat because they want to.

In John 6, Jesus references the analogy of eating Him and taking Him in as food (Jn. 6:33, 35, 48, 51, 55). Jesus says that He Himself is "the bread of life" and that "His body is true food and His blood is true drink." To walk after the Spirit is to receive the Lord Jesus into your heart just like you would take food, air, or water into your body. God is telling you that you need to eat of the Lord Jesus Christ. The Lord Jesus has set before you a huge banquet of food for you to enjoy. He is the appetizer, the main course, and the dessert. Yes, I am sorry, but you have to eat your ice cream.

Again, look at Rom. 10:4:

> *"For Christ is the end of the law for righteousness to everyone who believes."*

When we say that having to eat food is a law, you must understand that it is not a law for righteousness. Eating physical food has nothing to do with making you righteous. In other words, your right standing, acceptance, and value to God is not based on anything you do or don't do, but is because of the blood of Jesus. God will love you just the same if you starve yourself and die. You will still be incredibly valued by your heavenly Father if you go on a hunger strike and wither away. In the same way, if you do not humble yourself and receive His love, you will still be incredibly valued, and you will still be loved by your Father. But if you do not receive His love, you will wither and die spiritually (Jn.

15:6, Gal. 6:8). No, you do not *have to* do anything. You are still loved no matter what.

Enjoying the fact that you have been made clean before God, receiving His smile toward you, taking in His love, and trusting God from your heart are all wonderful things. But it does require the death of your flesh and your position of control. Your flesh will always view God's gifts as negative things, and it will always turn the beautiful benefits of salvation into "I have to."

Concluding Thoughts

Moving biblical concepts and ideas into experiential reality within the heart hinges on being according to the Spirit. Only as you are after the Spirit will you experience the reality of spiritual things.

Furthermore, being according to the Spirit hinges on childlike humility. Childlike humility causes your heart to hunger and need; and is therefore the prerequisite to trust. Without a childlike humility, you don't truly feel the need for God in your heart. As you find childlike humility, and therefore a dependent hunger comes up within your heart - submit yourself under the person of Jesus Christ and trust your entire self to Him. Trust Him by giving Him complete rule and power over you. Find enjoyment of His love for you, enjoyment of who He is, and bask in the freedom of His parental care for you.

Obviously, there are many other subjects that are related to the brief summary above. There are many things that can hinder and get in the way of the above process. Legalism and self-effort are extremely common dynamics that hinder; and many of these are subtle. Secondly, it is always imperative that you daily trust in the truth of the good news of what Jesus has done for you and how He has changed you. As a Christian, your spirit is who you truly are, not the flesh. You have been completely cleansed and God's love continually abounds toward you.

God has made Himself available to you. May you find Him daily, and the inexpressible joy, peace, and freedom that come from the life of His Spirit filling your heart.

Questions for Understanding and Discussion

1. Is walking after the Spirit a law?
2. Do your righteousness, acceptance and value to God change when you walk after the Spirit?
3. Do you have to walk after the Spirit or eat food? What will happen if you don't?
4. Is it negative to you that you have to walk after the Spirit?